Radical Theologies and Philosophies

Series Editors
Michael Grimshaw
Department of Sociology
University of Canterbury
Christchurch, New Zealand

Michael Zbaraschuk
Pacific Lutheran University
Tacoma, WA, USA

Joshua Ramey
Grinnell College
Grinnell, IA, USA

Radical Theologies and Philosophies is a call for transformational theologies that break out of traditional locations and approaches. The rhizomic ethos of radical theologies enable the series to engage with an ever-expanding radical expression and critique of theologies that have entered or seek to enter the public sphere, arising from the continued turn to religion and especially radical theology in politics, social sciences, philosophy, theory, cultural, and literary studies. The post-theistic theology both driving and arising from these intersections is the focus of this series.

More information about this series at
http://www.palgrave.com/gp/series/14521

Jordan E. Miller

Resisting Theology, Furious Hope

Secular Political Theology and Social Movements

Jordan E. Miller
Independent Scholar
Newport, RI, USA

Radical Theologies and Philosophies
ISBN 978-3-030-17390-6   ISBN 978-3-030-17391-3 (eBook)
https://doi.org/10.1007/978-3-030-17391-3

© The Editor(s) (if applicable) and The Author(s), under exclusive licence to Springer Nature Switzerland AG 2019
This work is subject to copyright. All rights are solely and exclusively licensed by the Publisher, whether the whole or part of the material is concerned, specifically the rights of translation, reprinting, reuse of illustrations, recitation, broadcasting, reproduction on microfilms or in any other physical way, and transmission or information storage and retrieval, electronic adaptation, computer software, or by similar or dissimilar methodology now known or hereafter developed.
The use of general descriptive names, registered names, trademarks, service marks, etc. in this publication does not imply, even in the absence of a specific statement, that such names are exempt from the relevant protective laws and regulations and therefore free for general use.
The publisher, the authors and the editors are safe to assume that the advice and information in this book are believed to be true and accurate at the date of publication. Neither the publisher nor the authors or the editors give a warranty, express or implied, with respect to the material contained herein or for any errors or omissions that may have been made. The publisher remains neutral with regard to jurisdictional claims in published maps and institutional affiliations.

Cover credit: The Picture Art Collection / Alamy Stock Photo
Cover image: Hilma af Klint: Chaos, Nr. 2, 1906

This Palgrave Macmillan imprint is published by the registered company Springer Nature Switzerland AG
The registered company address is: Gewerbestrasse 11, 6330 Cham, Switzerland

For Charlie and Tom, my ancestors, the ghosts. And especially for their children.
And for Rhen, for whom the world changes.

PREFACE

My commitments begin with life, not with God, religion, or theology. Maybe that's just semantics—"the love of people is already the love of God"—or maybe it's some kind of heresy. Either way, I think the direction of that commitment matters. The theological method at work in this book arises out of an immanentist solidarity with real human beings, organizing and acting in real time, and with the Earth. Resisting theology emerges from people fighting against the instruments of death, whether biological, technological, political, theological, economic, or bureaucratic. The first concerns in this work are always people and the Earth. And, though this is a work of radical political theology, I risk theology for them. When it's necessary—when theology and its partners become an instrument of death—I resist theology for them. All of life is a risk and, today more than ever, it seems like those wagers are increasing in value. If we are going to have any use for theology in the world to come, it will only be as life's accomplice.

I was a student during the George W. Bush years. That is when I first became an activist and community organizer. I have been teaching about religion, politics, and social movements since 2008. Partly as a way of coping with the horrors of the world, I began to develop a method for using my training in philosophy of religion to interpret and equip resistance to those horrors. In turn, my study of resistance movements began to change the way I understand the operations of religion and philosophy. These things have developed into what I call *resisting theology*: a radical, political theology engaged with movements of resistance.

While I have worked on a number of projects since that time, *Resisting Theology* has remained a constant concern. The Afghanistan and Iraq wars that began within the first year and a half after September 11, 2001, the economic crisis that began in 2007 and 2008, and racist policing had been the most visible concerns of leftist movements over those years. Though leftist organizing has continued to grow and develop since Vietnam, there has been an almost constant discourse circling back to the Civil Rights and student movements of the 1960s to uncover lessons for current struggles. Some even harken back to the labor movement. Many on the left suffer from nostalgia for a golden age of activism, however they understand it. Even regarding the current chief executive, activists continue to compare him and this new situation to Richard Nixon. There is a temptation to look for footholds for the current struggle in previous struggles. It assumes a symmetry between that time and this one. Yet as Mark Twain is reputed to have said, "history doesn't repeat itself but it often rhymes."

In June 2016, I participated in a conference put on by The International Society for Heresy Studies (heresystudies.org). It was also the 50th anniversary of the famous TIME Magazine issue from April 1966 whose cover asked, "Is God Dead?" I facilitated a conversation with Thomas J. J. Altizer and Jeffrey W. Robbins about the legacy of the death-of-God theology and movement and its politics. The 1950s and 1960s were a politically charged time. I suggested to Altizer, the most significant prophetic voice within the radical theological tradition, that from my position as a scholar of religion and theology there is a connection between the social and political changes going on at that time with the theological development in the radical tradition and its neglect of politics until the War on Terror began.

An early reader of this manuscript commented that no one takes radical theology seriously these days. Somewhat ironically, in commenting on a movement whose heyday was in the 1960s, that reader reveals themselves to be behind the times. It is true that the death-of-God theology waned in popularity over the course of the 1970s. But it did not go away. In the 1980s, radical theology, as it calls itself, was reinvigorated by an injection of deconstruction and postmodernism by its interlocutors. In 1982, Thomas J. J. Altizer, Max A. Meyers, Carl A. Raschke, Robert P. Sharlemann, Mark C. Taylor, and Charles Winquist collaborated on a conference devoted to radical theology and contemporary continental philosophy. The conference produced the book, *Deconstruction and Theology*, which reignited scholarly interest in radical theology.[1] A spate of influential and widely read books was published after that, bringing radical theology into literary and philosophical conversations through the gateway of deconstruction. Again, this wave of radical theology began to fade around the end of the last century. However, there has been a second reinvigoration and a third wave.

I am the co-editor, with Christopher D. Rodkey, of *The Palgrave Handbook of Radical Theology*[2] that includes essays from 54 contributors from around the world. *An Insurrectionist Manifesto*, by Ward Blanton, Clayton Crockett, Jeffrey W. Robbins, and Noelle Vahanian[3]; *Radical Theology: A Vision for Change*, by Jeffrey W. Robbins[4]; *Radical Political Theology*, by Clayton Crockett[5]; *Radical Democracy and Political Theology*, by Jeffrey W. Robbins[6]; and *A Materialism for the Masses*, by Ward Blanton,[7] have been published in recent series by Columbia University Press and Indiana University Press. *Resurrecting the Death of God*, edited by Daniel J. Peterson and G. Michael Zbaraschuk,[8] presents radical death-of-God theology as a response to contemporary theological conservatism. In 2012, Palgrave Macmillan launched the "Radical Theologies" book series, edited by Mike Grimshaw, Michael Zbaraschuk, and Joshua Ramey. The series is described as a call for transformational, "post-theistic" theologies and includes this book. In 2011 and 2013, conferences were held in Springfield, MO under the title, "Subverting the Norm." These conferences have brought together leading progressive church

---

[1] Thomas J. J. Altizer, Max A. Meyers, Carl A. Raschke, Robert P. Sharlemann, Mark C. Taylor, and Charles Winquist, *Deconstruction and Theology* (Spring Valley, NY: Crossroad Publishing Company, 1982).

[2] Christopher D. Rodkey and Jordan E. Miller, eds. *The Palgrave Handbook of Radical Theology* (New York: Palgrave Macmillan, 2018).

[3] Ward Blanton, Clayton Crockett, Jeffrey W. Robbins, and Noelle Vahanian, *An Insurrectionist Manifesto* (New York: Columbia University Press, 2016).

[4] Jeffrey W. Robbins, *Radical Theology: A Vision for Change* (Bloomington, IN: Indiana University Press, 2016).

[5] Clayton Crockett, *Radical Political Theology* (New York: Columbia University Press, 2011).

[6] Jeffrey W. Robbins, *Radical Democracy and Political Theology* (New York: Columbia University Press, 2011).

[7] Ward Blanton, *A Materialism for the Masses* (New York: Columbia University Press, 2014).

[8] Daniel J. Peterson and G. Michael Zbaraschuk, eds., *Resurrecting the Death of God* (Albany: SUNY, 2014).

practitioners with academics working in the fields of postmodern thought and radical theology. The events have been well attended and widely discussed in social media, representing an important emerging market. At both conferences, many attendees lamented the lack of serious political engagement there. Finally, the Westar Institute's Seminar on God and the Human Future—"the God Seminar"—is entering its fourth year of collaborative work. The Westar Institute is the organization responsible for the Jesus Seminar from the 1980s and 1990s—the most important interpreter of historical Jesus scholarship in the twentieth century. The God Seminar has explored varieties of post-theism for its first two years of meetings. All of this is to say that rumors of the death of radical theology—the death of the death of God—have been greatly exaggerated.

Radical theologians are busy. And they're newly politically engaged. But what radical theology has not done thus far is put its political variant into discussion with actual, lived social movements. This is my task in this book. Historically, there has been a close relationship between atheism and anarchism—"no Gods, no masters," being an old anarchist slogan. But regardless of the historical connections, it would seem that atheism—the absence of a sovereign—would have significant political consequences. There are a few essays and chapters that touch upon political revolution, but to my knowledge, Altizer has never written a work of political theology until what will likely be his final book,[9] despite gesturing toward a critique of sovereignty in the early part of his career. In 1966, he wrote that "Once the Church had claimed to be the body of Christ, it had already set upon the imperialistic path of conquering the world, of bringing the life and movement of the world into submission to the inhuman authority and power of an infinitely distant Creator and Judge" and that the radical Christian "knows that either God is dead or that humanity is now enslaved to an infinitely distant, absolutely alien, and wholly other epiphany of God. To refuse a deity who is a sovereign and alien other, or to will the death of the transcendent Lord, is certainly to risk an ultimate wrath and judgment." The only explicitly political article he's written states that death-of-God theology does not have any obvious or immediate political meaning or implications and in the end, comes off as quietist,

---

[9] Thomas J. J. Altizer, *Satan and Apocalypse: And Other Essays on Political Theology* (Albany: SUNY Press, 2017).

suggesting that politics is fickle.[10] And yet, while academic theology has been losing influence on the public, the last few decades have seen the development of globalization and religion as a politically galvanizing and radicalizing force. Especially in the last five years, there has been a massive increase in movements of resistance and protest. If the death-of-God movement was somehow related to the social and political upheaval of the 1960s, I wondered to Altizer at the Heresy Studies conference in 2016 what role there is for the death of God today, if there is one at all. In one sense, this book is a stab at answering that question.

In another sense, this book reflects the reversal of that question. Rather than looking for clues about religious or theological positions in movements that set out to change the world, I started to recognize a kind of radical theology that develops out of those movements. I inverted my priorities and my critical lens. It isn't that theological truths pre-exist social movements in which that theological content is revealed; it's that the movements themselves generate new theological insights. This first began for me in the fall of 2011 after the Arab Spring and the 15 M movement in Spain had kicked off some months earlier and the occupation began in lower Manhattan. In the world-construction that the occupiers were performing at Zuccotti Park, I began to notice the work of religion being performed. I didn't start with religion and look for it at Occupy. Occupy created something unique to its time and place that only theological language could fully explain. Then I began looking at other social movements.

I wrote the majority of this book before Donald Trump became president of the United States. He was inaugurated a month ago and has taken every opportunity to follow through on his racist, xenophobic, anti-environmental, and misogynistic promises through issuing an executive order to ban Muslim immigrants from countries that American military intervention destabilized, to putting Scott Pruitt, one of the Environmental Protection Agency's (EPA's) most strident critics, an opponent of climate change science, and someone with intimate ties to the fossil fuel industry in charge of the EPA. The last few weeks have felt like they've proceeded incredibly quickly. But even before Trump was installed, the American public inaugurated a resistance to him and his program.

---

[10] Thomas J. J. Altizer, "Radical Theology and Political Revolution," pp. 5–10 in *Criterion* 7 (Spring, 1968).

Still, that is shortsighted. History doesn't start and stop. It isn't convenient. And every time is new, built on what came before. I hope that in studying the secular theologies of ACT UP, Occupy Wall Street, and #BlackLivesMatter, the present resistance for this new period in American history can recognize its roots. *Resisting Theology* is something of a theopoetics of resistance politics. It's a theopoetics that rhymes, but doesn't repeat. So today, I hope that *Resisting Theology* can attune our ears to the internal schemes and the uneven stanzas pulsing and driving us forward. I want *Furious Hope* to serve as a way of aiding in the resistance to come.

Newport, RI
February 19, 2017

Jordan E. Miller

ACKNOWLEDGMENTS

First, I need to acknowledge my deepest gratitude to Jeff Robbins for being an inspiration and showing me the power of critical, creative thought; for his support and guidance all these years; and for demonstrating to me what an academic life can be. Jeff introduced me to academia and has shown me how to devote myself to the pursuit of a thinking that will not disappoint. It is a lonely business, but Jeff remains a steadfast companion along the way.

Thanks to Clayton Crockett for his encouragement, patience, and charity of both thought and time. Also, I want to express my special gratitude to Mike Grimshaw and Burke Gerstenschlager who saw the value in this project at its outset and have encouraged and pushed me along the way. I would not have done this without you.

Thanks to my colleagues Ryan Marnane, Fred Abong, Ali AlAbri, and Al Antosca. My conversations with them have been frustrating, exciting, and productive (often, though not always in that order). They have been paramount in creating a challenging and rewarding environment where I live. They have pushed me to think better and have challenged me to communicate more clearly and effectively. Special thanks to Ryan and Fred for their careful readings of drafts and sections. Ryan and Fred's questions, comments, and insistences have been invaluable. Thanks also to Tim Snediker for his patience and generous critiques and for his hospitality the night I defended my dissertation.

I taught a number of classes during the time I was crafting this manuscript wherein I workshopped arguments and road-tested arcs of ideas with the help of my students. In particular, Corey Whalen and Brandon

Harrington have had a hand in what you read in these pages. In addition to them, I'd like to thank three special groups of students: The Utopians, The Sisterhood, and Dean Wollenberg, Dakota Williams, and Patty Socarras. You are not merely inspirations but life rafts in a world that should be better than it is.

I consulted with a number of experts, activists, and witnesses along the way. Alan J. Richard, Grady Crittendon (may he rest in power), and Ben Shepard were instrumental in fine-tuning my thoughts about the AIDS Coalition to Unleash Power (ACT UP). George Schmidt gave me new insights and challenged my old ones about Occupy. I am indebted to him for being my pastor and comrade. James Howard Hill, Jr., has kept my eyes open and my mouth honest. Netta Elzie, Pamela Lightsey, Zachary Smith, and Chris Parr were extremely generous with providing new insights surrounding #BlackLivesMatter and policing. Chris Parr is also the reason I began thinking about religion and politics, order and disorder in this way in the first place.

Thank you to Drs. Adam Seligman and Robert Weller whose seminars on ritual I attended at Boston University in 2005 and 2006. It was through them that I was first introduced to the work of Roy A. Rappaport and the concept of subjunctivity as it relates to ritual and religion. This idea has clearly had a profound influence on me and I'm deeply grateful to Drs. Seligman and Weller for the care they took and the passion they exhibited in their teaching. I've done something here with the concept of the subjunctive that departs from their work, but I certainly want to give them all due credit for setting certain ideas in motion. I am also indebted to Michael Anton Budd and Debra Curtis for reading early sections of this book.

Callid Keefe-Perry and the leadership of ARC: A Creative Collaborative for Theopoetics have helped provide me with numerous opportunities to continue to work out the relationship between political theology, radical theology, and social movements. I have published in their journal, presented at their conference, and helped to organize and run their working group at the American Academy of Religion Annual Meeting. Theopoetics is not my home, but it is a welcoming place that has supported me in ways the academy more generally has not. Similarly, Gregory Erickson and Bernard Schweizer, in their capacity as leaders of The International Society for Heresy Studies, have also been immensely encouraging and supportive.

I am also grateful for the opportunities to have presented a number of components of this book in various stages of development at conferences.

I am especially thankful to have been able to test out some rather controversial ideas about Rappaport at American University's Public Anthropology Conference in October 2013 that helped me to develop Chap. 2. I also presented some of that chapter at Concordia University's "In/Tangibility" conference in Montreal in March 2014 and at the Inaugural Conference of the Society for Heresy Studies, New York University, in May. I presented early sections of Chap. 5 at the American Academy of Religion Annual Meeting for the Theopoetics Working Group in San Diego in November 2014. I presented early versions of components of Chap. 6 at the University of Rhode Island's "Innovations & Anxieties" conference in March 2012; Villanova University's Inaugural Graduate Theology Student Conference, "Faith and Culture: Theologians of the Future in Dialogue," in April 2012; West Chester University's philosophy conference, "Ethics in Dialogue," also in April 2012; the American Academy of Religion Annual Meeting in Chicago on the "Irreligion, Secularism, and Social Change" panel in November 2012; the TELOS conference, "Religion and Politics in a Post-Secular World," in February 2013; and the Roger Williams University Conference on Religion and the State in March 2013. And finally, I presented early work on Chap. 7 at the Society for Heresy Studies conference on "Heresy, Belief, and Ideology: Dissent in Politics and Religion" at New York University in June 2016 and at the American Academy of Religion Annual Meeting for the ARC Theopoetics Working Group in Boston, MA, in November 2017.

Finally, some sections of this book have been adapted from previously published essays. Components of Chap. 2 originally appeared in my essay "Making the World: Against Spirituality" in the volume *Reading Heresy: Religion and Dissent in Literature and Art*, edited by Gregory Erickson and Bernard Schweizer (De Gruyter, 2017). Parts of Chap. 4 appeared in "A book review of Mark Lewis Taylor, *The Theological and the Political: On the Weight of the World*" in *Theopoetics: A Journal of Theological Imagination, Literature, Embodiment, and Aesthetics* (vol. 1, no 2, 2015) and in "Secular Theology, Political Poetics, and ACT UP: On Meaning-Making and Resistance," *Theopoetics: A Journal of Theological Imagination, Literature, Embodiment, and Aesthetics* (vol. 2, no. 1, 2016). Components of Chap. 6 appeared in "Silence and the City: Political Theology and Occupy Wall Street," in *Decentering Discussions on Religion and State: Emerging Narratives, Challenging Perspectives*, edited by Sargon Donabed and Autumn Quezada-Grant (Lexington Books, 2015). Parts of Chap. 7 originally appeared in "A Book Profile of Walter D. Mignolo, *The Darker*

Side of Western Modernity: Global Futures, Decolonial Options," in *Journal for Cultural and Religious Theory* (vol., 13 no. 1, Winter 2014: 162–164).

In the end, this book is about hope and creativity—albeit a furious hope and creativity. So finally, at the conclusion of this very long list of acknowledgments, as much as this book is about beginnings and as much as it is about possibilities not yet realized, it is for my daughter, Rhen. *Resisting Theology* and she are the same age.

Contents

1 Introduction to Resisting Theology — 1

2 Subjunctivity — 19
 Religion, Not Spirituality — 19
 Manufacturing the World — 27
 Introduction to Illustrations — 34

3 Political Theology — 51
 Political Theology Otherwise — 51
 Sovereignty or Authority — 59
 From Theory to Application — 65

4 Resisting Theology Part 2 — 69
 Toward a Radical Theology of Politics — 69
 Resisting Theology (Again) — 71
 Modernity, Politics, and Religion — 81
 Theology Today — 87
 Tactics and Liberation — 91
 Democracy, or Anarchy — 97
 The City — 101

5 Act Up — 111
 The AIDS Coalition to Unleash Power — 111
 Subjunctivity: Crisis of Meaning — 114

	Subjunctivity: Poetry	117
	Subjunctivity: Desire	118
	Ghosts	122
	Theopoetic Utopianism	125
6	**Occupy Wall Street**	127
	Seasons	127
	Spirit	133
	Silence	143
7	**#BlackLivesMatter**	153
	Impropriety, Resistance	153
	Property Destruction	155
	Baltimore	162
8	**Conclusion: Standing Rock**	165
	Benediction	168

Bibliography   169

Index   187

LIST OF TABLES

Table 4.1   Religion and politics at modernity's start   85
Table 4.2   Heuristic proposal for religion and politics after modernity   89

CHAPTER 1

Introduction to Resisting Theology

The world always appears new. Politics and religion, sovereignty and theology, resistance and ritual play key roles in the making, maintaining, and remaking of that world. This may be counterintuitive. According to conventional wisdom, the world had been losing its religion. From the nineteenth century until the last few decades, in both scholarly and popular outlets, the proponents of this secularization thesis seemed to dominate the discourse about religion. Science and technology, through the twin legacies of the Enlightenment and industrialization, would ultimately erode the sphere of human meaning typically occupied by religion, thus bringing humanity into a new, secular-humanist epoch. Modernity would destroy religion.[1] But despite exponentially advancing technological and

---

[1] The secularization thesis has taken a variety of forms. The Enlightenment's repositioning of reason as superior to theology began a trend that culminated in the late nineteenth and early twentieth centuries. The most significant expressions of that early secularization thesis came from thinkers such as Sigmund Freud ("Obsessive Actions and Religious Practices," pp. 429–435, published in 1907, *The Future of an Illusion,* pp. 685–721, published in 1927, and *Civilization and Its Discontents,* pp. 722–771, published in 1930, collected in Peter Gay, ed., *The Freud Reader,* New York and London. W. W. Norton and Co., 1989), Karl Marx ("Theses on Feuerbach," pp. 569–575 in *The German Ideology,* with Friedrich Engels, Amherst, NY: Prometheus Books, 1998, originally 1845), Auguste Comte (*The Positive Philosophy of Auguste Comte. Freely Translated and Condensed by Harriet Martineau,* London: George Bell & Sons, 1896, originally 1830–46), Emile Durkheim (*The Elementary Forms of the Religious Life,* New York: Free Press, 1995, originally 1912), and Max Weber (*The Protestant Ethic and the Spirit of Capitalism,* New York: Scribner, 1930, originally 1904).

scientific change and vast improvements in world literacy and education, the world has not secularized as it had been predicted. Especially since the Iranian Revolution, the rise of the Moral Majority and Christian evangelicalism in American politics, the rise of religious extremism and violence, and the Arab Spring, it has become increasingly clear that the secularization thesis, while ubiquitous in the middle of the twentieth century, was—quite simply—wrong. Religion did not disappear. And yet neither is this a simple case of a return. The religion that seems to have returned is different than it had been. The relationship between religion and the secular has thus proven to be more complex and nuanced than previously imagined.

In response to this so-called return of religion, there has been a growing body of scholarship that, over the last 30 years or so and increasing in volume and frequency, has attempted to re-conceive religion, politics, the

---

Each thinker had a different take on what was effectively the same argument. Freud argued that religion had lost its ability to contribute to the forward march of human civilization. While religion may have once contributed to social or moral development, scientific and intellectual progress had eclipsed religion revealing it to be nothing more than neurotic superstition. Marx's version of the secularization thesis began with the presupposition that religion is a product of social forces. The inevitability of the collapse of capitalism and the ensuing transition to socialism would remove any social need humanity may have once had for religion. Comte thought that theology was superstition and humanity's ability to think about religion at a critical and abstract distance would eliminate it. Interestingly, he appreciated religion's ritual and ethical functions and attempted unsuccessfully to create a positivist-humanist church as a result. Durkheim argued that industrialization was eroding the social functions that religion had traditionally played such as in education, social control, and welfare. Finally, Weber argued that science and education would continue to produce an increasingly rational worldview in industrialized societies, thus ultimately eradicating religion.

The secularization thesis peaked in the 1960s, most notably in the work of Peter L. Berger (*The Sacred Canopy: Elements of a Sociological Theory of Religion*, Garden City, NY: Doubleday, 1966) and Bryan Wilson (*Religion in Secular Society: A Sociological Comment*, London: C. A. Watts, 1966). Berger and Wilson each argued that the secularization thesis had become both a descriptive and a normative project explaining both that religion was being pushed out of society and that modernity had cast this as a desirable outcome in its own right, rather than simply as a consequence of other developments. Berger and Wilson lamented this movement. They both warned of dire consequences of religion's disappearance such as declines in both morality and social cohesion. For surveys of the development of the secularization thesis and accompanying debate, see Steve Bruce, ed., *Religion and Modernization* (Oxford: Oxford University Press, 1992); William H. Swatos Jr. and Daniel V. A. Olson, eds., *The Secularization Debate* (Lanham, MD and Oxford: Rowman and Littlefield Publishers, Inc., 2000); and the first chapter in *Sacred and Secular: Religion and Politics Worldwide*, entitled "The Secularization Debate," by Pippa Norris and Ronald Inglehart (New York and Cambridge: Cambridge University Press, 2004), 3–32.

secular, and the relationships between them.[2] Talal Asad's *Formations of the Secular: Christianity, Islam, Modernity* is a prominent and important example. In it, Asad explains that the growing academic disenchantment with the secularization thesis is not just a result of the new importance that religion seems to be playing in politics. He writes:

---

[2] The list of texts that fit this bill is too long to chronicle here. Let it be sufficient to say that included among the most important for this project are Peter Berger, ed. *The Desecularization of the World: Resurgent Religion and World Politics* (Grand Rapids, MI: Wm. B. Eerdmans Publishing Company, 1999); Judith Butler, Jürgen Habermas, Charles Taylor, and Cornel West, *The Power of Religion in the Public Sphere*, eds. Eduardo Mendieta, Jonathan VanAntwerpen, and Craig Calhoun (New York: Columbia University Press, 2011); Craig Calhoun, Mark Juergensmeyer, and Jonathan VanAntwerpen, eds. *Rethinking Secularism* (Oxford and New York: Oxford University Press, 2011); William T. Cavanaugh, *Migrations of the Holy: God, State, and the Political Meaning of the Church* (Grand Rapids, MI: Wm. B. Eerdmans, 2011); Clayton Crockett, ed. *Religion and Violence in the Secular World: Toward a New Political Theology* (Charlottesville, VA: University of Virginia Press, 2006); Philip Gorski, David Kyuman Kim, John Torpey, and Jonathan VanAntwerpen, eds. *The Post-Secular in Question: Religion in Contemporary Society* (New York and London, New York University Press, 2012); Jürgen Habermas, *An Awareness of What is Missing: Faith and Reason in a Post-secular Age* (Cambridge, UK and Malden, MA: Polity Press, 2010); Joseph Ratzinger and Jürgen Habermas, *The Dialectics of Secularization: On Reason and Religion*, ed. Florian Schuller (San Francisco: Ignatius Press, 2006); Charles Taylor, *A Secular Age* (Cambridge, MA: The Belknap Press of Harvard University Press, 2007); Mark L. Taylor, *The Theological and the Political: On the Weight of the World* (Minneapolis: Fortress Press, 2011); Hent De Vries and Lawrence E. Sullivan, eds. *Political Theologies: Public Religions in a Post-Secular World* (New York: Fordham University Press, 2006); and Michael Warner, Jonathan VanAntwerpen, and Craig Calhoun, eds. *Varieties of Secularism in a Secular Age* (Cambridge, MA: Harvard University Press, 2010).

These recent works of the last few decades are not without precedent. A number of philosophical and theological thinkers in the early and mid-twentieth century argued effectively that religion and politics and the sacred and the secular or profane were not as opposed to one another as the secularization thesis might have us believe. Texts in this vein that have inspired this project include Ernst H. Kantorowicz, *The King's Two Bodies* (Princeton, NJ: Princeton University Press, 1997); Karl Lowith, *Meaning in History. The Theological Implications of the Philosophy of History* (Chicago and London: University of Chicago Press, 1957); H. Richard Niebuhr, *Christ and Culture* (New York: Harper Collins, 1996) and *Radical Monotheism and Western Culture* (Louisville, KY: Westminster/John Knox Press, 1993); Carl Schmitt, *The Concept of the Political*, trans. George Schwab (Chicago and London: University of Chicago Press, 2007) and *Political Theology: Four Chapters on the Concept of Sovereignty*, trans. George Schwab (Chicago and London: University of Chicago Press, 2006); Paul Tillich, *Theology of Culture*, ed. Robert C. Kimball (Oxford, UK: Oxford University Press, 1959); and Gabriel Vahanian, *The Death of God: The Culture of Our Post-Christian Era* (New York: George Braziller, 1961).

In a sense what many would anachronistically call "religion" was *always* involved in the world of power. If the secularization thesis no longer carries the conviction it once did, this is because the categories of "politics" and "religion" turn out to implicate each other more profoundly than we thought, a discovery that has accompanied our growing understanding of the powers of the modern nation-state. The concept of the secular cannot do without the idea of religion.[3]

This is a typical example of the ways in which a traditional understanding of the secular needs to be frustrated and reexamined. For Asad, both are expressions of power and the State. So not only do the secular and the religious depend on one another, but the religious and the political implicate each other as well. Studying the religious, the secular, or the political thus requires studying all three. As a result, this has profound implications for both political philosophy and theology, as well as for their hybrid, political theology.

We are living through a time of renewed emphasis on religion. Further, it is not coincidental that we are also living in a time of increasingly accelerating political and social change around the world. Most notably, recent phenomena such as the Arab Spring, the Occupy Movement, the Zapatista Rebellion, the 15-M Movement in Spain, the activities in Gezi Park in Istanbul, the Umbrella Revolution in Hong Kong, Idle No More in Canada, #BlackLivesMatter, and the encampments at Standing Rock in North Dakota have demonstrated a trend of peoples' unwillingness to accept the imposition of injustice through neoliberal globalization and its allies. Increasing wealth disparity, the depletion of natural resources, and political and social violence through racism, misogyny, and homophobia are all features of the emerging, dominant political-economic system on the planet. There has been an explosion in political theory in recent years attempting to resist neoliberalism through rethinking such tried and true political concepts as democracy, anarchy, and socialism.[4] In light of Asad's connection of

---

[3] Talal Asad, *Formations of the Secular: Christianity, Islam, Modernity* (Stanford: Stanford University Press, 2003), 200.

[4] The list of texts in this conversation is far too long to include here. To take one example covered here in this book, there is a large number of thinkers writing about Occupy Wall Street. These texts were all published since 2012 and include Alain Badiou, *The Rebirth of History: Times of Riots and Uprisings,* trans. Gregory Elliott (London and New York: Verso, 2012); Mark Bray, *Translating Anarchy: The Anarchism of Occupy Wall Street* (Winchester, UK: Zero Books, 2013); David Graeber, *The Democracy Project: A History, a Crisis, a Movement* (New York: Spiegel and Grau, 2013); David Harvey, *Rebel Cities: From the Right*

religion and the secular to the political sphere, any understanding of the human condition in today's world requires an understanding of resistance movements occurring within the contexts of religion, the secular, and neoliberalism.

Political theology is a way of thinking that has the potential to shed light on this matrix of religion, politics, and social change. Political theology is not theology that is political or has political implications. It is a hybrid branch of political philosophy, philosophy of religion, and theology that investigates ways in which religious concepts, postures, and thinking underlie political, social, economic, and cultural discourses and institutions. Perhaps its most famous proponent is Carl Schmitt whose *Political Theology*, written in 1922, lays out the theory that political sovereignty is a secularization of divine sovereignty and, thus, political theory and theology are disciplinary cognates.[5] The social-creative powers of religion and politics thus lend themselves to a political-theological understanding.

The principal questions guiding the trajectory of this book are: (1) how might political theology understand contemporary political resistance? and its reciprocal, (2) how will an examination of contemporary resistance force a reconsideration of political theology? To answer these questions, the project begins by investigating the historical development of the relationship between religion and politics and their common foundations. I propose certain ways in which religion works to create a meaningful, political world in which one might live. I then critically investigate the relationship between radical theology and its relationship to the construction of community and political activity. The culmination of this project takes place in its second half: experimental and creative performances of resisting theology. The relationship, tension, and translatability between religion and politics are constant points of reference.

Subjunctivity is common to both religion and political resistance. In using that term, I'm appropriating a concept that refers to the grammatical mood of a verb used to express uncertainty, hypothesis, contingency, possibility, desire, potentiality, necessity, or hope and extrapolating it out

to the *City to the Urban Revolution* (London and New York: Verso, 2012); Chantal Mouffe, *Agonistics. Thinking the World Politically* (London and New York: Verso, 2013); Nathan Schneider, *Thank You, Anarchy: Notes from the Occupy Apocalypse* (Berkeley: University of California Press, 2013); and Slavoj Žižek, *The Year of Dreaming Dangerously* (London and New York: Verso, 2012).

[5] Carl Schmitt, *Political Theology: Four Chapters on the Concept of Sovereignty*, trans. George Schwab (Chicago and London: University of Chicago Press, 2006).

into a concept.[6] This idea has been theorized most fully in Adam B. Seligman, Robert P. Weller, Michael J. Puett, and Bennett Simon's *Ritual and Its Consequences: An Essay on the Limits of Sincerity*, in which they develop one of the anthropologist Roy A. Rappaport's most significant insights: that the work of any given ritual, regardless of its particular meaning, is to create an order that is self-consciously distinct from other possible social worlds.[7] In short, the subjunctive describes the world, not as it is, but as it might be. This "might be" is the root of both movements of political resistance which seek to model life differently than the status quo and of religious world-construction through theology, myth, and ritual. This book argues that the common ground between resistance and religion is the subjunctive; as such, it is appropriate to theologize political resistance. One of the primary points of entry into this line of thinking is an insistence on theology as a mode of interrogation. When considering the work of religion—what religion does, rather than what it says or means—we begin to understand the various ways religion underlies, or at least partners, with the political. It is first necessary to establish theology as a mode.

The variety of radical theology I employ is concerned with desire; political resistance is concerned with possibilities and improvement; subjunctivity encompasses both. Religion's desire is an urge or a drive. Political possibility is a creativity, but that possibility is found most clearly in the form of politics that resists the current order of things. Religion is an inspiration, a mode, or a method, and politics is about content and material (would-be) reality—the future. In my view, these both—the former as the why and whence, and the latter as the what or how—hinge on the same concept: subjunctivity. But not only do both political resistance and religion *hinge* on the subjunctive, but they both also *need each other* so as not to remain empty. The inspiration remains empty as long as it remains unfulfilled. Thus, theology relies on the political for its realization. The

---

[6] See *The Oxford English Dictionary*, second edition, prepared by J. A. Simpson and E. S. C. Weiner, Volume XVII: Su-Thrivingly (Oxford: Clarendon Press, 1991), 35–36: "Designating or relating to a verbal mood that refers to an action or state as conceived (rather than as a fact) and is therefore used chiefly to express a wish, command, exhortation, or a contingent, hypothetical, or prospective event."

[7] See Adam B. Seligman, Robert P. Weller, Michael J. Puett, and Bennett Simon, *Ritual and Its Consequences: An Essay on the Limits of Sincerity* (Oxford and New York: Oxford University Press, 2008) and Roy A. Rappaport, *Ritual and Religion in the Making of Humanity* (Cambridge, UK: Cambridge University Press, 1999).

subjunctive makes the world. The Earth may exist independently, but there would be no world without the subjunctive. Reality itself drives toward its own difference.

The initial question about the relationship between religion and politics may now be reframed in a subjunctive way. What steps are required to adequately perform a theology of resistance? Proceeding *as if* theology of resistance is both appropriate and fertile, what are the steps one might take? What points might one identify as loci of affinity? What are the ideas, thinkers, and concepts that might assist in advancing this line of thinking? As this line of thinking is interested in resistance and theology, it is fitting that political theology is its general framework. In his *Radical Democracy and Political Theology*, Jeffrey W. Robbins writes, "What political theology brings is a sustained focus on the nature of sovereign power. …democracy fundamentally alters the experience and understanding of sovereign power. In this way, it is not only the political instantiation of the death of God but also a theological affirmation of the political power particular to humanity."[8] Robbins also argues that radical democracy is the political instantiation of the death of God.[9] With intimacy between theology after the death of God and radical democratic resistance in mind, I undertake a theological approach to understanding radical democratic activity. That is, this book engages directly with the question of political resistance as radical theological activity. In the end and throughout, I argue for a political theology based on an openness to the construction of alternative worlds in which one might live as read through the lens of theological thinking that affirms—insists upon—God's absence.

Religion and political resistance are two of the most significant and timely human activities. An analysis of how they inform each other could not be more urgent. Suggesting that at the beginning of the twenty-first century, an investigation into the ways in which neoliberal capitalism and secularity provide a backdrop for acts and movements of political resistance is appropriate and profoundly important. Further, this project is not just an attempt to describe those conditions, but to respond to them. Both intellectual pursuits, generally, and work within the academy, particularly, are best when engaged with the world and the living that goes on in it.

---

[8] Jeffrey W. Robbins, *Radical Democracy and Political Theology* (New York: Columbia University Press, 2011), 190.
[9] This is Robbins's overarching claim in *Radical Democracy and Political Theology*.

I've written this book in that spirit: it is a dialogue between the world as it is and the creation of a vision for how it might be otherwise.

Regarding this project as an intervention into the field of political theology, its emphasis on alternatives is particularly important. Carl Schmitt's political theology is a ubiquitous point of reference in that field—so much so that it has prompted Antonio Negri to remark that there is "just one political theology, the one at whose opposite ends stand Bodin and Stalin, with Carl Schmitt occupying a slot somewhere in between."[10] But Negri is wrong. While one cannot—and should not try to—erase Schmitt and his dominance in the field of political theology from history and memory, it may be possible however to attempt to get under him (or maybe to try to get one over on him). This book is such an attempt. It is the proposal of alternative political theology.

So I'm doubling down. This is a work of political theology. Again, political theology is not theology that is political. Political theology is a hybrid mode of interpretation that investigates ways in which religious concepts, postures, and thinking underlie political, social, economic, and cultural discourses and institutions. Further, this book—my intervention into the contemporary conversation surrounding political theology—takes the death of God as axiomatic. In combining a creative and critical reading of subjunctivity against Schmitt's influence on the field, and insisting upon radical theology in the lineage of American death-of-God thought, the variety of political theology that appears in this work may appear positioned peripherally to the tradition or even transformed to a point on the edge of recognition.[11] For these reasons, I find it useful to name the variety

---

[10] Antonio Negri, *Spinoza for Our Time: Politics and Postmodernity,* trans. William McCuaig (New York: Columbia University Press, 2013), 32.

[11] The thinkers within the American death-of-God lineage that I have in mind include Thomas J. J. Altizer, Paul van Buren, William Hamilton, and Richard Rubenstein. They began their work in the 1960s. Altizer and Hamilton's *Radical Theology and the Death of God* (Indianapolis and New York: Bobbs-Merrill Company, Inc., 1966) is the most representative of this first generation of death-of-God theologians. Paul Tillich, Rudolph Bultmann, and Dietrich Bonhoeffer were significant influences on their work. And they, in turn, influenced Carl A. Raschke, Robert P. Scharlemann, Mark C. Taylor, Victor Taylor, and Charles E. Winquist who put their stamps on the legacy of death-of-God theology beginning in the late 1970s and the 1980s. The most representative text for this second generation is undoubtedly *Deconstruction and Theology* (New York: The Crossroad Publishing Company, 1982) by Thomas J. J. Altizer, Max A. Myers, Carl A. Raschke, Robert P. Scharlemann, Mark C. Taylor, and Charles E. Winquist. These thinkers loom in the background of this project—especially the dual notions of the social and existential experience of God's absence and theology after the death of God as a kind of methodological theology, driven by desire.

of radical, subjunctive, political theology appearing here something different: *resisting theology.*

Resisting theology is a *methodological* political theology. Rather than examining existing phenomena for their hidden theological underpinnings or unacknowledged influences—as if theology is the key to understanding what's really been happening all along—resisting theology instead applies theological thinking, through subjunctivity, as a way of understanding and interpreting acts, movements, and events of political resistance. It is not an attempt to chart a shift from theology to politics or vice versa, but rather to take these two together. It remains political-theological in its frames of reference, but also takes the death of God as axiomatic, and thus reads subjunctivity more openly than orthodox theological expressions might accept. Its understanding of religious ritual stretches to include a variety of human activities that are only counterintuitively so-described. I argue that religious community is only truly possible in God's absence. This means that the most appropriate places to look for religious community are the ones wherein nothing explicitly religious appears at first glance.

This all begins with subjunctivity as its foundation. In that spirit, I take Kierkegaard's comment about Hegel—that if he had introduced his project with the comment that everything to follow would be an experiment, it would have been the greatest work of philosophy ever created—very seriously.[12] I insist that there is an experimental thread running throughout this project. And I also wager that not only is such an experiment valuable in its own right, but performing such experiments is the imperative of the humanities within the academy.

Subjunctivity is both the foundation for the religious and the social. By extension, it is thus the foundation of the political. There is a deep current running under both religion and politics, feeding them both, creating the conditions of the possibility of both. I explain this more fully in Chap. 4, "Resisting Theology Part 2." But one needn't appeal solely to what is prior to do this work. I wager it is useful to proceed *as if a theology of resistance were already meaningful.* Afterward, in retrospect, it will be possible and appropriate to judge the quality of the performance. The second half of the

---

[12] See Søren Kierkegaard, *Søren Kierkegaard's Papers and Journals Vol. 1*, trans. Howard V. Hong, Edna H. Hong, and Gregor Malantschuk (Bloomington: Indiana University Press, 1967–1978), from an entry in 1844, p. 87. "If Hegel had written the whole of his logic and then said, in the preface or some other place, that it was merely an experiment in thought in which he had even begged the question in many places, then he would certainly have been the greatest thinker who had ever lived. As it is, he is merely comic."

book is devoted to this experiment in reading real cases of resistance theologically. I'm not interested in the supersessionism of trying to discover a kind of crypto-theology lurking underneath secular political movements. I'm arguing that theology does not exist on its own but is rather generated within resistance. Resistance doesn't reveal the theological underneath.

This book is an interdisciplinary approach to religion and politics because the topic suggests such an approach. To attempt a thinking of religion and political resistance together without a supersessionist agenda, one must cross disciplinary boundaries with regard, but without respect. This is why the book is constructed along two fronts: the first is descriptive, comparative, and interpretive, and the second is constructive. The fields of political theology, radical theology, political theory, philosophy, anthropology, social theory, and history provide insight into the basic foundations of the key concepts under investigation. Specifically, this book depends on Carl Schmitt's understanding of political theology and sovereignty,[13] Roy A. Rappaport's anthropology of authority and the development of religion and language in early humanity,[14] and Paul Tillich, Dietrich Bonhoeffer, Thomas J. J. Altizer, and Charles Winquist's work on radical theology.[15] As the interdisciplinary approach purports, no single vantage point provides a clear picture of any complex subject. A compendium of several views taken from diverse perspectives is necessary to build a more comprehensive understanding of complex and interrelated phenomena. Then I proceed with a constructive work by using radical political theology as a hermeneutic to better understand various cases of resistance in our current, neoliberal milieu. The end of the project experiments with the construction of a radical political-theological understanding of important political events occurring in the world today.

---

[13] Carl Schmitt, *Political Theology: Four Chapters on the Concept of Sovereignty*, trans. George Schwab (Chicago and London: University of Chicago Press, 2006) and *The Concept of the Political*, trans. George Schwab (Chicago and London: University of Chicago Press, 2007).

[14] Roy A. Rappaport, *Ecology, Meaning, and Religion* (Berkeley, CA: North Atlantic Books, 1979) and *Ritual and Religion in the Making of Humanity* (Cambridge, UK: Cambridge University Press, 1999).

[15] Paul Tillich, *Theology of Culture*; Dietrich Bonhoeffer, *Letters and Papers from Prison*, ed. Eberhard Bethge (New York: Touchstone, 1997); Altizer and Hamilton, *Radical Theology and the Death of God*; Thomas J. J. Altizer, *The Call to Radical Theology*, ed. Lissa McCullough (Albany: SUNY Press, 2012), *The Gospel of Christian Atheism* (Philadelphia: The Westminster Press, 1966), and *Living the Death of God* (Albany: State University of New York Press, 2006); Winquist, *Desiring Theology*.

This book is a work of theory. It broadly introduces a new theoretical framework based in interdisciplinary research. That is, this book argues that subjunctivity is at the root of both political resistance and religion. The bulk of the first half of it is devoted to justifying that claim. In the end, its final step is to apply radical political-theological methods within this context to illuminate and describe some of the ways in which seemingly disparate phenomena are more closely connected than they might appear. To do so, it explains contributing and conflicting theories, refining and critiquing them as necessary, and attempts to set an agenda for thinking differently about them and applying them in creative ways. While this is a theoretically driven book, I nevertheless turn to the practical in the second half and apply the theoretical work to the cases of AIDS Coalition to Unleash Power (ACT UP), Occupy Wall Street, and #BlackLivesMatter. This is to say that, while theoretical, this book also works toward a practical application of its ideas.

The central argument of Chap. 2 is that religion is a force that makes the world, and that religious community operates best without God. This chapter investigates the meaning of religious practice in light of the developments arising from my reading of Rappaport. I argue that subjunctivity short-circuits sovereignty producing a reorientation of political theology. The chapter begins with an in-depth analysis of the term "subjunctivity" by way of a comparison of subjunctivity with sovereignty and subjectivity. I then investigate the power of religion to create and harness illusion—a paradigmatic expression of subjunctivity—whether for good or for ill. Chapter 2 engages with Karl Marx, Sigmund Freud, and Dōgen Zenji in an attempt to arrive at positive resources of the subjunctive in religion.[16] This prompts a need for a more significant investigation of religious language due to the inability to adequately define religion fully. Paul Tillich's understanding of religion as orientation toward what ultimately concerns us is significant here for its circumvention of traditional theism. Next, the chapter investigates two different expressions of what I take to be subjunctive, liberatory religious practice: craft and apophatic mysticism. Taken together with the need for an investigation into religious language, this section

[16] Marx, "Theses on Feuerbach" and Karl Marx and Friedrich Engels, *On Religion* (Atlanta: Scholars Press, 1964); Sigmund Freud, *New Introductory Lectures on Psychoanalysis* (New York: Vintage, 2001), *The Future of an Illusion*, and *Civilization and Its Discontents*; and Dōgen and Thomas F. Cleary, *Shōbōgenzō: Zen Essays by Dōgen* (Honolulu: University of Hawaii Press, 1991).

examines subjunctive apophaticism and world-construction through these two possibilities. It argues, through craft and negative theology, that love is a religious expression of subjunctivity that creates social bonds. It then turns to figures firmly rooted in their respective traditions and draws atheological insights from them. Martin Buber argues that we find God in each other person and that the traditional image of God may function as an idol, and René Girard suggests that the God of the Christian Bible slowly withdraws from the realm of human interaction leaving us alone with ritual, but not God in the end.[17] Both of these are essentially descriptive claims as to how religious community might understand itself without God in its midst.

This second chapter also makes a methodological claim about the role of theology. That is, I argue based on my reading of Paul Tillich's *Theology of Culture*, that theology may be cleaved from any particular object of study (traditionally, God) and it should instead be understood as a way of thinking.[18] This way of thinking—this radical theology—is oriented toward its ultimate concern in such a way that it is simultaneously relentless and iconoclastic, paradoxically desirous of that which might stand up to its suspicion of ultimacy, and scrutinous of theological claims. Radical theology is ultimately concerned with being suspicious of claims of ultimacy. So, in this chapter, I argue that both religious practice and theological thinking operate best in the absence of God.

In Chap. 3, I engage with Carl Schmitt's political theology as both descriptive and normative. He uncovers and examines the ways in which theological concepts became secularized into modern political concepts, and he valorizes sovereignty. Schmitt's political theology is therefore quite specific in its parasitism on the modern nation State. Schematically, the normative claim in Chap. 3 is that (a) political theology should be founded upon a non-theistic concept of religion, which (b) has at its center the ability of ritual to construct the bonds of social solidarity, which (c) in turn is the seat of religion's authority and the condition of political possibility, which (d) operates through open, critical, and creative imagining of the way the world might be—subjunctivity.

In Chap. 4, "Resisting Theology Part 2," I chart the historical development of the relationship between religion and politics. I begin with the early modern formation of the State. I argue that the medieval and modern

---

[17] Martin Buber, *I and Thou*, trans. Walter Kaufmann (New York: Simon and Schuster, 1996); and René Girard, *Things Hidden Since the Foundation of the World*, trans. Stephen Bann and Michael Metteer (Stanford: Stanford University Press, 1987).
[18] Tillich, *Theology of Culture*.

understanding of politics and religion was founded upon an underlying, animating concept of sovereignty. Understanding modernity as perpetual disintegration and renewal, I take politics to be the principal force behind disintegration and religion the principal force behind renewal or maintenance during this period. Politics, the realm newly dominated by the State, was a disordering force in the world. Its process during modernity is a disordering one. It's the force of war and State-making. Religion, on the other hand, develops in modernity into a private affair, still based on and inspired by sovereign power, as a way of ordering social life and maintaining a sense of meaning in a rapidly changing world. I argue that our contemporary situation lies at the end of modernity, where this relationship between religion and politics has changed. Rather than conceiving of modernity as a proper stage in its own right, I understand modernity to have been a transition from a period of sovereignty as the animator of social life to our current period when sovereignty has been dissolved into the market. Liberalism is the vehicle of this transition.

After the transitional phase of modernity, in our time, resistance is the theological enacted politically. It is the expression of the theological—of desire for an alternate, less disappointing world—within the political sphere. Theology is the impulse toward resistance brought into the political ordering of life. Resistance takes up the meaning-making function of religion within the sphere of the political. Resistance is the political act through which the desire for a world that does not disappoint becomes expressed. Resistance is the activity through which theology animates the political. Theology itself is thus insurrectionary. This lays the groundwork for the examination of resistance movements that come next.

The second half of this book is a performance of resisting theology. To do so, it sets the stage through an examination of the concept of the city in its first section. It draws significantly on Thomas Merton, Michel de Certeau, and David Harvey.[19] Harvey helps to lay out the city as the site of subjunctive politics and Certeau provides a way for reading and understanding urban activity. In short, Certeau argues that methods of interpreting language may be applied to urban activities such that one

---

[19] Thomas Merton, *Love and Living*, ed. Naomi Burton Stone and Brother Patrick Hart (San Diego: Harcourt, Inc., 1979); Michel de Certeau, *The Practice of Everyday Life*, trans. Steven Rendall (Berkeley: University of California Press, 1988); and David Harvey, "The Right to the City," *New Left Review* (53: September/October 2008), and edited and reprinted in *Rebel Cities* (London: Verso, 2012).

might read a pedestrian's walk through a city like a text. Further, Certeau provides a hermeneutic of thinking about the city theologically. The connections between urban resistance and theology will thus begin to become clear. Merton argues for the city as the site of celebration and communion, further solidifying this link and harkening back to Rappaport in the process.

"Resisting Theology Part 2" concludes by examining the concept of the city as it relates to both the political and the theological. Through critical readings of Michel de Certeau and Thomas Merton's work on how people perform acts of resistance in cities, I argue that the city is both a theological object and produces political resistance.[20] The city is the site of the theology I have been constructing. The chapter then briefly discusses Jeffrey W. Robbins's claim that radical democracy is the political instantiation of the death of God through a critical engagement with the idea of anarchism, as an alternative to the language of radical democracy.[21] I compare the radical democracy described by Jeffrey W. Robbins with anarchism as described by Maia Ramnath. In short, Robbins argues that democracy is the very principle of politics, while—based on Ramnath—I suggest that anarchy is the political expression that most self-consciously exhibits that principle. Radical democracy thus *is* anarchy. I argue here that anarchic resistance is theological activity.

Chapter 5 builds upon each of the previous chapters, synthesizing their arguments and applying them to the case of the AIDS Coalition to Unleash Power (ACT UP). Chapter 5 is oriented toward the poetic act of meaning-making, political resistance, and theology of desire exhibited by ACT UP. ACT UP was a non-religious and at times anti-religious organization, so it might seem odd at first to write a theology of it. I justify this endeavor broadly by arguing for a theological thinking oriented toward desire, meaning-making, and the creation of alternate possible worlds. The implication is that theology is always already political. That allows for both political readings of the theological and, perhaps more controversially, theological readings of the political. In that spirit and examining ACT UP's general engagement with death and political funerals specifically, this chapter examines a secular political organization like ACT UP through a theological lens.

---

[20] Michel de Certeau, *The Practice of Everyday Life*, trans. Stephen Rendall (Berkeley: University of California Press, 1988); and Merton, *Love and Living*.
[21] Robbins, *Radical Democracy and Political Theology*.

Chapter 6 is about Occupy Wall Street. After the development of the concept of subjunctivity out of Rappaport, as understood regarding craft and apophaticism, and as it constructs religious community in God's absence, the political commitments that arise out of this theological thinking find their application in the event of Occupy Wall Street. Occupy is the occasion for understanding what a theology of resistance might look like. The first part of the chapter details the events and conditions of late 2010 and the first half of 2011 that led up to the occupation of Zuccotti Park on September 17. Included are the Arab Spring, the Wisconsin State House takeover, and the 15-M Movement in Spain. The next part examines Slavoj Žižek's claim that Occupy is the Holy Spirit by using theology as a method to interpret the general structure and quality of Occupy Wall Street. Occupy's modeling of social relations differently—specifically through anarchic modes of organization and participatory democracy—is exemplary of the kind of subjunctive creation of social solidarity, arising out of my appropriation of Rappaport in Chap. 2. The third part examines Occupy Wall Street's refusal to make concrete demands through a methodological transposition that attempts to think of Occupy as politically apophatic.

Chapter 7 is on the movement for Black lives. The #BlackLivesMatter movement's most controversial moments have centered on the destruction of property. Freddie Gray was killed in Baltimore by police on April 19, 2015. On April 27, what the media reported as a "riot" began at the Mondawmin Mall. Many of #BlackLivesMatter's most notable actions have involved direct interference with the normal operations of businesses. Beginning with a theoretical reading of the role of property in American life, this chapter reads the act of property destruction as a decolonial act—a kind of iconoclasm against colonial structures of power. In the movement for Black lives, such acts force us to choose which we value more: human life or property. The destruction of property by people whose ancestors had been owned—who *were* property—should be understood as a direct and obvious reclaiming of their very humanity. Far from being nihilistic, property destruction is an affirmation of life. Riots are thus theological and property destruction is a deeply theological act.

There is a consciousness-raising component to all of this. That is, it is widely speculated that the future of the academy is in interdisciplinarity. I don't anticipate the longevity of the liberal arts. But insofar as the university has a future outside of professional studies, that future is interdisciplinary. We are living in a time of what appears to be increasingly accelerating change in all facets of life: economics, politics, religion, science, technology, art, and education. This book is an attempt at a performance within that context for the sake of illuminating it more fully. It suggests that politics and religion need to be thought together, but not in the traditional ways in which this has been done. The dominant categories for understanding the relationship between religion and politics are fast becoming outdated. This book attempts to contribute to the burgeoning of a new understanding of how that might be approached.

Regarding contributing to the disciplines of philosophy of religion and theology, I follow Jeffrey W. Robbins' charge. He has argued at length that political theology has been insufficiently radical and radical theology has been insufficiently political while politics itself has been insufficiently theological.[22] A constructive and interdisciplinary research project that connects global capitalism, secularity, and political resistance is sorely needed. This project attempts to take up that challenge and combat that problem.

Political theology has tended, in the wake of Carl Schmitt, toward the anti-democratic. Radical theology, especially through its engagement with deconstruction, has become so focused on text, language, and aesthetics that it has become politically apathetic. And with the rise of religious fanaticism, political theory has had a tendency toward writing off the religious as aberrant, violent, and unhelpful in the political sphere. Religion, so goes the logic, is best when it remains private.[23] But each of these perspectives is fantastic. Each prefers selective blindness to the reality of our condition. This book attempts to think the reality of the relationship between each—political theology, radical theology, and political theory, action, and power—without cynicism in a creative, forward-moving way.

If the primary theme of this project is subjunctivity, I hope to perform it as well. That is, not only should this book demonstrate what subjunctivity is and what its implications for politics and religion are, I hope it *acts subjunctively* as well. I hope for it to be a performance of the subjunctive in its own right. Given my view about the subjunctive, that means that this book is both a political project and a theological one. As Robbins asks, "What if the very imagination of a more democratic future is itself a political act?"[24]

---

[22] See Robbins, *Radical Democracy*.

[23] John Rawls may be the most significant proponent of this view. He argues that one's private religious convictions may be translated into the language of public reason in order to be expressed politically and publicly, but that one's religion must remain, fundamentally, in the private sphere. See John Rawls, *A Theory of Justice* (Cambridge, MA and Oxford: Harvard University Press, 1971).

[24] Robbins, 49.

With that question in mind, this book's meditation on imagination demonstrates its desire for a thinking that does not disappoint, but also one that makes the world anew. "Politics-as-democracy consists in the belief that this world could be otherwise," continues Robbins.[25] The need for subjunctive living and thinking is becoming increasingly more critical.

Immanuel Kant once wrote, "He who would know the world must first manufacture it."[26] The theorist, who would know the world, must first make the world by hand. Marx said that philosophers have endeavored to understand the world, but our goal should be to change it. Theologians have endeavored to understand the world and God. The imperative, then, is to make them anew. The work of political theology is to inform both religion and politics in their manufacture of alternate worlds. Lest the reader gets the impression that this emphasis on alternate futures, possibility, and the world as if it were otherwise is a kind of escapism, neglect, or abandonment of the present, we would be wise to remember that to resist the present, you've got to be there.

---

[25] Robbins, 63.
[26] Immanuel Kant, *Opus Postumum*, ed. Eckart Förster, trans. Eckart Förster and Michael Rosen (Cambridge, UK: Cambridge University Press, 1993), 240.

CHAPTER 2

Subjunctivity

RELIGION, NOT SPIRITUALITY

Religion is subjunctive. In using "subjunctive," I'm referring to the grammatical mood of a verb used to express uncertainty, hypothesis, contingency, possibility, desire, potentiality, necessity, hope, or action that has not yet occurred.[1] Experimentally extrapolated out into a concept, the subjunctive points to a void. In short, the subjunctive describes the world, not as it is, but as it might be. This "might be" is the root of religious world-construction through theology, myth, and ritual. Subjunctivity uproots the world the way it has been and plants new possibilities in its place. The world becomes meaningful through subjunctivity. As a result, subjunctivity has clear political implications in addition to its religious ones. I would like to investigate some of the ways in which subjunctivity might be thought in terms of lived religion—regarding the material conditions in everyday life—and in terms of political resistance. I conclude that religion creates the illusion of the social order in which we all might participate and that such work is usefully construed in terms of craft—the material building and repairing of the world in which we live.

---

[1] See *The Oxford English Dictionary*, second edition, prepared by J. A. Simpson and E. S. C. Weiner, Volume XVII: Su-Thrivingly (Oxford: Clarendon Press, 1991), 35–36: "Designating or relating to a verbal mood that refers to an action or state as conceived (rather than as a fact) and is therefore used chiefly to express a wish, command, exhortation, or a contingent, hypothetical, or prospective event."

Sigmund Freud understood the subjunctive component of religion, if incompletely. He wrote, "Religion is an attempt to get control over the sensory world, in which we are placed, by means of the wish-world, which we have developed inside us as a result of biological and psychological necessities."[2] Here is the recognition of the subjunctive possibilities of religious belief, but as a danger, rather than a boon. Religion, for Freud, is a flight from life. Similarly, Karl Marx recognized this "wish-world" component of religion but framed it in terms of protest. He famously wrote:

> Religious distress is at the same time the expression of real distress and the protest against real distress. Religion is the sigh of the oppressed creature, the heart of a heartless world, just as it is the spirit of a spiritless situation. It is the opium of the people. The abolition of religion as the illusory happiness of the people is required for their real happiness. The demand to give up the illusion about its condition is the demand to give up a condition which needs illusions.[3]

Religion is a protest. Religion is what people turn to when their material conditions are intolerable. The implication of Marx's insight is that instead of focusing on religion, one should be more concerned with the material conditions in which people live and upon which they depend. For Marx, if one changes the conditions, beliefs will follow, and illusions will evaporate. As religion is the expression of distress, if the cause of the distress is removed, so will be the need for religion. Abolish poverty and religion will disappear. This is particularly appropriate today in the marketplace of ideas wherein religion has itself become an object of consumption.[4] Only since the twentieth century with the widespread use of information technology, mass communications, and mass transit has it become possible to shop the marketplace of religions the way one would shop for most any other consumable object. Religion's ties to communities, traditions, and geographies are loosening. Today, religion has become a product, bought, sold, and consumed. Religious paraphernalia and practices have become

---

[2] Sigmund Freud, *New Introductory Lectures on Psychoanalysis* (New York: Vintage, 2001), 215.

[3] Karl Marx, "Contribution to the Critique of Hegel's Philosophy of Right." Karl Marx and Friedrich Engels. *On Religion*. Atlanta: Scholars Press, 1964. 41–58. 42.

[4] See, for instance, "Religion and Consumption: The Profane Sacred," a special issue of *Advances in Consumer Research*, ed. Güliz Ger, Vol. 32 (2005). http://www.acrwebsite.org/volumes/v32/acr_vol32_44.pdf.

commodified. Illusory happiness is much more effective when it can be purchased.

The anthropologist Roy A. Rappaport is no stranger to these types of critiques of religion, of which both Freud's and Marx's focus on the psychological component of religious belief. There is, of course, much more to religion than its adherents' beliefs. For instance, Emile Durkheim distinguishes between belief which he argues is private, and religion which is social. But even more recently, there has been an explosion of interest in the study of "lived religion": emphasis on the experiential and material aspects of religious practice while deemphasizing issues of doctrine. Rappaport's focus on ritual action as the solution to anxiety produced by language and rationality makes for an interesting point of contact with Freud and Marx on this point. Interestingly, belief is not necessary for ritual to create a sense of alienation in its performers. Rappaport explains that insofar as anxieties, but not their causes, are alleviated by participation in ritual, then ritual is just as Freud and Marx argued: a neurosis or opiate. Rituals function as benevolent lies, reinforcing suffering while deluding the faithful, promising salvation.

> But the cost is great even for those who are not deluded. For them ritual becomes empty and meaningless, indeed the very term "ritual" comes to denote empty form (Douglas 1970: 19). The act of ritual acceptance, once more profound than belief, becomes a proverbial form of hypocrisy. But in refusing to participate hypocritically no less than in hypocritical participation, the conscious minds of men and women become divorced from those deep and hidden portions of themselves to which ritual participation introduced and bound them. The self becomes fragmented and some of the fragments may be lost. The consciousness that remains is likely to remain trapped in its radical separation. For those not deluded there is alienation.[5]

Freud wanted to heal suffering, and Marx wanted to change the world. And they both thought the abolition of religion was a necessary precondition for significant progress to occur. But here we see that Rappaport is not so narrow in his understanding of religion. For him, religion creates the possibilities for both alienation and liberation, while the refusal to participate in the subjunctivity of ritual will indeed lead to alienation. Of course, given the right conditions, religion both causes and is the result of

---

[5] Roy A. Rappaport, *Ecology, Meaning, and Religion* (Berkeley, CA: North Atlantic Books, 1979), 241.

alienation and neurosis. But religion might also provide us with a way out. Again, Rappaport argues "...that aspects of religion, particularly as generated in ritual, ameliorate problems of falsehood intrinsic to language to a degree sufficient to allow human sociability to have developed and to be maintained."[6]

I should be clear that illusion is not the same thing as delusion or deception. Rappaport's commenters—Adam B. Seligman, Robert P. Weller, Michael J. Puett, and Bennett Simon—write, "Illusions are not lies—they are a form of the subjunctive. Illusion is what can be, as indeed so many different symbolic worlds can."[7] Further, Seligman and his coauthors continue explaining that rituals "create an illusion, but with no attempt to deceive. This is a crucial difference from a lie, which is an illusion with a clear attempt to deceive the other. In this ritual is much more like play, which is the joint entrance into an illusionary world."[8] Contrary to Freud and Marx, this understanding of ritual may now provide us with the ability to say that the work of religion is precisely and necessarily to create the illusion of the social order in which we all might participate. This implicitly requires an understanding of the world as inherently meaningless and requiring of our investing of meaning in it. Ritual is the method through which one makes such an investment. Religion's illusions, if overcome, would result in social disintegration.

Zen Buddhism is a religious tradition that self-consciously takes on its own illusions, promoting them as both useful and illusory. Rather than trying to establish its doctrines and practices as true, Zen owns up to the idea that religion plays with illusions and instead appropriates what has amounted to a critique for its own uses. Zen doesn't deny that religion produces illusions; it *emphasizes* it. Eihei Dōgen, the medieval Zen philosopher, understood the power of illusion within religious thinking and its relationship to the inherent meaninglessness of the world very well. That is, Dōgen understood what Rappaport has been telling us—that the world means nothing until we create it subjunctively. It is useful to read Dōgen as a religious source for some of the positive possibilities of religion. For him, even religion's illusions are beneficial, but in a counterintuitive way. Paradoxically,

---

[6] Roy A. Rappaport, *Ritual and Religion in the Making of Humanity* (Cambridge, UK: Cambridge University Press, 1999), 15–16.

[7] Adam B. Seligman, Robert P. Weller, Michael J. Puett, and Bennett Simon, *Ritual and Its Consequences: An Essay on the Limits of Sincerity* (Oxford and New York: Oxford University Press, 2008), 22.

[8] Seligman et al., 22.

religion's illusions confront the world as it really is—not as a therapeutic avoidance or existential flight from the absurdity or trauma of life. But— and this is the paradox—that *as it really is* is illusory. The world is subjunctive.

Dōgen uses the phrase "flowers in the sky" as a metaphor for illusion. He recounts that having an accurate outlook, "Shakyamuni Buddha said, 'It is like someone with cataracts seeing flowers in the sky: when the affliction of cataracts is removed, the flowers perish in the sky.'"[9] Dōgen's translator and commentator, Thomas Cleary, explains that to make sense of Dōgen's preoccupation with this phrase, one must understand that "Reality, in Kegon [Buddhist] terms, means the interdependence of all things, which also means the 'emptiness' of things in themselves."[10] Cleary continues:

> The word for "sky" in the expression "flowers in the sky" is the same Sino-Japanese as the word for the Buddhist term "emptiness," so this expression could also be read from Chinese as "empty flowers" or "flowers of emptiness." Dōgen stresses that everything without exception is "flowers in the sky." The traditional saying that "flowers in the sky" are due to cataracts or obstructions in the eye is here [in Dōgen's essay] presented positively, with "cataracts" being used to refer to compassion, or nonextinction, the acceptance and recognition of life as it is.[11]

With all of this in mind, one should consider that Dōgen interprets the Buddha's parable differently than might be intuitive.

> Know that the person with cataracts spoken of by the Buddha is the originally enlightened person, the ineffably enlightened person, the person of the Buddhas, the person of the three worlds, the person beyond Buddha. Do not ignorantly consider cataracts to be delusive factors and thus study as if there were something else which is real—that would be a small view. If cataract flowers are delusions, the agent and action wrongly clinging to them as delusions would have to be delusions. If they are all delusions, there can be no logical reasoning. If there is no reason established, the fact that cataract flowers are delusions cannot be so.[12]

---

[9] Dōgen and Thomas F. Cleary, *Shōbōgenzō: Zen Essays by Dōgen* (Honolulu: University of Hawaii Press, 1991) 64.
[10] Dōgen and Cleary, 68.
[11] Dōgen and Cleary, 65.
[12] Dōgen and Cleary, 69.

Illusion, then, is Enlightenment. These two categories cannot be separated in Dōgen's Zen Buddhism. The older school of Theravada Buddhism stresses individual liberation through the annihilation of the illusion of permanence. This is the small view. But Dōgen's variety of Mahayana Buddhism—the great vehicle—focuses instead on universal liberation by a different approach.

Trying to annihilate illusion suggests that the illusion exists—that it is a thing to be annihilated. The annihilation of illusion requires the *reality* of the illusion. Dōgen suggests instead that everything, without qualification, is illusion—everything is flowers in the sky. The goal of religious practice, as Dōgen would have it, is to attain liberation through comprehending illusion, not annihilating it. Cleary writes, "…instead of treating illusion as something to be annihilated, Dōgen points out that all is illusion, and being empty in its very essence is in that sense identical to absolute reality." He further writes:

> This is like saying that all existence is relative and therefore empty of absolutes, so to realize emptiness it is not necessary to annihilate existence. In fact, the very idea of annihilating presumes existence as something in itself real, hence is illusion within illusion. Dōgen points out that not only mundane things are 'flowers in the sky,' but so are the Buddhist teachings themselves.[13]

This kind of emptiness is the precondition for creativity. A blank page makes a drawing, a letter, or origami possible. For my purposes here, Dōgen should be understood as arguing that religious subjunctivity is a creative enterprise. Religion's illusions create the world. Or, in Dōgen's own words, "Therefore know that flowers in the sky have the meaning of causing both earth and sky to bloom."[14]

This is why contrary to Marx and Freud, illusion is not pathological in and of itself. In fact, illusion is one of religion's most useful and powerful tools. Reinhold Niebuhr wrote in *Moral Man and Immoral Society* that "the truest visions of religion are illusions which may be partially realized by being resolutely believed, for what religion believes to be true is not wholly true but ought to be true; and may become true if its truth is not doubted."[15] The last comment about doubt is evidence of Niebuhr's Protestantism and is not correct. The truth of religion's illusions is not a matter of their being

---

[13] Dōgen and Cleary, 64.
[14] Dōgen and Cleary, 74.
[15] Reinhold Niebuhr, *Moral Man and Immoral Society* (Louisville, KY: Westminster John Knox Press, 2002), 81.

believed, but being lived. Truth is not here an issue of belief and doubt, but of performance. Enacted illusions are real. Taking Niebuhr together with Rappaport—belief with self-referential action—the truth, the method, and the hope of religion are its performed subjunctivity.

Underneath it all, religion is humanity's subversive force. Religion's subjunctivity has the potential—the charge, even—to undercut the status quo. That is, subjunctivity's insistence upon alternatives is as much about the way the world is and might be as it is about the opposite. Subjunctivity has an apophatic component as well. The world might be otherwise. It also might not be. Subjunctivity allows the thinking of both what the world might be changed into and what it should be changed from. So subjunctivity has a dual perspective. Subjunctivity aims toward alternatives, but for another world to be possible, subjunctivity must also be in negative relation to the way the world is. This is why religion not only makes the world, it remakes it. Another world is possible, indeed. And religion is the method of its construction.

The great twentieth-century theologian Paul Tillich might help us think religion more fully by beginning with a liberatory conception of religion, rather than an oppressive one. Tillich takes Jesus' great commandment as his point of reference. In the Synoptic Gospels, Jesus is asked what the greatest commandment is.[16] Jesus appeals to Deuteronomy 6: 4–5 and says the *Shema*. Jesus explains that the greatest commandment is to love God fully and—in almost the very same breath—supplements the Deuteronomic code with the requirement to love one's neighbor as well. In contemporary language, one might say that the greatest commandment in the Gospels is to "love God and love each other." Indeed, it appears that these two cannot be separated. For Tillich, this is the beginning of how one might think about religion itself. He explains:

> If we abstract the concept of religion from the great commandment, we can say that religion is being ultimately concerned about that which is and should be our ultimate concern. This means that faith is the state of being grasped by an ultimate concern, and God is the name for the content of the concern. Such a concept of religion has little in common with the description of religion as the belief in the existence of a highest being called God, and the theoretical and practical consequences of such a belief. Instead, we are pointing to an existential, not a theoretical, understanding of religion.[17]

---

[16] See Matthew 22:35–40, Mark 12:28–31, and Luke 10:25–28.
[17] Paul Tillich, *Theology of Culture*, ed. Robert C. Kimball (New York: Oxford University Press, 1959), 40.

This might seem counterintuitive. The great commandment insists that one must love God, but Tillich is concerned that we do not get too fixated on God's existence as a matter of theoretical concern. I am arguing for an appropriation of Tillich—possibly his radicalization—to argue that a definition of religion abstracted from the great commandment has little to do with theistic belief. It is not a spirituality or a transcendence. These are the things that theistic belief points toward.

Instead (to take Tillich and run with him), I argue that existential religiosity is a matter of binding ourselves to what concerns us in our practices and immediate existential conditions. It is an immanent religiosity, first and foremost. This is not necessarily a denial of transcendence or spirituality *tout court*, but rather a reemphasis on the immediacy and close proximity of religious concern. It does not happen over there in that holy place or oriented by a time we call eternity; religion happens here and now in front of us. This radicalization of Tillich is thus a call to reorient transcendence and to emphasize it as a horizontal structure, rather than a vertical one. To love one's neighbor is to drop one's eyes from their heavenly gaze and to look out—perhaps infinitely—over the world.[18]

There, faith becomes possible through theological method rather than its object. Once one becomes open to the idea of a theology of culture, rather than a theology of propositional statements about a being called "God," one may recognize that the unconditional element that is constituent of religion for Tillich may, of course, be found in traditional mythological symbols like the gods, but that it may also appear in

> prophetic-political demands for social justice, if they are the ultimate concern of religious and secular movements. It can occur in the honesty and ultimate devotion of the servants of scientific truth. It can occur in the universalism of the classical idea of personality and in the Stoic (ancient and modern) attitude of elevation over the vicissitudes of existence. *In all these cases the risk of faith is an existential risk, a risk in which the meaning and fulfillment of our lives is at stake, and not a theoretical judgment which may be refuted sooner or later.*[19]

---

[18] Jacob Taubes locates this call in Paul. In Romans 13:8–10 wherein Paul summarizes Jesus' comments on the greatest commandment (Matthew 22:36–40), Paul argues that all of the law is summed up by the command, "Love your neighbor as yourself." Paul continues, writing "Love does no wrong to a neighbor; therefore, love is the fulfilling of the law." On this point, Taubes remarks that Paul has taken Jesus' dual commandment—to love God and love each other—and made them equivocal. "No dual commandment, but rather *one* commandment. I regard this as an absolutely revolutionary act" (Jacob Taubes, *The Political Theology of Paul*, trans. Dana Hollander (Stanford: Stanford University Press, 2004), 53.

[19] Tillich, 20. My emphasis.

This final critical line, of course, includes theologically liberal theoretical judgments like religious holism—that underneath it all, the world's religions all aim at the same divinity, like different approaches to climbing the same mountain that nevertheless all arrive at a single peak. Theological holism, or the perennialist position, is thus both naive and existentially trite according to this reading, because it attempts to keep the winnings without the wager. My point here is sustained: that theology and religion are possible without any explicitly religious or theological content. Theology, for Tillich, is a way of thinking and experiencing rather than the study of a specific object in an attempt to open up to the need for an investigation of religious language. "God" does not carry the kind of currency it once did. We have thus arrived at the oddly heretical claim that it is not God, but religion that makes the world.

MANUFACTURING THE WORLD

Matthew B. Crawford's *Shop Class as Soulcraft* describes the deep satisfaction of working with one's hands, building, and fixing things.[20] It is a religious text. As much as it is about making and repairing things—engaging in craft or trade—it is about the ritual construction of the world. Working in a trade is not terribly far from Rappaport's definition of ritual: "the performance of more or less invariant sequences of formal acts and utterances not entirely encoded by the performers."[21] Further, both religious ritual and tradecraft—being useful—require a particular stance toward language. As I demonstrated with Rappaport, self-referential acts cannot be argued because they stand outside of language. Crawford is working in a similar, but more familiar problematic. In the background of his text is the existential angst brought on by postmodernism and pluralism. It is difficult to discern meaning in the world. Similar to Rappaport who posits ritual self-reference as the solution to dishonesty, Crawford's solution to the problem of a world in which multiple authorities compete with one another putting values into question is to *act objectively*. This is objective and satisfying. It is technology-as-solution. Acts do not need reason or language to make sense or be meaningful.

The problems of language might still be approached from a different angle. Rappaport and Crawford are both interested in acting to produce

---

[20] Matthew B. Crawford, *Shop Class as Soulcraft* (New York: Penguin, 2009).
[21] Rappaport, *Ritual and Religion*, 24. I should note that Rappaport admits that "this definition encompasses much more than religious behavior."

meaning. Apophatic mysticism—or negative theology—starts with a similar problematic, but challenges it differently. That is, apophaticism advocates the use of iconoclasm through negative language to self-consciously illuminate language's shortcomings. Language might be honest about its potential for dishonesty by certain tactics.

Qushayri, the great medieval Sufi, writes in his *Principles of Sufism*, that "Those engaged in striving [*mujahada*] prefer silence because they know the dangers of words."[22] He explains that one of the major dangers of speaking is that the speaker tends to find comfort and pride in words. This wariness of speaking exists because—not only does it rationalize and produce confusion—language reifies. It creates things out of no-thing. As such, language can never adequately express any experience, according to Qushayri. This is the same with emotions such as sorrow, fear, and desire which serve to ground us and force us to remember our contingency and the arbitrary nature of language and the constructed nature of culture. Silence, fear, sorrow, and desire are all opposed to institutional religion which reifies scripture, sermons, songs, tradition—praises aimed toward and descriptions of God—all the while forgetting that these are not actually God, Godself.

Language conceptualizes the material world and our experiences, and concepts lose specificity. Any abstraction loses the specific idiosyncrasies of any particular. The problem is one of meaning and language. Language is a system of concepts and always falls short of what it attempts to describe. One can use countless words to describe an event or object, but one will never be able to describe everything adequately, not to mention the additional and unintending connotations that each word would carry to its audience that would be unfairly attributed to that event or object. Language both falls short in accuracy and adds extras to what it describes.

This is why one cannot say what is; one can only do what is.[23] Reason, based in language, always breaks down to the point that a new and unencumbered authority becomes necessary. Farid ud-Din Attar, in *The Conference of the Birds*, writes, "Whoever is grounded firm in love renounces faith, religion, and unbelief."[24] All propositions and institu-

---

[22] Al-Qushayri, *Principles of Sufism*, trans. B. R. von Schlegell (Oneonta, NY: Mizan Press, 1990), 49.

[23] See Ralf Dahrendorf: "Homo Sociologicus: On the History, Significance, and Limits of the Category of Social Role," *Essays in the Theory of Society* (Stanford, CA: Stanford University Press, 1968).

[24] Farid ud-Din Attar, *The Conference of the Birds*, trans. C. S. Nott (Accord, NY: Pir Press, 1998), 33.

tional structures crumble before love. Love cannot be proposed or institutionalized. Love is anarchic. The Hoopoe bird in that same text comments that

> reason cannot live with the folly of love; love has nothing to do with human reason. If you possessed inner sight, the atoms of the visible world would be manifested to you. But if you look at things with the eye of ordinary reason you will never understand how necessary it is to love. Only a man who has been tested and is free can feel this. He who undertakes this journey [to find God] should have a thousand hearts so that he can sacrifice one at every moment.[25]

Love becomes the doing of what is when language loses its meaning. Love, then, is much closer to authoritative self-referentiality—an authority that holds its authority by appealing to itself, rather than to another outside authority—than it might seem.

As a result, language itself is the ultimate idol, just as representatives of the self-referential—charismatic, sovereign figures—are prone to be idolized. Maybe this is why God's name is unpronounceable. Words are power and power corrupts.[26] Words divide and God is unified. To name God would be to cut God into parts. This is why mysticism seeks to move beyond language. Mysticism itself is the image of God in that it allows for possibility, resists definitional confinement, defies conclusion, and yet nonetheless creates and impassions. Meister Eckhart—the mystic who was tried for heresy before the Inquisition and Pope John XXII in the 1320s—wrote that

> God is nameless, for no one can speak of him or know him. ... Accordingly, if I say that "God is good," this is not true. ... If I say again that "God is wise," then this too is not true. ... Or if I say that "God exists," this also is not true. He is being beyond being, he is a nothingness beyond being. Therefore St Augustine says: "The finest thing that we can say of God is to

---

[25] Attar, 102. Another lovely quote on this point regards the seemingly reckless action that devoted mystics take. Attar writes, "His boldness then is good and laudable, because he is an idiot of love, on fire" (81).

[26] Incidentally, this also seems to relate to God's preference for the poor—those with less power—fewer words—testified to by liberation theologians. Furthermore, perhaps this is why so many have vilified sexuality—often, traditional sexual relationships are relationships of domination and submission. As God sides with the downtrodden, a system which dominates is rendered corrupt.

be silent concerning him from the wisdom of inner riches." Be silent therefore, and do not chatter about God, for by chattering about him, you tell lies and commit a sin. ... If you wish to be perfect and without sin, then do not prattle about God. Also you should not wish to understand anything about God, for God is beyond all understanding. A master [Augustine, in sermon 117] says: If I had a God that I could understand, I would not regard him as God.[27]

Eckhart explains "that we should forsake God is altogether what God intends, for as long as the soul has God, knows God and is aware of God, she is far from God. This then is God's desire—that God should reduce himself to nothing in the soul so that the soul may lose herself."[28] Language does not provide comfort; only God can do that—the God beyond all words. Furthermore, Pseudo-Dionysius writes that "[God] is neither contained nor comprehended by anything. He reaches out to everything and beyond everything and does so with unfailing generosity and unstinted activity."[29] It is impossible to rest in uncontainment. This is the profound paradox of religious passion. How can one settle on that which shifts? Language inevitably falls short and disintegrates. Someone needs to come along and fix things. The negative path of the mystics points not to nihilism, but rather to possibility.

Crawford's craftsman is a religious character in this sense. The repairman "...seems to pose a challenge to our self-understanding that is somehow fundamental. We are not as free and independent as we thought. Street-level work that disrupts the infrastructure (the sewer system below or the electrical grid above) brings our *shared* dependence into view."[30] It is this simultaneous issue of material dependence and the impotence of language that makes craft religious. "Because craftsmanship refers to objective standards that do not issue from the self and its desires, it poses a challenge to the ethic of consumerism...."[31] The repairman and the mystic illuminate uncomfortable subjunctivity. And subjunctivity is what creates the world.

---

[27] Meister Eckhart, *Meister Eckhart: Selected Writings*, ed. Oliver Davies (NY: Penguin, 1994), 236–7.

[28] Eckhart, 207.

[29] Pseudo-Dionysius, "The Divine Names," in *Light from Light: An Anthology of Christian Mysticism*, eds. Louis Dupré and James A. Wiseman, OSB (New York/Mahwah, NJ: Paulist Press, 2001), 82.

[30] Crawford, 17.

[31] Crawford, 17.

Let us not forget that in the Bible, God's first appearance is as a creator. It is true, initially, God creates through speech.[32] But this speech-creation is not enough for the authors and editors of Genesis. After God speaks, God sculpts and gardens.

> Then the Lord God formed man of dust from the ground, and breathed into his nostrils the breath of life; and man became a living being. The Lord God planted a garden toward the east, in Eden; and there He placed the man whom He had formed. Out of the ground the Lord God caused to grow every tree that is pleasing to the sight and good for food; the tree of life also in the midst of the garden, and the tree of the knowledge of good and evil.[33]

Within the narrative, God's creative power of speech is not enough. When it comes to the details, God does not leave creation to speech. God becomes a craftsperson, molding and cultivating creation with divine hands and breath. One cannot ever say what is. One can only do what is. Language only takes us so far before it breaks down requiring self-referential action.

Apophatic mysticism leverages this approach to language in its understanding of the way religion should work. Mysticism is the critique of institutional religion, subjunctively, on the grounds of uncertainty. The mystic and the priest each represent these two broad categories of mysticism and institutional religion, respectively. The priest is official (because of ordination and the de facto way that the institutional powers that be view the priestly office), upholds the status quo, and functions within a prescribed role—that is, the priest is entirely contingent upon his institution. The priest, to use Rappaport's categories, acts within the canonical component of religious practice. The mystic, on the other hand, is not usually officially sanctioned by anyone, often makes radical or even heretical claims, and serves the institution by attempting to revive its un-institutionalizable passion. The mystic is attuned to the subjunctive at the outset. Mysticism is wary of those things which limit us and language is their foundation.

---

[32] In Genesis 1:3, "God said: 'let there be light.'" This "God said" becomes a refrain, repeated nine times throughout the first chapter of Genesis. The Gospel of John echoes the Creation in Genesis in chapter 1, verses 1–4: "In the beginning was the Word, and the Word was with God, and the Word was God. He was with God in the beginning. Through him all things were made; without him nothing was made that has been made. In him was life, and that life was the light of all humankind."

[33] Genesis 2:7–9 (NASB).

While the priest is a pillar of what is, the mystic is the usher of what might be. The priest and the mystic, when engaging in priestly and mystical activities, are always engaged in a struggle with each other. The priest is the champion of orthodoxy, struggling to reign in religious belief and the experiences that stem from those beliefs. The mystic dabbles in heterodoxy, heresy, apostasy, something as-yet undefined in orthodox terms, or even something not contrary to orthodoxy, but deeper than what orthodoxy will allow. The priest and the mystic complement each other through this tension.

The term "mysticism" itself is rather muddy and begs for clarification. However, it functions well muddily because to dry it up would make it crumble. Mysticism's very essence is fluid. It always stands against institutions and, thus, cannot be clearly demarcated as institutions can. When Henri Bergson discusses mysticism, he means

> mystic experience taken in its immediacy, apart from all interpretation. True mystics simply open their souls to the oncoming wave. Sure of themselves, because they feel within them something better than themselves, they prove to be great men of action, to the surprise of those for whom mysticism is nothing but visions, and raptures, and ecstasies. That which they have allowed to flow into them is a stream flowing down and seeking through them to reach their fellow-men; and the necessity to spread around them what they have received affects them like an onslaught of love. A love which each one of them stamps with his own personality.[34]

Mysticism, because it is religious, must always be seen in relationship to institutional religion. And, in the sense that I am using the term here, mystics always come from within institutional religion and consider themselves religious (*re-ligare*), in the vocational sense of the word (i.e., bound). I am content to let the definition of mysticism remain indistinct as the crux of this argument depends on mysticism's adaptability. To box it in with words and to make it finite would suffocate it as it would any living organism cut off from amenities.

One positive or definite thing I can say for mysticism, however, is that it is not entirely separate from institutional religion. These two overlap but retain distinctions. This overlapped area where the two come in contact with each other is my interest. Furthermore, it seems that institutional

---

[34] Henri Bergson, *The Two Sources of Morality and Religion* (Westport, CT: Greenwood Press, 1935 and 1963), 90.

religion and mysticism are mutually dependent. As institutional religion and mysticism—the canonical and the self-referential—are inherently in relationship with each other; they cannot ever be separated, or they would each lose their identities. Both are necessary for a balance of power. For one of these to take complete control would be tyranny on either side—a tyranny of rigid totalitarianism or of spiritual depths so deep, most religious adherents would drown. To put it another, mundane, way, not everyone would make either a good priest or a good mystic. These two vocations are highly selective. However, there is an element of the priestly and the mystical each in all religious adherents. The mystical critique of religion is not necessarily intentional; often mystics do not mean to directly criticize religion. But since mystics are more concerned with a relationship with God than with other people, a criticism of other people tends to come about. In Rumi, for instance, there is a profound sense of humor coupled with humility.[35]

The mystical and priestly roles are similar to Max Weber's two forms of charisma.[36] Weber divided charisma into a pure form and an institutional form. The pure form, loosely speaking, looks a lot like mysticism. It is extraordinary, outside of the realm of daily life; it stands opposed to ordinary structures such as the family and religious institutions, rebellious; and it is individualized. In other words, it sounds a lot like the mystical path. On the other hand, Weber asserts that institutional charisma, which is characterized by social roles, is contained within structures of authority, thus legitimated by the existing structures of society. Yet again, this looks a lot like institutional religion. For Weber, the two cannot exist without each other. A people's need for order, says Weber, and the simultaneous desire to overcome that order always come together because each is insufficient to keep a community going individually. Order (read: religion) is always constraint, but is always necessary—otherwise, at the most basic

---

[35] In his poem on Moses and the Shepherd, Rumi has God saying that "I am not made any purer by [humanity's] praise/Their own impurities these prayers erase/And I pay no attention to their speech/But their intention and the heights they reach: Pure, humble hearts are what I seek/Regardless of the haughty words they speak." And then the narrator continues, "The heart's the essence, words are mere effects/The heart's what counts, the cackle he neglects!/I'm tired of fancy terms and metaphors/I want a soul which burns so much it roars!/It's time to light one's heart with pure desire/Burn thought and contemplation with this fire!/How far apart the meek and well-behaved/From ardent lovers who may seem depraved!" And finally, *"Lovers stand beyond religion's hold,"* (my emphasis).
[36] Weber, Max, *Economy and Society* (Berkley, CA: University of California Press, 1975).

level, no one would be producing food. On the other hand, because order is constraining, people hungrily desire to break free of their restraints.

Still, the two types of charisma, structure and anti-structure, religion and mysticism, need to co-exist. They correct each other. Albert Schweitzer once wrote to his (scandalously) Jewish girlfriend, referring to the Pauline dimension of Friedrich Nietzsche's philosophy, that "in the end, only the blasphemous is true."[37] For this reason, the mystical impulse is necessary to keep religion from strangling itself. Or, in the words of Paul Tillich:

> In its prophetic role the Church is the guardian who reveals dynamic structures in society and undercuts their demonic power by revealing them, even within the Church itself. In so doing the Church listens to prophetic voices outside itself, judging both the culture and the Church in so far as it is a part of the culture. We have referred to such prophetic voices in our culture. Most of them are not active members of the manifest Church. But perhaps one could call them participants of a 'latent Church,' a Church in which the ultimate concern which drives the manifest Church is hidden under cultural forms and deformations.[38]

The iconoclastic, apophatic mystic-craftsman might not be as obvious and visible a character as one might expect. And yet this counter-intuition might be the most significant evidence of its accuracy. One might consider that the one who rails against religion—or who doesn't feel the necessity of recourse to religious terminology and concepts while nevertheless acting subjunctively—is radically religious *precisely for that refusal.*

But while craftsmen and mystics may work by themselves, their work is socially constructive. So the irony has compounded: religious community arises from atheistic religiosity. It is this paradoxical posture to which I turn in the next chapter. While this chapter has argued that religious practice and conviction work best without God, the next argues that religious community works best when God is not its object.

INTRODUCTION TO ILLUSTRATIONS

In the illustrations that follow, I rely on the term "radical theology" throughout. I take radical theology to refer broadly to relentless and iconoclastic thought, paradoxically desirous of that which might stand up to its

---

[37] Albert Schweitzer, *The Albert Schweitzer–Helene Bresslau Letters: 1902–1912,* eds. Rhena Schweitzer Miller and Gustav Woytt, trans. Antje Bultmann Lemke with Nancy Stewart (Syracuse: Syracuse University Press, 2003), 24.

[38] Tillich, 50–51.

suspicion of ultimacy, and scrutinous of theological claims. In the words of Thomas J. J. Altizer,

> a genuinely radical theology is a theological thinking that truly rethinks the deepest ground of theology, a rethinking that is initially an unthinking of every established theological ground; only through such an unthinking can a clearing be established for a theological thinking, and that is the very clearing that is the first goal of radical theology. Nor can this be accomplished by a simple dissolution of our given theological grounds, for those are the very grounds that must here be ultimately challenged, and challenged in terms of their most intrinsic claims.[39]

Radical theology thus takes as one of its most serious concerns suspicion toward any claims to ultimacy. As I showed above, Dōgen's iconoclastic understanding of the traditional Buddhist teachings surrounding illusion is a good example of radical theological thinking. So in Dōgen's case, his is a religious thinking that subverts even traditional Buddhist doctrines surrounding impermanence and desire. I claim, perhaps tendentiously, that Matthew B. Crawford, Farid ud-Din Attar, and Qushayri, referred to previously, and Martin Buber, Paul Tillich, Thomas J. J. Altizer, William Hamilton, and Dietrich Bonhoeffer, to whom I refer later, are all resources for radical theology due to their willingness to think theologically without God.[40] In the move toward a radical political theology, I take these thinkers as resources, to appropriate Altizer, for rethinking the deepest ground of both theology—which is the principal concern here in Chap. 2—*and* politics, which I take up in the next chapter.

The illustration below on Martin Buber discusses the relationship between religion and community. My claim is that at bottom, religion is about two things: communion and the subjunctive mood. Religious

---

[39] Thomas J. J. Altizer, *The Call to Radical Theology*, ed. Lissa McCullough (Albany: SUNY Press, 2012), 1.
[40] See Matthew B. Crawford, *Shop Class as Soulcraft* (New York: Penguin, 2009); Farid ud-Din Attar, *The Conference of the Birds*, trans. C. S. Nott (Accord, NY: Pir Press, 1998); Al-Qushayri, *Principles of Sufism*, trans. B. R. von Schlegell (Oneonta, NY: Mizan Press, 1990); Martin Buber, *I and Thou*, trans. Walter Kaufmann (New York: Simon and Schuster, 1996); Paul Tillich, *Theology of Culture*, ed. Robert C. Kimball (New York: Oxford University Press, 1959); Thomas J. J. Altizer and William Hamilton, *Radical Theology and the Death of God* (Indianapolis and New York: Bobbs-Merrill Company, Inc., 1966); Dietrich Bonhoeffer, *Letters and Papers from Prison*, ed. Eberhard Bethge (New York: Touchstone, 1997); and Philip Hallie, *Lest Innocent Blood Be Shed* (New York: HarperCollins, 1979).

subjunctivity functions, as I demonstrated through my reading of Rappaport, as a way of producing the bonds of social solidarity. Subjunctivity creates community and religion hinges on transcendence. Communion is a kind of self-transcendence wherein the religious person transcends their own solipsism through an experience of entering into a relationship with the divine and/or their community of practitioners. Likewise, the subjunctive—that is, the grammatical mood centered upon what *might be* rather than *what is*—is about transcending any particular reality itself, as it is presented. This may sound otherworldly, but I mean it as a subjunctive claim. Another world is possible and ritual creates a subjunctive world. Quite literally, religion is otherworldly. But this claim should not be taken in its colloquial sense. The otherworldliness of religion is precisely its deep concern with creating the social order here and now.

Ritual—liturgy, prayer, Eucharist, meditation, baptism, confession, Lent, Ramadan, Yom Kippur, as well as shaking hands upon greeting someone, happy hour at the bar, and one's monthly trip to the barber—is one of the most direct expressions of the religious subjunctive. Using the work of Martin Buber and René Girard,[41] I demonstrate later that religious communion is only really possible—however paradoxically—when God is absent. Ritual, not God, makes a community. But we'll go further: God gets in the way. Rappaport demonstrated how ritual subjunctivity creates the social. But the social is only possible in God's absence. So there is a paradox that *religion creates community*, but also that *religious community works best without God*.

In the third illustration, I elaborate upon the notion of radical theology—theology suspicious of and rethinking the deepest ground of theology—theology in the absence of God more fully. The fundamental consideration there is Tillich's theology of culture and definition of religion as ultimate concern.[42] The most significant insight here is that theology might be employed as a method, divorced from any particular object of investigation. Reading Tillich together with Rappaport, the third illustration arrives at a position from which to think of religious language as concerning itself with subjunctive world creation. These are significant resources for my appropriation of theology for secular ends.

---

[41] Buber, *I and Thou*; and René Girard, *Things Hidden Since the Foundation of the World*, trans. Stephen Bann and Michael Metteer (Stanford: Stanford University Press, 1987).

[42] Tillich, *Theology of Culture*.

Illustration 1: Martin Buber and Communion Without God

In the first chapter of Genesis, God speaks creation into existence. And then God separates light from darkness; day from night; land from water; and water from air. God creates through language that divides creation. Then God creates humanity in God's image. The first human's first task as a creation in the image of God is to name the animals (Genesis 2:19). The divine power of creation and the uniquely human quality in this most foundational of Western creation myths is *language* which controls the environment and divides it into pieces. To put it differently, subjunctive technology is an inherently spiritual—even divine—quality. And yet, the relationship between human activity and receptivity in a religious context is complicated by their respective mediation through language—that which is both a divine, active, creative technology—and silence—that most profound and apophatic of religious experiences. Speech and silence, action and reception, creation and withdrawal, presence and absence, the sacred and the profane, the watching and waiting of Advent and the arrival of the nativity, transcendence and immanence: these dynamics and tensions are all paramount to religious experience. These distinctions collapse in mystical experience. Withdrawal is an activity. A mystic actively experiences her receptivity. A mystic experiences the transcendent immanently. In an unsettling irony, God's silence becomes a kind of speech while words become emptied of their meaning.[43] What remains in the silence is the experience of the sacred.

For Martin Buber, religion is about communion. But even more fundamentally, Buber's phenomenology causes him to argue that all human life happens dialectically—within and between tensions—in relation. This is why he writes, "Basic words do not signify things but relations."[44] And, "There is no I as such but only the I of the basic word I-You and the I of the basic word I-It."[45] Nothing exists without already being interconnected to other things. This echoes the Buddhist concept of dependent origination which is related to the concept of emptiness described in regards to Dōgen above. All things are always already in and a part of the world—they exist together, dependent upon one another. One cannot

---

[43] Incidentally, the Occupy Movement—counterintuitively—may then be seen as a contemporary mystical movement, for instance, despite its lack of any language about God whatsoever and its deep engagement with—rather than withdrawal from—the world. I will take up this line of thinking again in Chap. 6.
[44] Buber, 53.
[45] Buber, 54.

withdraw from the world in passivity. "Man becomes an I through a You," explains Buber.[46] We only exist at all in relation with others. So theology is always already social.

One's existence in the world and with others is not oppositional, but dialectical. It only works as a field of relations. Contemplation—which might appear as a kind of religious withdrawal from the world or a passivity—is thus just another type of action. These kinds of terms are all variations on different types of human activities within a field of possibilities. They are not opposites or even points on a fluid scale. This is not two-dimensional, but wide open. Buber writes, "Those who experience do not participate in the world. For the experience is 'in them' and not between them and the world." But then he goes further to suggest, "The world as experience belongs to the basic word I-It. The basic word I-You establishes the world of relation."[47] So while experience is not participatory in Buber's sense, it is nevertheless still dependent upon interconnection. Religion creates the conditions for the social and, I argue by extension, the political. Buber is arguing here that experience and relation are opposed to one another, not in structure, but in quality. This isn't a matter of acting or receiving, of doing or contemplating—these kinds of distinctions cease making sense in Buber's context. Instead, it's a matter of precisely *how* one acts, receives, does, or contemplates. Buber wants to reframe the binary. It's not the difference between action and contemplation or between speech and silence, but rather between relation and experience. And by "experience," Buber is referring to using something as an object—I enter into I-It. This is why, "The improvement of the ability to experience and use generally involves a decrease in man's power to relate."[48]

Buber's understanding of religion is not about God as such, but rather about relation. Louis Auguste Sabatier was quoted by the theorist of religion, William James, as arguing that, "Religion is an intercourse, a conscious and voluntary relation, entered into by a soul in distress with the mysterious power upon which it feels itself to depend, and upon which its

---

[46] Buber, 80.
[47] Buber, 56.
[48] Buber, 92. Buber is using "relate" and "experience" in idiosyncratic ways here. By "relate," Buber means to signify a reciprocity between those who relate to one another. By contrast, Buber understands "experience" unidirectionally. One experiences an object. The experiencer is active while the object of experience is a passive recipient of that which acts upon it.

fate is contingent."⁴⁹ Religion is a feeling, a relationship, and a dependence. This resonates with Tillich's state of being grasped by an ultimate concern.⁵⁰ Religion is about how we interact with each other—how we *relate*. This is a scandal. After Buber, one might radically redefine theology such that it is no longer about an object of investigation or description (God), but rather is about a *method* of how one lives *in the world*. Buber writes, "The relation to a human being is the proper metaphor for the relation to God...."⁵¹ And in his Afterword, he clarifies that much of the misunderstanding of *I and Thou* arose from "...the central significance of the close association of the relation to God with the relation to one's fellow-men, which is my most essential concern."⁵² Religion is not about relating to God, per se, but rather about relating to other people. Every other person might as well be God as far as the religious relation is concerned. To be very clear: religion does not require God; only other people. God is not necessary.

To say that God is not necessary for theology is to put it softly. God has actually become *problematic* for religion. In Western culture, God has generally—to use Buber's language—become an It. Relations are not permanent. They happen in real time and are fleeting. This births in the religious practitioner an anxiety about the relation's end and a desire for its perpetuation. This is why,

> ...God becomes an object for faith. Originally, faith fills the temporal gaps between the acts of relation; gradually, it becomes a substitute for these acts. The ever new movement of being through concentration and going forth is supplanted by coming to rest in an It in which one has faith. The trust-in-spite-of-all of the fighter who knows the remoteness and nearness of God is transformed ever more completely into the profiteer's assurance that nothing can happen to him because he has the faith that there is One who would not permit anything to happen to him.⁵³

---

⁴⁹ As quoted by William James in *The Varieties of Religious Experience: A Study in Human Nature*, fwd. Jacques Barzun (New York: Mentor/New American Library, 1958), 352. Originally from Auguste Sabatier, Esquisse d'une philosophie de la religion, 2me éd. (1897), 24–26, abridged.

⁵⁰ Paul Tillich, *Theology of Culture*, ed. Robert C. Kimball (New York: Oxford University Press, 1959), 40.

⁵¹ Buber, 151. The scandal might go all the way to the greatest commandment—theology is about love before it is about love's object.

⁵² Buber, 171.

⁵³ Buber, 162.

And then, Buber puts it succinctly: "Thus, God becomes a cult object."[54] Rather than God providing the conditions for the religious relation, God becomes a hindrance. God now hinders one's ability to be religious because God—as an object—pulls the rug out from under the possibility of communion. This may be why Meister Eckhart once wrote, "...*I pray God to rid me of God*."[55] The following section is an attempt to go beyond Buber's passive lack of a need for God to a positive, active willing of God's absence, and God's role in the creation of community.

Illustration 2: René Girard and God's Withdrawal

It has become a cliché that if there is no God, all things are permitted.[56] Note the usage of the conditional verb and passive voice. The statement is subjunctive, but its emphasis is weak. I will go further in light of Buber and suggest that *only if* God is absent, then all things are possible. And not just all things, but specifically religious communion becomes possible. In God's absence, one might find religion's possibility anew. The way God's absence affects religious communion is important for René Girard in *Things Hidden Since the Foundation of the World*. There, he fleetingly refers to the Gospels as "having established a kind of practical atheism."[57] He writes of the importance of the passage in the Sermon on the Mount where Jesus tells his listeners to love their enemies:

> Beside this text we can put all the texts denying that God is responsible for the infirmities, illnesses and catastrophes by which innocent victims perish— in particular, of course, for conflict... The Gospels deprive God of his most essential role in primitive religions—that of polarizing everything mankind does not succeed in mastering, particularly in relationships between individuals.[58]

---

[54] Buber, 162.

[55] Meister Eckhart, *Meister Eckhart: Mystic and Philosopher*, ed. Reiner Schürmann (Bloomington: Indiana University Press, 1978), 218. Quoted from Eckhart's 52nd sermon, "Beati Pauperes Spiritu."

[56] Slavoj Žižek examines this idea in his inimitable way in, "If There Is a God, Then Anything is Permitted." ABC Religion & Ethics. April 17, 2012 http://www.egs.edu/faculty/slavoj-zizek/articles/if-there-is-a-god-then-anything-is-permitted/.

[57] Girard, *Things Hidden*, 183.

[58] Girard, *Things Hidden*, 183.

To appropriate a phrase from Thomas J. J. Altizer, Girard seems to be advocating the gospel of Christian atheism here.[59] God's absence is good news. And it is even good news *for religion*. When God is absent, God cannot be responsible for atrocity. This, of course, goes well beyond Buber for whom the relation with any other You is a window into a relation with the Absolute You. Girard is useful here in reminding us of how God—whose principal historical identity has been as a prohibitor—has become an object for use in violence and therefore been emptied of religious value.

Girard's work is built upon his theory of mimetic violence.[60] All human behavior has its roots in mimesis. We imitate each other. But according to Girard, we not only imitate each other's activities but each other's emotions and desires as well. This eventually leads us to a problem of resources. That is, if we want the same things, what happens when there's a scarcity? Initially, we seek mediation. But this leads to greater rivalry and eventually violence. When a community of people are imitating each other to such a degree that their similarities lead to shared desires and rivalry climaxes, that community will seemingly have no choice but to self-destruct in a war of all against all. However, argues Girard, the community will more often than not shift its violent impulses away from a kind of dispersed rivalry between each of the members to a locus on a single person. This is the scapegoat. For Girard, community can reestablish itself—it can bond—over hatred of a single entity. Former rivals become friends in being united against a single common enemy. This is the very foundation of human civilization for Girard: human beings unite and form community through a process of mimesis that results in ritualized violence toward a scapegoat. The resonances with both Rappaport and Schmitt on this point should be clear. For Schmitt, politics depends upon the friend/enemy distinction and is most evident in its hyperbolic expression of war. Girard supplements this idea by arguing that to maintain itself, a community will develop a system of prohibitions that mediates, normalizes, and channels the desire for violence. In Schmittian terms, this is the law. And in regards to Rappaport, Girard sees the *ritual act* of sacrificial violence as socially constructive. Rappaport, of course, emphasizes the ritual act, while Girard

---

[59] Thomas J. J. Altizer, *The Gospel of Christian Atheism* (Philadelphia: The Westminster Press, 1966).

[60] See René Girard, "Mimesis and Violence: Perspectives in Cultural Criticism," *Berkshire Review* 14 (1979): 9–19; *Violence and the Sacred*, trans. Patrick Gregory (Baltimore: Johns Hopkins University Press, 1977), 36; and *Things Hidden*, 26–27, 93–94, and 338–347.

focuses on the violence. In this sense, he's a bit more Schmittian. After a scapegoat is sacrificed, the behavior that precipitated the scapegoating is prohibited. Thus, the scapegoaters appear to have restored order to the community. This entire process, for Girard, is unconscious. And, as such, it is destined to repeat itself.

Girard argues that mimetic rivalry and the subsequent creation of rituals to alleviate the violent tension in which it results have unraveled over time. The traditional scapegoating sacrificial ritual no longer works. Biblically, God enacted the cathartic violence directly on humanity's behalf in the beginning. God destroyed Sodom and Gomorra; God caused the great flood; God caused the confusion at Babel. But, as the mechanisms of this divine violence proceeded and repeated, they became illuminated over time and began to lose their efficacy since they were no longer purely unconscious. This is why God started to allow humanity itself to enact the violence while merely associating with the righteous from a distance. Job and the prophets can directly attest to this.[61] Ultimately, after passing through Jesus' teachings in the Gospels, we arrived at the Crucifixion in which God had absolutely no part whatsoever. The mob, the religious establishment, and the Romans killed Christ who, in turn, cried out for a God who wasn't there to listen. For Girard, the cross is where God had become completely absent from the cycle of mimetic, ritual violence. God died, freeing us.

It has become a truism that the death of God requires the death of the death of God. It took quite a few centuries, but the West lost its faith, only to get it back again in corrupted form. Girard writes:

> The omnipresent victim [has] already been delayed from time immemorial by sacrificial processes that are now becoming exhausted, since they appear to be more and more transparent and less and less effective—and are proportionately more and more to be feared in the domains of politics and sociology. To make these processes effective once again, people are tempted to multiply the innocent victims, to kill all the enemies of the nation or the class, to stamp out what remains of religion or the family as the origins of all forms of "repression," and to sing the praises of murder and madness as the only true forces of "liberation."[62]

Freedom has resulted in cataclysm. The hopes of the Enlightenment crescendoed in the Reign of Terror. American destiny was most manifest on

---

[61] Girard, *Things Hidden*, 422.
[62] Girard, *Things Hidden*, 287. The recent celebrations of Osama bin Laden's death could not be more blatant and appropriate evidence of this claim.

the Trail of Tears. The great utopian genius of Marxism was most fully realized in the gulags. The brilliance of science glowed most brightly on the civilians of Hiroshima. Emmanuel Levinas once commented that "General and generous principles can be inverted in their application. Every generous thought is threatened by its own Stalinism."[63] Liberal democracy is thus most triumphant in Guantanamo Bay.

Secularization, which had been the end, has been transcended. It has resulted in the return of and to religion. Our freedoms have failed to keep the violence at bay, but there's no turning back. Mubarak's fall and Saddam Hussein's death were both inevitable because communities desire the deaths of their respective tyrants. This is what makes a community. And yet, after the Muslim Brotherhood was elected to power and then deposed, the military is back in control in Egypt. In the United States, some of the strongest antigovernment voices come from advocates of God's return to a tyrannical throne. One yearns for the sovereign and the exception. So one witnesses the revolt against government in the name of restoring the prohibitions which we have illuminated and destroyed. These prohibitions continually disintegrate and plunge us further toward the absurdity of true and ultimate freedom.[64]

There thus appears to be an ambivalence about tyranny. Girard "[finds] it absurd to hear people calling for a return to constraints, which is impossible." And yet, in the same breath, Girard states, "From the moment cultural forms begin to dissolve, any attempt to reconstitute them artifi-

[63] Emmanuel Levinas, "The Pact," in *The Levinas Reader*, trans. Seán Hand (Oxford: Basil Blackwell, 1990), 220.

[64] As the celebrations in the wake of Osama bin Laden's death demonstrated, the American public seems not to have noticed that Christ illuminated the emptiness of the scapegoat mechanism. Either that, or it noticed, but doesn't care. We have moved beyond the imitation of each other. We are a step removed, just like God. The first step for Girard was to remove the object of our rivalry from the mimetic equation, but we've since moved beyond that simple removal. Girard might be surprised that *we've become absent from our own mimesis*. We are now imitating what we think the other will imitate. We are imitating *as if.* This was Obama's problem regarding the Egyptian Revolution in 2011. He wouldn't actively take a position. His mimetic rivalry didn't result in direct competition. Instead, it attempted to react to some then-unseen actor. It was a subjunctive, predictive mimesis, not a reactive one. Incidentally, this is also how we ended up with a housing bubble when no one thought houses were a good investment: we didn't think houses were a good investment, but we assumed everyone else did think so. We invest in that in which we think others will invest. See "Ranking Cute Animals: A Stock Market Experiment," NPR: Planet Money, accessed August 18, 2012, http://www.npr.org/blogs/money/2011/01/14/132906135/ranking-cute-animals-a-stock-market-experiment?ft=1&f=93559255.

cially can only result in the most appalling tyranny."⁶⁵ Absurdity has arrived. Contemporary society has made "no more taboos" the highest taboo.⁶⁶ Or, as Žižek explains, "Today, nothing is more oppressive and regulated than being a simple hedonist."⁶⁷ Girard's argument is that "At the present moment, sacrifice is being sacrificed; culture in its entirety, especially our own culture, historic Christianity, is playing the role of the scapegoat."⁶⁸ So what then to think of the photoshopped images of Osama bin Laden's head hanging from the Statue of Liberty's hand? It's a loop of sacrificing sacrifice only to fall back into scapegoating the other once again.

Desire is fully dependent upon the sustenance of the prohibition. "He dreams continually of the moment of this conquest and represents it to himself as if it had already taken place."⁶⁹ But something changes after it *does* take place. The husband desires the resurrection of his wife so that he might again resume the affair with his mistress. So, politically, the United States moves through a series of tyrannical enemies, from Mubarak to Gaddafi to Assad, never sustaining any particular one, but maintaining the abstraction of the exceptional enemy all the while.

Nostalgia changes the direction of desire. One desires one's former lack—that is, one comes to desire the moment before the satisfaction of that desire. But it goes even deeper than that. One never lacked in the first place. It is an ironic or paradoxical desire for privation. Once God's vacancy has been filled with the immanence of all one's taboos, one comes to desire that impossible absence once again. Or is it transcendence? In either case, one's desire has become deferred or differentiated from its object.

One desires because the object of desire is taboo or impossible to attain.⁷⁰ Prohibition creates desire for the prohibited. With God's death, all things have become permissible. Prohibition has disappeared. Ivan's Grand Inquisitor would rather Christ give us freedom through the absence than the presence of the benevolent tyrant.⁷¹ But this freedom has also carried entropy along with it. It is something akin to the anti-Absolute

---

⁶⁵ Girard, *Things Hidden*, 286.
⁶⁶ Girard, *Things Hidden*, 291.
⁶⁷ Žižek, "If There Is a God, Then Anything is Permitted."
⁶⁸ Girard, *Things Hidden*, 399.
⁶⁹ Girard, *Things Hidden*, 398.
⁷⁰ God is both of these things.
⁷¹ Fyodor Dostoevsky, *The Grand Inquisitor*, ed. Anne Fremantle (New York: Continuum, 2003).

Spirit of the Hegelian dialectic. God has become increasingly more absent; we have become increasingly more free. And yet this is not a synthesizing move in any Hegelian sense. It is a negative Hegelianism. Rather than arriving at the culmination of human history and potential, we have arrived instead at absurd, apocalyptic desiring of nostalgia. We aren't nostalgic. We're too well-educated for that. Instead, *we wish we were nostalgic.* "From this point, desire seeks only to find a resistance that it is incapable of overcoming."[72] Our desire has turned to prohibition itself. We long for the return of the sovereign, but we are all too aware that "the exception" has become an impossible category.

Illustration 3: Paul Tillich's Theology of Culture

If religion works best today without God, theology might best be applied to profane human endeavors. Paul Tillich's work analyzing the theological expressions of secular culture was groundbreaking. He writes, "If you start with the question whether God does or does not exist, you can never reach Him; and if you assert that He does exist, you can reach Him even less than if you assert that He does not exist. A God about whose existence or non-existence you can argue is a thing beside others within the universe of existing things."[73] Tillich explains that science's demonstration of the lack of evidence for God's existence is a "considerable service" provided to religion. "[Scientists] have forced [religion] to reconsider and to restate the meaning of the tremendous word *God*."[74] Unfortunately, Tillich says, theologians have the same issue:

> They begin their message with the assertion that there is a highest being called God, whose authoritative revelations they have received. They are more dangerous for religion than the so-called atheistic scientists. They take the first step on the road which inescapably leads to what is called atheism. Theologians who make of God a highest being who has given some people information about Himself, provoke inescapably the resistance of those who are told they must subject themselves to the authority of this information.[75]

---

[72] Girard, *Things Hidden*, 297.
[73] Paul Tillich, *Theology of Culture*, ed. Robert C. Kimball (New York: Oxford University Press, 1959), 4–5.
[74] Tillich, 5.
[75] Tillich, 5.

Tillich insists that his task is to affirm both critical voices—scientific and theological. He wants to appropriate the elements of truth and avoid the pitfalls of both. He wants to collapse conceptions of the secular and the sacred.

Religion needs to be redefined. "Religion is the dimension of depth in all [functions of man's spiritual life]." Tillich continues:

> What does the metaphor *depth* mean? It means that the religious aspect points to that which is ultimate, infinite, unconditional in man's spiritual life. Religion, in the largest and most basic sense of the word, is ultimate concern. And ultimate concern is manifest in all creative functions of the human spirit. It is manifest in the moral sphere as the unconditional seriousness of the moral demand. Therefore, if someone rejects religion in the name of the moral function of the human spirit, he rejects religion in the name of religion. Ultimate concern is manifest in the realm of knowledge as the passionate longing for ultimate reality. Therefore, if anyone rejects religion in the name of the cognitive function of the human spirit, he rejects religion in the name of religion. Ultimate concern is manifest in the aesthetic function of the human spirit as the infinite desire to express ultimate meaning. Therefore, if anyone rejects religion in the name of the aesthetic function of the human spirit, he rejects religion in the name of religion. You cannot reject religion with ultimate seriousness, because ultimate seriousness, or the state of being ultimately concerned, is itself religion. Religion is the substance, the ground, and the depth of man's spiritual life. This is the religious aspect of the human spirit.[76]

Religion, language, and humanity are the same age. "The passionate longing for ultimate reality" as a manifestation of ultimate concern is another way of saying that religion's power is its subjunctivity. And Tillich is making it clear that it is as possible to get away from religion as it is to stop being human or to excise language from history. Religion is a part of our humanity—what makes us who we are.[77]

---

[76] Tillich, 7–8.

[77] Walter Sobchak, John Goodman's character in the 1998 Coen Brothers' film, *The Big Lebowski*, expresses nicely just how tight our bonds to religion are. He cannot fathom a world in which his religious commitments would no longer apply. His religion is an integral component of his identity. When Jeff Bridges's character, the Dude, suggests that Walter should break the Sabbath since he is no longer married to his Jewish ex-wife, Walter responds, shouting, "So what are you saying? When you get divorced you turn in your library card? You get a new license? You stop being Jewish?!" Like our driver's licenses, it is religion that gets us through the day. It is integral to our very identities, not simply some consumable object we may choose to use or not.

Tillich provides us with a way of thinking differently about God. Rather than the object of theology, theological method becomes a way of relating to power. As a result, atheism, incredulity, and doubt become theological tactics par excellence. Resistance is divine. Again, and concerning apophaticism, Tillich writes:

> God is no object for us as subjects. He is always that which precedes this division. But, on the other hand, we speak about him and we act upon him, and we cannot avoid it, because everything which becomes real to us enters the subject-object correlation. Out of this paradoxical situation the half-blasphemous and mythological concept of the "existence of God" has arisen. And so have the abortive attempts to prove the existence of this "object." To such a concept and to such attempts atheism is the right religious and theological reply. This was well known to the most intensive piety of all times. The atheistic terminology of mysticism is striking. It leads beyond God to the Unconditioned, transcending any fixation of the divine as an object. But we have the same feeling of the inadequacy of all limiting names for God in non-mystical religion. Genuine religion without an element of atheism cannot be imagined. It is not by chance that not only Socrates, but also the Jews and the early Christians were persecuted as atheists. For those who adhered to the powers, they were atheists.[78]

Here, Tillich points a way to theological connection to human political structures. One might be an atheist depending upon one's relation to the powers that be. At first glance, Tillich would seem to be echoing Schmitt's comment about the secularization of theological concepts into politics. But this goes much deeper because Tillich views theology as method, not object.

If theology is a method, not inherently connected to any particular object of investigation, then, "…in every cultural creation—a picture, a system, a law, a political movement (however secular it may appear)—an ultimate concern is expressed, and … it is possible to recognize the unconscious theological character of it."[79] Tillich is explaining that one *may* use theology as a way of understanding any cultural creation as it expresses ultimate concern. I take Tillich's descriptive or permissive statement as an imperative. Not only *may* culture be theologized, but *it should*. One *should* look simultaneously at culture, political resistance movements, secular

---

[78] Tillich, 25.
[79] Tillich, 27.

appearances, and their theological character. That is what this project is humbly attempting. That is, it is working out a theology of political resistance.

If political resistance is theological—if radical democracy is the political instantiation of the death of God—then in what might one have faith? "The risk of faith is not that it accepts assertions about God, man and world, which cannot be fully verified, but might be or might not be in the future. The risk of faith is based on the fact that the unconditional element can become a matter of ultimate concern only if it appears in a concrete embodiment."[80] This is why subjunctivity must be *enacted* in Rappaport and why Crawford fixes machines. This is why illusions must be made real. Faith only means something when it appears, embodied. Even the New Testament epistle writer James recognized this when he wrote:

> What good is it, my brothers and sisters, if you say you have faith but do not have works? Can faith save you? If a brother or sister is naked and lacks daily food, and one of you says to them, "Go in peace; keep warm and eat your fill," and yet you do not supply their bodily needs, what is the good of that? So faith by itself, if it has no works, is dead.[81]

The superficial understanding of this passage is that that one achieves salvation through an accumulation of moral deeds. To the contrary, James exhibits Tillich's definition of religion as ultimate concern. One demonstrates faith by feeding the hungry not to reserve a place in heaven, but to allow one's ultimate concern to become embodied. It is a risk to clothe the naked. Faith must risk being made real to be worth anything. To put it differently, James is advocating that faith should be made materially manifest by living subjunctively. Faith without works risks nothing. The absence of risk empties belief of its faith. Radical theological faith, on the other hand, risks both God and the world. Both become subject to interrogation and reevaluation. Radical theological faith is a subjunctive faith. God might not be, and the world might be otherwise.

Putting both God and the existing order of the world into question is an honest religious response to our contemporary post-secular condition. Tillich's redefinition of religion is an attempt at taking such a condition seriously for faith. He explains that one of the consequences of this move

---

[80] Tillich, 28.
[81] James 2:14–17 (NRSV).

...is the disappearance of the gap between the sacred and secular realm. If religion is the state of being grasped by an ultimate concern, this state cannot be restricted to a special realm. The unconditional character of this concern implies that it refers to every moment of our life, to every space and every realm.... In all preliminary concerns, ultimate concern is present, consecrating them. Essentially the religious and the secular are not separated realms. Rather they are within each other.[82]

Effectively, risk is compounded exponentially. The faith that becomes possible when religion is rethought as the state of being grasped by an ultimate concern is a faith that risks the sacred and the secular. The secular is revealed as sacred, and the religious is shown in all its profanity. The eradication of the distinction between religious and secular comes from both directions. And yet faith remains. Again, Tillich writes:

Religion as ultimate concern is the meaning-giving substance of culture, and culture is the totality of forms in which the basic concern of religion expresses itself. In abbreviation: religion is the substance of culture, culture is the form of religion. Such a consideration definitely prevents the establishment of a dualism of religion and culture. Every religious act, not only in organized religion, but also in the most intimate movement of the soul, is culturally formed.[83]

For Tillich, culture forms religious acts. This demonstrates a reciprocity with Rappaport for whom religious acts form society. This should not be surprising when meaningful distinctions between the religious and the secular are dubious.

The link between religion and culture in Tillich dovetails nicely with Rappaport's understanding of the ritual construction of the social and their respective relationship to language. So we've come back around again to this issue of *speaking religion*. That is, Tillich has returned to the issue raised at the beginning of this chapter regarding how one might talk about religion and what religion might say. "The form of religion is culture. This is especially obvious in the language used by religion. Every language, including that of the Bible, is the result of innumerable acts of cultural creativity. All functions of man's spiritual life are based on man's power to speak vocally or silently."[84] Rappaport might say instead that all functions

---

[82] Tillich, 41.
[83] Tillich, 42.
[84] Tillich, 47. Also, earlier on 42 and 43, Tillich explains: "...language is the basic cultural creation. On the other hand, there is no cultural creation without an ultimate concern

of a human's spiritual life are based on humanity's power to *act self-referentially*, vocally or silently. The subjunctive component of Tillich's theology should no longer be a surprise. He writes, "*Language is the expression of man's freedom from the given situation and its concrete demands. It gives him universals in whose power he can create worlds above the given world of technical civilization and spiritual content.*"[85] He continues: "religious language is ordinary language, changed under the power of what it expresses, the ultimate of being and meaning."[86] Now we are in a position to think of religious language through Rappaport and Tillich together as concerning itself with subjunctive world creation.

Religious language is ordinary language changed under the power of its self-referentiality by which the subjunctive expresses ultimate concern. Religious language is thus methodical language. It speaks ways and possibilities through a faith that radically risks both the world and God. Before frustrating the construction of Babel, God admits this very situation by saying of the remarkable success of humanity, "There is now one people and they all have one language. This is what they have begun to do, and now all that they plan to do will be possible for them."[87] Ivan Karamazov's assertion that God's death made all things permissible might make new sense in this context.[88] And yet Jesus said, "For God, all things are possible."[89] When theology is method, religion is ultimate concern, and faith is existential risk, one doesn't have to choose one over the other. Nothing escapes possibility.

---

expressed in it. This is true of the theoretical functions of man's spiritual life, for example, personal and social transformation of reality. In each of these functions in the whole of man's cultural creativity, an ultimate concern is present. Its immediate expression is the style of a culture. He who can read the style of a culture can discover its ultimate concern, its religious substance."

[85] Tillich, 47. Emphasis added.
[86] Tillich, 47.
[87] Genesis 11:6 (CEB).
[88] See the previous section.
[89] Matthew 19:26, Mark 10:27, Luke 1:37 (NRSV).

CHAPTER 3

Political Theology

POLITICAL THEOLOGY OTHERWISE

Carl Schmitt begins *Political Theology: Four Chapters on the Concept of Sovereignty* with the proclamation: "Sovereign is he who decides on the exception."[1] Counterintuitively, it is not the creator of the law that is sovereign, but the one who can suspend the pre-existing law. Further, the sovereign determines the exception to the law in the name of the law. The law is made legitimate by the decision on the exception. Schmitt explains, "The exception is more interesting than the rule. The rule proves nothing; the exception proves everything: It confirms not only the rule but also its existence, which derives only from the exception. In the exception, the power of real life breaks through the crust of a mechanism that has become torpid by repetition."[2] It takes a sovereign to periodically reach out from within the legal machine to remind us all that the law exists for us who live. The sovereign wields power over the law in the name of maintaining the State. Without the sovereign—the one with the ability to decide the exception to the law—there would be no law at all and, indeed, no State. The profound and disturbing implications of such a suggestion should not go unnoticed. Law is only legitimate when the sovereign suspends it. Politics is born of sovereign violence.

---

[1] Schmitt, *Political Theology*, 5.
[2] Schmitt, *Political Theology*, 15.

Schmitt's political theology advocates the abuse of power in the name of political stability. Schmitt sees the political most clearly in its polemical expressions. The most evidently sovereign rule would then appear to be tyrannical. And so politics itself, in Schmitt's formulation, would seem to have its very foundation in tyranny. Simon Critchley explains: "For Schmitt, the concept of sovereignty finds its definition with the notion of *iustitium* or state of exception (*Ausnahmezustand*), where the sovereign is that subject who is capable of a decision on the state of exception. This entails that dictatorship reveals the essence of the political insofar as the latter is identified with the power of decision."[3] In a time of Congressional deadlock, one might be tempted to praise Schmitt's willingness to sidestep bureaucracy through authoritative action. There's a certain satisfaction derived from such an argument. One hears its echoes on both the left and right.[4] Executive authority sometimes appears to be the only solution to an utterly ineffective process that is removed from day-to-day life.

And so we find ourselves entertaining the idea that authoritarianism might not be all that bad. At least not all the time. Maybe, when the State's interest is at risk, the decision on the exception might be wielded benevolently. This is a problem with liberalism in general. Checks and balances sound nice in theory, but they tend to require an immense amount of time and compromise for anything to be accomplished. The casuistry of liberal democracy can be painful. Laws build upon laws built upon laws which get teased out in an almost infinitely nuanced and tedious debate. Liberal democracy is seemingly obsessed with its own process at the expense of what that process is supposed to accomplish. Schmitt despised liberal pluralism for good reason, it seems. If the sovereign decides the exception, creating the possibility of politics, constitutional democracy is about as far away from politics as we might get. Again, Critchley writes:

> Schmitt's problem with liberalism is that it is anti-political. What this means is that for the liberal every political decision must be rooted in a norm whose ultimate justification flows from the constitution. Within liberalism, political

---

[3] Simon Critchley, *The Faith of the Faithless: Experiments in Political Theology* (London and New York: Verso, 2012), 67.

[4] See, for instance, Slavoj Žižek's tribute to Margaret Thatcher after her death in *New Statesman*, "The Simple Courage of Decision: A Leftist Tribute to Thatcher," from April 17, 2013. http://www.newstatesman.com/politics/politics/2013/04/simple-courage-decision-leftist-tribute-thatcher. Žižek writes, "What we need today, in this situation, is a Thatcher of the left: a leader who would repeat Thatcher's gesture in the opposite direction, transforming the entire field of presuppositions shared by today's political elite of all main orientations."

decisions are derived from constitutional norms and higher than the state stands the law and the interpretation of the law. This is why the highest political authority in a liberal state rests with the supreme court or its equivalent. Political action is subordinated to juridical interpretation. Lawyers and not philosophers are kings in a liberal democracy.[5]

It is no real surprise then that George W. Bush was effectively appointed to the presidency by the Supreme Court only to go on to develop a governing philosophy of Schmittian sovereignty. Writing in 2006, Glenn Greenwald explains, "What we have in our Federal Government are not individual acts of law-breaking or isolated scandals of illegality, but instead, a culture and an ideology of lawlessness. It cannot be emphasized enough that since September 11, the Bush Administration has claimed the power to act without any constraints of law or checks from the Congress or the courts."[6] Citing a memorandum from the Justice Department, published on September 25, 2001, Greenwald continues:

> That decisions about what actions our country takes "are for the President alone to make"—without any interference from the Congress, the courts, or anything else—is not a fringe academic theory. It is a definitely authoritarian and lawless ideology that has truly—expressly—become the governing philosophy of George Bush and his Administration. And it is not something the Administration has merely embraced in theory. It has been aggressively exercising these limitless powers.[7]

The sovereign must break the law for our own good. We should be grateful.

But we must not stop here. The authoritarianism that reveals the essence of the political is a theology. Schmitt is not simply explaining the way politics works. He is making theological claims. In one of his most famous and oft-quoted arguments, Schmitt writes:

---

[5] Critchley, 104.
[6] Glenn Greenwald, "Unclaimed Territory," http://glenngreenwald.blogspot.com.br/2006/01/ideology-of-lawlessness.html.
[7] Greenwald, "Unclaimed Territory." The memorandum may be accessed at http://www.justice.gov/olc/warpowers925.htm. Among other comments, the Justice Department claims, "In both the War Powers Resolution and the Joint Resolution, Congress has recognized the President's authority to use force in circumstances such as those created by the September 11 incidents. Neither statute, however, can place any limits on the President's determinations as to any terrorist threat, the amount of military force to be used in response, or the method, timing, and nature of the response. These decisions, under our Constitution, are for the President alone to make."

> All significant concepts of the modern theory of the state are secularized theological concepts not only because of their historical development—in which they were transferred from theology to the theory of the state, whereby, for example, the omnipotent God became the omnipotent lawgiver—but also because of their systematic structure, the recognition of which is necessary for a sociological consideration of these concepts. The exception in jurisprudence is analogous to the miracle in theology. Only by being aware of this analogy can we appreciate the manner in which the philosophical ideas of the state developed in the last centuries.[8]

We must read theology and politics together here. Schmitt is revealing something of his sense of who God is. God's only qualities in this passage are the miraculous possession of unlimited power and legal beneficence. The sovereign theistic God has, according to Schmitt, been secularized into political form. As the theological is secularized into the political, God becomes the sovereign. But the people are also implicated in this transference. Our subjectivity is affected. So, how do we recognize the political sovereign? Who do we become as its subjects? Who is the sovereign and what does it make of us? Critchley writes:

> The question "who?" is answered by the decision itself. That is, the decision on the state of exception, the moment of the suspension of the operation of law, brings the subject "who?" into being. To put it into a slogan, the subject is the consequence of a decision. The subject that is revealed by the decision on the state of exception is the personage of the state, and the core of Schmitt's theory of the political is to show that the true subject of the political is the state, and that the state must always stand higher than the law.[9]

We, the people, are thus a consequence. We are fallout. We would not exist as a politically constituted people without the sovereign's decision. As God created humanity in God's image, the polis is the consequence of the sovereign decision on the exception.

Schmitt seems to get it right. He makes sense of Congress's gridlock and Bush's "with us or against us" foreign policy. "In a time of war, in dark times ... Carl Schmitt will always appear to be right."[10] This all seems accurate except that Schmitt's theology is flawed. Something more profound

---
[8] Schmitt, *Political Theology*, 36.
[9] Critchley, 105.
[10] Critchley, 222.

has happened than a simple transference of God into the political sovereign. Schmitt's theology is insufficient. "God emptied Godself, taking the form of a servant, and became like humanity. As a human, God was humble and obedient even to the point of death by political execution."[11] There is real theological precedent for the idea that sovereignty has been emptied out into the world and that divine power is, by definition, anti-authoritarian. One might even go so far as to suggest that to be a Christian—a follower of Christ—is to be an enemy of the State.[12]

If we follow Schmitt, suggesting that all modern political concepts are secularized theological ones, and then go further to the conclusion that God is dead, then—as McKenzie Wark suggested in his interview with *The Occupied Times*—we must recognize that politics is dead, too. In both cases, sovereignty has been emptied into the multitude.[13] In his article, "How to Occupy an Abstraction," Wark explains Occupy Wall Street's diagnosis of the contemporary American political condition. He writes that

> ...the most interesting thing about Occupy Wall Street is its suggestion that the main thing that's lacking is not demands, but process. What is lacking is politics itself. It may sound counterintuitive, but there really is no politics in the United States. There is exploitation, oppression, inequality, violence, there are rumors that there might still be a state. But there is no politics. There is only the semblance of politics. It's mostly just professionals renting influence to favor their interests. The state is no longer even capable of negotiating the common interests of its ruling class. ... So the genius of the occupation is simply to suggest that there could be a politics, one in which people meet and propose and negotiate. This suggestion points to the great absence at the center of American life: a whole nation, even an empire, with no politics.[14]

Why is this so? In a way, Schmitt has indeed been correct, but insufficiently so. His theology certainly does not go far enough, but neither do his politics. As we no longer live in the first decades of the twentieth century and much has changed since, we might update Schmitt's critique of liberalism to a critique of neoliberalism. As our condition has changed, so

---

[11] My gloss on Philippians 2:7.
[12] This is effectively Søren Kierkegaard's argument in *Attack upon "Christendom"* (Walter Lowrie, tr. Princeton: Princeton University Press, 1944).
[13] McKenzie Wark, "Preoccupying: McKenzie Wark," http://theoccupiedtimes.org/?p=6451.
[14] McKenzie Wark, "How to Occupy an Abstraction." http://www.versobooks.com/blogs/728-mckenzie-wark-on-occupy-wall-street-how-to-occupy-an-abstraction.

must our understanding of Schmitt. According to David Harvey in *Spaces of Global Capitalism*, Margaret Thatcher might be an ironic but appropriate theorist for understanding our current neoliberal theo-politico-economic context. Quoting her, Harvey explains:

> There is, she famously ... declared, "no such thing as society, only individuals and," she subsequently added, "their families." All forms of social solidarity were to be dissolved in favor of individualism, private property, personal responsibility and family values. The ideological assault along those lines that flower from Thatcher's rhetoric was relentless and eventually broadly successful. "Economics are the method," she said, "but the objective is to change the soul."[15]

Thatcher was a public architect of where we find ourselves today, taking the role of politics and sovereignty further than Schmitt may have predicted.

We appear to live in a society undoing itself in which politics is dead. In a way, Schmitt saw the potential for our current situation when he warned:

> The pluralist theory of state is in itself pluralistic, that is, it has no center but draws its thoughts from rather different intellectual circles (religion, economics, liberalism, socialism, etc.). It ignores the central concept of every theory of state, the political, and does not even mention the possibility that the pluralism of associations could lead to a federally constructed political entity. It totally revolves in a liberal individualism. The result is nothing else than a revocable service for individuals and their free associations. One association is played off against another and all questions and conflicts are decided by individuals.[16]

Thatcher might as well have quoted Schmitt directly. Schmitt argued, "In its literal sense and in its historical appearance the State is a specific entity of a people."[17] But in a neoliberal context, individuals' associations are disintegrating, and the State is withdrawing from view. This is all rather ironic. History has changed its object of investigation. Traditionally understood, history has focused on recording the progress of societies. But in a neoliberal context, focus on economics has come at the expense

---

[15] Quoted in David Harvey, *Spaces of Global Capitalism* (London: Verso, 2006), 17.
[16] Carl Schmitt, *The Concept of the Political*, trans. George Schwab (Chicago and London: University of Chicago Press, 2007), 45.
[17] Schmitt, *The Concept of the Political*, 19.

of society itself. "The fundamental mission of the neo-liberal state is to create a 'good business climate' and therefore to optimize conditions for capital accumulation no matter what the consequences for employment or social well-being," writes Harvey.[18] And, "Internally, the neo-liberal state is hostile to (and in some instances overtly repressive of) all forms of social solidarity..."[19] Our understanding of society through time is focused on socioeconomic progress as its driving force. But socioeconomic progress has brought us to a situation in which socioeconomics is undoing that very society itself.

With the breakdown of social solidarity coupled with the rise of global capitalism—in short, neoliberalism—one of Schmitt's other most famous and important concepts becomes distorted as well. Schmitt argues that politics is dependent upon the friend/enemy distinction.[20] Politics is based upon at least two opposing collectivities. We are only a political body when we are differentiated from another political body. Once again, Schmitt sees concepts most clearly in their polemical expressions. As sovereignty is most evident through tyranny, politics is most evident in war. In *The Concept of the Political*, Schmitt writes, "An enemy exists only when, at least potentially, one fighting collectivity of people confronts a similar collectivity. The enemy is solely the public enemy, because everything that has a relationship to such a collectivity of men, particularly to a whole nation, becomes public by virtue of such a relationship."[21] And then later, "A world in which the possibility of war is utterly eliminated, a completely pacified globe, would be a world without the distinction of friend and enemy and hence a world without politics."[22] But this is more complicated than it might seem. We now live in a world of perpetual war against no enemy in particular (an enemy called "terrorism"). Coupled with the hastening disappearance of social institutions (such as the decline in church attendance, the closure of veterans' clubs, and drastically reduced union membership), war is certainly not eliminated—in fact, it is exacerbated—but friendship has disappeared. On this point, Wark demonstrates the dialectical reversal of Schmitt. The friend/enemy distinction has become so hyperbolized that it has rendered politics impossible. In neoliberalism, everyone in particular is an enemy and

---

[18] Harvey, 25.
[19] Harvey, 25.
[20] Schmitt, *The Concept of the Political*, 26. "The specific political distinction to which political actions and motives can be reduced is that between friend and enemy."
[21] Schmitt, *The Concept of the Political*, 28.
[22] Schmitt, *The Concept of the Political*, 35.

everyone in the abstract is a friend. We are all potential customers and no one can be trusted.

Following Giorgio Agamben's reading of Schmitt in light of contemporary politics, we appear to be living in a time of permanent exception. Agamben writes, "*The state of exception thus ceases to be referred to as an external and provisional state of factual danger and comes to be confused to juridical rule itself.*"[23] God and politics are dead. Sovereignty appears to have become emptied out into global capitalism. Transnational corporations are a kind of disembodied sovereign. But the certainty provided by Schmitt's modern sovereign is a far cry from the radical uncertainty of the global market. The king may have two bodies, but the market has none; only an invisible hand. God seems to have turned into the market. Walter Benjamin, writing at roughly the same time as Schmitt, explained this clearly when he argued that, "Christianity…did not encourage the emergence of capitalism, but rather changed itself into capitalism."[24]

Schmitt's predictions and warnings have come true. But they have arrived in radicalized form. Schmitt explains, "Universality at any price would necessarily have to mean total depoliticization and with it, particularly, the nonexistence of states."[25] This appears to be an apt and prophetic description of the neoliberal project. An unregulated, global market capitalism, unrestricted by State boundaries has arrived. Functionally, neoliberalism would have the State become as nonexistent as possible, relegated only to ensuring that the market runs at peak efficiency. The neoliberal State enables the market and its social and political suicidality. Again, the prescient Schmitt:

> If, in fact, all humanity and the entire world were to become a unified entity based exclusively on economics and on technically regulating traffic, then it still would not be more of a social entity than a social entity of tenants in a tenement house, customers purchasing gas from the same utility company, or passengers traveling on the same bus. An interest group concerned exclusively with economics or traffic cannot become more than that, in the absence of an adversary.[26]

---

[23] Giorgio Agamben, *Homo Sacer: Sovereign Power and Bare Life*, trans. Daniel Heller-Roazen (Stanford: Stanford University Press, 1998), 168. Italics in original.
[24] Walter Benjamin, "Capitalism as Religion," trans. Chad Kautzer in *Reflections: Essays, Aphorisms, Autobiographical Writings*, ed. Peter Demetz (New York: Harcourt Brace, 1978), 261.
[25] Schmitt, *The Concept of the Political*, 55.
[26] Schmitt, *The Concept of the Political*, 57.

So the neoliberal world is an interest group—a kind of cooperative ownership—renting to the people who live in it. We have to pay to live in a world we were born into. And the price is high. Financially, this is obvious. But we also pay the cost of the disintegration of social solidarity.

Schmitt has defined the problem well. It's just that his solution leaves something to be desired. He seems to have predicted with relative accuracy, if underestimation, the development of liberalism into neoliberalism, the pluralist destruction of the political coupled with the disintegration of social solidarity, and the rise of economics—or resistance to this very process—as the only human rallying point of real global significance. This, at first, might appear like a contradiction. On the one hand, I have been arguing here that neoliberalism has been loosening the bonds of social solidarity. On the other hand, I argue that the last few decades have been witness to a marked rise in resistance movements. I argue that this is no contradiction, but the tension produced by neoliberalism itself. That is, most of the resistance movements erupting around the world today are direct reactions against neoliberal policies and procedures. In other words, neoliberalism has succeeded in destroying traditional forms of social solidarity. This has left few options but to find or create solidarity negatively, over and against and in resistance to neoliberalism itself. One no longer finds significant examples of solidarity in American churches, unions, and social clubs. Such examples exist, but as exceptions, rather than the old rule. Instead, the last few decades have witnessed the development of the Tea Party, the campaign for Fair Trade, the Arab Spring, the protests at the World Trade Organization meeting in Seattle in 1999, and the like. The common thread running between most social movements today is neoliberal hegemony. Schmitt is of very little help to us here. Schmitt is a reactionary. His solution is tyrannical and violent. As Schmitt's diagnoses need updating, so does his concept of sovereignty and its place in political theology. Schmitt's theology is superficial and triumphalist and leads him to a politics of bravado.

Sovereignty or Authority

Carl Schmitt famously defines sovereignty by decision on the exception. And it is sovereignty, rather than law, that is the foundation of political stability. By contrast, Roy A. Rappaport argues that ritual self-referentiality is the foundation of social solidarity and authority. In certain ways, Rappaport would seem to mirror Schmitt. That is, Schmitt's sovereign decision and Rappaport's legitimate self-referential action each only come into play by a crisis—an emergency in the former, and a shortfall of language in the latter—and they both appear to be exceptional with respect to the established order and repetition of everyday life.

To be clear on the categories, Schmitt is concerned with the political while Rappaport focuses instead on the social. To compare these thinkers more directly requires a certain degree of appropriation and willingness to inhabit tensions rather than to attempt to resolve them. At first, it may seem odd to place the juridical-political theorist into conversation with the anthropologist. Odd, maybe, but certainly not without interdisciplinary warrant. However, one might note that Schmitt, himself, referred to his work on sovereignty as "a sociology of concepts."[27] So, at least on this point, social theory might function as a hinge allowing us to swing back and forth between these two thinkers.

Barring the question of method, Schmitt and Rappaport seem to share some significant concerns. They seem to agree on the problem: namely, that the law is insufficient. Occasionally, Schmitt sounds a lot like Rappaport: "The decision becomes instantly independent of argumentative substantiation and receives an autonomous value."[28] And, "After all, every legal order is based on a decision, and also the concept of the legal order, which is applied as something self-evident, contains within it the contrast of the two distinct elements of the juristic—norm and decision. Like every other order, the legal order rests on a decision and not on a norm."[29] So there appears to be a certain commonality between the ways Schmitt describes the relationship between the law and the exception on the one hand, and the ways Rappaport describes the relationship between the canonical and self-referential on the other. Both of their arguments rely upon how authority functions. Schmitt explains:

> The existence of the state is undoubted proof of its superiority over the validity of the legal norm. The decision frees itself from all normative ties and becomes in the true sense absolute. The state suspends the law in the

---

[27] Schmitt, *Political Theology*. On page 45, Schmitt writes, "...the sociology of concepts, which is advanced here and alone has the possibility of achieving a scientific result for a concept such as sovereignty. This sociology of concepts transcends juridical conceptualization oriented to immediate practical interest. It aims to discover the basic, radically systematic structure and to compare this conceptual structure with the conceptually represented social structure of a certain epoch."
[28] Schmitt, *Political Theology*, 31.
[29] Schmitt, *Political Theology*, 10.

exception on the basis of its right of self-preservation, as one would say. ...
The exception reveals most clearly the essence of the state's authority. The
decision parts here from the legal norm, and (to formulate it paradoxically)
authority proves that to produce law it need not be based on law.[30]

Schmitt's sovereign decision on the exception is conservative. That is, it seeks its own self-preservation. The exception is the State's way of maintaining itself. So while the State requires the exception for its own sustenance, the priority is reversed in Rappaport's parallel situation. The canonical is the vehicle for the self-referential, rather than the other way around. Agamben is helpful here:

> The exception is to positive law what negative theology is to positive theology. While the latter affirms and predicates determinate qualities of God, negative (or mystical) theology with its 'neither ... nor ...,' negates and suspends the attribution to God of any predicate whatsoever. Yet negative theology is not outside theology and can actually be shown to function as the principle grounding the possibility in general of anything like a theology. Only because it has been negatively presupposed as what subsists outside any possible predicate can divinity become the subject of predication. Analogously, only because its validity is suspended in the state of exception can positive law define the normal case as the realm of its own validity.[31]

Significantly, Schmitt is focused on decision, while Rappaport focuses on action. The former is still consigned to the realm of naming—of reference to the existing order, even if only to suspend it—and, thus, at least on this point, Rappaport supersedes Schmitt. Likewise, Schmitt is concerned with a movement of exception which legitimates the legal order and ultimately must return to it, while Rappaport is concerned with, quite literally, remaking the world other than it had been through self-reference. Rappaport's is a transformative action. Schmitt's, by comparison, is merely a commentary.[32] It is the difference between revolution and coup. And, of course, Schmitt is primarily interested in maintaining the status quo—preserving the State—not creating an alternative one.

---

[30] Schmitt, *Political Theology*, 12–13.
[31] Agamben, *Homo Sacer*, 17.
[32] The reason that Christ's sacrifice on the cross—arguably one of the foundations of political theology—works is not because it functions as a decision on the exception, but rather it creates a new world, full stop. The same could be said of the Akedah, to cite an even earlier example.

Rappaport, by contrast, does not shy away from the possibilities created by disorder. Whereas Schmitt's political theology is aimed at stopping disorder, the subjunctivity at play in Rappaport's understanding of ritual authority recognizes the potential creative powers of disorder. The hazardous and creative potentials of disorder are both necessary outcomes of subjunctivity. "The ability to imagine and establish alternative orders is not, on the face of it, problematic. Such an ability makes possible, or even itself constitutes, a quantum leap in adaptive flexibility, the capacity of a system to adjust or transform itself in response to changing conditions. This enhanced flexibility has, however, an unavoidable but dangerous concomitant: increased grounds for disorder."[33] He continues:

> No actual society is utopian. It may, therefore, be difficult for any society's members not to imagine orders in at least some respects preferable to those under which they do live and labor. If they can conceive of better orders, how are their actions to be kept in sufficient conformity to the prevailing order for that order to persist? The conception of the possible is always in some degree the enemy of the actual. As such it may be a first step toward the disruption of prevailing social and conceptual orders, whatever they may be, without necessarily being a first step toward their improvement or replacement by orders more acceptable to those subject to them.[34]

Rappaport has brought Schmitt's friend/enemy distinction to the subjunctive sphere. That is, we might consider an alternative politics based not on warring associations, but rather on a different tension: between the actual and the possible. In this sense, the moral weight typically ascribed to friends and enemies breaks down. The possible is problematic for the actual, but it might be better. The enemy might be right. Agamben again: "The rule applies to the exception in no longer applying, in withdrawing from it. The state of exception is thus not the chaos that precedes order but rather the situation that results from its suspension. In this sense, the exception is truly, according to its etymological root, taken outside (*ex-capere*), and not simply excluded."[35] Agamben illuminates for us the way in which Schmitt would have us focus on the suspension of the law for the State's sake and ultimately for the law itself. But, following Rappaport, we might instead attempt to investigate the way in which the law itself

---

[33] Rappaport, *Ritual and Religion*, 17–18.
[34] Rappaport, *Ritual and Religion*, 17–18.
[35] Agamben, *Homo Sacer*, 18. Italics in original.

produces chaos.³⁶ Reason is confusion. On this reading, disorder does not precede order, nor does it result from its suspension. Rather, the law itself leads to disorder on its own terms.

Further, Schmitt's sovereignty is enacted and embodied by the one. Ritual self-referentiality, by contrast, may be enacted by the many, cooperatively and collectively. Its very enactment produces social solidarity. Ritual rests on the circumscription of the wills of its participants. Sovereignty happens to a people. Ritual happens by a people. Sovereignty is violent while subjunctivity is generative. This is not to say that certain measures cannot be taken to translate Schmitt's unified sovereign into a plural (if not pluralistic) one. Many thinkers have certainly embarked upon this task.³⁷ But for my purposes here, it seems more fitting to appeal directly to a theory of legitimacy and authority derived from cooperation rather than to manipulate a theory of the sovereign into indirectly fitting into a conception of a sovereignty of the many.

Once again, it comes down to theology. Schmitt's theology is triumphalist, closed, and outdated. The theology implicit in Rappaport, on the other hand, is open and fertile. One possible move would be to follow Rappaport and suggest an alternative. That is, one might suggest a different conception of sovereignty than Schmitt's. Michael Hardt has looked to the notion of sovereignty deployed by Machiavelli and Spinoza, for instance, which "posits the autonomy of the multitude and its social relations against any pre-established or divine conceptions of social order or hierarchy. According to this conception, sovereignty is secondary; it arises only from a relationship between the rulers and the ruled, and in this relationship the multitude is always primary over the sovereign."³⁸ Referring to Hardt, Jeffrey W. Robbins writes:

> …if sovereignty is secondary to the constituent power of the multitude, 'resistance and rebellion actually have a positive, foundational role.' That is because it returns power to where it properly resides. In this sense, the preservation of the state form is not the first order of business for politics; on the contrary, because there are no 'preestablished or divine conceptions of social order,' the multitude is free to find its own coherence and structure. This is

---

³⁶ Maybe this is the social-scientific version of the Second Law of Thermodynamics.
³⁷ See David Pan, "Political Theology for Democracy: Carl Schmitt and John Dewey on Aesthetics and Politics" in *Telos*, Winter 2012, vol. 2012, no. 161, 120–140.
³⁸ Michael Hardt as quoted in Jeffrey W. Robbins, *Radical Democracy and Political Theology* (New York: Columbia University Press, 2011), 83.

a fluid conception of the state that, as recommended by Thomas Jefferson, is served well by periodic upheavals. Again, in the words of Hardt, "resistance (and the threat of it) is the constantly present constituent foundation of sovereignty. Against the primacy of sovereignty, then, stands the primacy of resistance."[39]

This is a conception of sovereignty much closer to being in line with Rappaport's notion of self-referentiality. Resistance is thus counterintuitively the source of the law and the State. The self-referential is the source for the canonical. This constant threat—resistance at the root of sovereignty—is the subjunctive. Holiness might thus be conceived not as unified, omnipotent law-giving, but alternatively as the drive toward difference itself. We might consider a subjunctive holiness when we read Rappaport:

> But if discursive reason and speech are unique on this earth to human life, human life remains more than reason and speech, and the generation of the lie is continuously challenged by the living—by prophets, mystics, youth, revolutionaries, and reformers—who, in their search for wholeness, restore holiness ever again to the breaking world by re-establishing the adaptive connection of the timeless sacred and the immediate numinous to the continuing here and now.[40]

Regarding theology, Schmitt's sovereign is the link between the transcendent and everyday life. But this is an exercise in nostalgia. If God is dead, the sovereign link to the transcendent is a redundancy. For the same reason that God died, Schmitt's sovereignty falls short. Sovereignty is disconnected from everyday life. Rappaport's understanding of ritual, however, couldn't be more intimately tied to the lived experience of its performers. He explains, "Although ritual's contents may be concerned with matters as trivial and inconsequential as the doings of tooth fairies, that which can be expressed in or achieved through the ritual form ... are neither trivial nor inconsequential but, on the contrary, are requisite to the perpetuation of human social life. I therefore take ritual to be the social act basic to humanity."[41] The sovereign decision on the exception—a kind of masculine assertion of virile power—tends to be viewed from below as an empty posture. One might think of the ways in which indigenous peoples virtually disregard national (imperialist) sovereignty in daily living, only

---

[39] Robbins, *Radical Democracy*, 83.
[40] Rappaport, *Ecology, Meaning, and Religion*, 243.
[41] Rappaport, *Ritual and Religion*, 31.

noticing it enough to give the sovereign or his representatives enough of a nod to feel acknowledged.

This brings to mind Robert Redford's 1988 film adaptation of John Nichols's 1974 novel, *The Milagro Beanfield War*. In the film, corporate interests weigh upon the small, New Mexico town of Milagro, pressuring the locals to sell their land and water rights. The town's oldest inhabitant, Amarante, played by Carlos Riquelme, is the conduit for the ancient beliefs and culture that have sustained it through centuries of impoverishment. Amarante prays each day to a shrine of supposedly Catholic saints—hybrids of the imperialist-imposed religious images and content and an ancient, indigenous polytheism. The subterfuge here is lovely. Amarante's "Catholic" saints—imposed upon him by a modern, European imperialist process, but appropriated by and filtered through his ancient and indigenous culture—are what give him the strength and support to resist the new, corporate imperialism. The location of authority and power may not always be as clear as the sovereign might like.

Rappaport's self-referentiality is preferable to sovereignty because it allows for a more nebulous understanding of authority and power. It is dependent upon the subjunctive, rather than the inevitable violence of the decision by the exception. Further, sovereignty is parasitic on the State. In a neoliberal global capitalist context, the State is in question. Sovereignty has been dislocated from State centers. Ritual self-referentiality, on the other hand, is the stuff of life. The sovereign decision is necessarily a very poor reflection of what the people have always known. Power comes from below. Exceptional circumstances only remain exceptional insofar as the people accept the exception. Self-referential subjunctivity is a more accurately descriptive, open, and fertile concept than Schmitt's sovereignty. Subjunctivity lends itself to people-power and democracy and to creation and cooperation, rather than destruction. In Robbins's words, "In the place of Schmitt's political theology, which follows from the idea of a sovereign and transcendent God, what I am proposing here is an immanent political theology predicated on the constituent power of the multitude."[42]

FROM THEORY TO APPLICATION

This project has been a deliberate and interdisciplinary investigation into, on the one hand, the common subjunctive foundation of both the political and the religious as well as, on the other, a construction of a theology

---

[42] Robbins, *Radical Democracy*, 84.

of resistance. The first two chapters marked out the conceptual terrain upon which I've wanted to work. In short, I began by establishing subjunctivity as an alternative foundational concept for political theology. Then I argued for an understanding of religion without God—both in terms of personal practice and in the construction of religious community. I concluded that radical theology—a name for thinking theologically in the absence of God—contains within it a latent political imperative. At that point, the project had laid out the tools necessary to undertake a theology of contemporary political resistance—this is the task of the chapters that follow. So its focus will now shift: this project has justified the methodological legitimacy of thinking theologically about resistance, and it now begins to experimentally perform that theology of resistance. The project is both arguing for subjunctivity and performing it.

This project has set out to situate itself within the field of political theology, but in an atypical way. Contrary to Carl Schmitt's dominant conception of political theology which is based upon a conception of the sovereign-as-tyrant, this work has proposed that Roy A. Rappaport's anthropology of ritual and the religious construction of social solidarity is a better, more fitting and fertile, and also democratic foundation for political theology. The key concept I have appropriated from Rappaport (and as expanded upon by his commenters, Adam B. Seligman, Robert P. Weller, Michael J. Puett, and Bennett Simon) is subjunctivity: the structure within human thinking and activity that conceives of the world's possibilities and alternatives to its existing realities. Schematically, the normative claim in Chap. 2 is that (a) political theology should be founded upon a nontheistic concept of religion, which (b) has at its center the ability of ritual to construct the bonds of social solidarity, which (c) in turn is the seat of religion's authority and the condition of political possibility, which (d) operates through open, critical, and creative imagining of the way the world might be—subjunctivity.

Then, Chap. 2 turned to an understanding of subjunctivity's world-construction through illusion and craft. In short, one of religion's most useful and important activities is world creation through deployment of illusion. As Seligman et al. explain, "Of course, by presenting our actions in this light [as productive of illusions]—more precisely, by constructing a symbolic universe where our activities with one another can be understood in this manner—we are also in a sense actually denoting the construction of the illusion as the real nature of our interaction. The 'as if' quality of the ritual invocation, its subjunctive sense, is also what makes it real. What is, is what can be."⁴³ Chapter 2 included an examination of the affinities between negative-theological mysticism and craft. Though these two examples of religious expression and activity might not seem to have much in common at first glance,⁴⁴ in my view, both participate in the religious construction of the world through subjunctive activity that circumvents religious language. As such, this project began to open the door to the possibilities of non-theistic religion.

Next, I argued that religious communion is best when God is absent. This section began with a reading of Martin Buber's idea of finding God in every other person. If God is in the person in front of you or even on the other side of the world, what need is there for a god in heaven? Further, as my reading of René Girard showed, one of the hidden—though deeply important—core concepts of the Jewish and Christian traditions is that God gradually withdraws from interaction with the world and religious adherents, ultimately becoming absent from human affairs entirely. At this point, I introduced one of the theologians most significant to this project: Paul Tillich. While I have certainly not remained faithful to Tillich's own theological convictions, I have nevertheless taken his understanding of theology as orientation to what ultimately concerns us as a point of constant reference and departure. Religion-as-ultimate-concern effectively allows us to abstract theological method from its traditional content, thus performing methodological theology. Theology no longer needs the theistic God after Tillich.

This chapter made the critical argument that the concept of subjunctivity, developed out of Roy A. Rappaport's study of ritual and language, is a more fitting foundation for political theology than Carl Schmitt's concept of sovereignty because the ritual act toward authority is more fundamental than the sovereign act of decision. Subjunctivity is the technology that builds society and the world.

The second half of this book continues to apply the theoretical insights garnered from the first half through interpretations of AIDS Coalition to Unleash Power (ACT UP), Occupy Wall Street, and #BlackLivesMatter. It is here that I first begin to deploy resisting theology. Resisting theology

---

⁴³ Adam B. Seligman, Robert P. Weller, Michael J. Puett, and Bennett Simon, *Ritual and Its Consequences: An Essay on the Limits of Sincerity* (Oxford and New York: Oxford University Press, 2008), 22.

⁴⁴ Do a twenty-first-century barber and a thirteenth-century Sufi have much to discuss? Perhaps if the Sufi is sufficiently hirsute.

takes the concerns of the tradition of political theology, but reads them in light of both ritual subjunctivity and radical theology. It is a methodological political theology. Rather than examining existing phenomena for their hidden theological underpinnings or unacknowledged influences, resisting theology instead applies theological thinking, through subjunctivity, as a way of understanding and interpreting acts, movements, and events of political resistance. It is not an attempt to chart a shift from theology to politics or vice versa, but rather to take these two together. It remains political-theological in its frames of reference, but also takes the death of God as axiomatic, and thus reads subjunctivity more openly than orthodox theological expressions might accept. Its understanding of religious ritual stretches to include a variety of human activities that are only counterintuitively so-described.

CHAPTER 4

Resisting Theology Part 2

Toward a Radical Theology of Politics

I take radical theology broadly to mean relentless and iconoclastic thought, paradoxically desirous of that which might stand up to its suspicion of ultimacy. It is theology suspicious of any claims to ultimacy. In political terms, radical theology is the theological resistance to theology. As I understand the term, theology resists itself. Figures rooted firmly within their own traditions, such as Buber, Tillich, Winquist, Bonhoeffer, Altizer, and Hamilton, but also Dōgen, Crawford, Attar, and Qushayri, each qualify as radical theological thinkers. Their respective willingness to examine the material, immanently experienced world, their recognition of Nietzsche's caution against religiosity that contradicts life, and their insistence upon humanity's role in creating the world anew are indeed both radical and theological. Further, their radical theology is a theopolitics. It cannot distinguish neatly between the religious and the political. If loving God is loving the other person, then theology is already an engagement and relationship between people. Radical theology is already political theology.

Carl Schmitt's sovereign determines the exception to the law in the name of the law, in order to preserve the legal order. But his theology is backward. Schmitt's Christianity betrays him. Jesus came not to destroy, revoke, or abolish the law, but to fulfill it.

> Do not think that I have come to abolish the law or the prophets; I have come not to abolish but to fulfill. For truly I tell you, until heaven and earth pass away, not one letter [one iota], not one stroke of a letter, will pass from the law until all is accomplished. Therefore, whoever breaks one of the least of these commandments, and teaches others to do the same, will be called least in the kingdom of heaven; but whoever does them and teaches them will be called great in the kingdom of heaven.[1]

For the Christian, Jesus—or the spirit Jesus' death looses upon the world, into it—is sovereign not because it is the exception that shores up and validates the legal order, but *because it fulfills the legal order once and for all.* Kenosis is the death (not the abolition) of the law; it is the law's completion. Only the living may die. The law, which has been fulfilled, may now be emptied. Christian resistance to political authority has long been a contentious issue. Paul wrote in Romans 13:

> Let every person be subject to the governing authorities; for there is no authority except from God, and those authorities that exist have been instituted by God. Therefore whoever resists authority resists what God has appointed, and those who resist will incur judgment. For rulers are not a terror to good conduct, but to bad. Do you wish to have no fear of the authority? Then do what is good, and you will receive its approval; for it is God's servant for your good. But if you do what is wrong, you should be afraid, for the authority does not bear the sword in vain! It is the servant of God to execute wrath on the wrongdoer. Therefore one must be subject, not only because of wrath but also because of conscience. For the same reason you also pay taxes, for the authorities are God's servants, busy with this very thing. Pay to all what is due them—taxes to whom taxes are due, revenue to whom revenue is due, respect to whom respect is due, honor to whom honor is due. Owe no one anything, except to love one another; for the one who loves another has fulfilled the law. The commandments, "You shall not commit adultery; You shall not murder; You shall not steal; You shall not covet"; and any other commandment, are summed up in this word, "Love your neighbor as yourself." Love does no wrong to a neighbor; therefore, love is the fulfilling of the law.[2]

This passage has been used since Constantine to provide legitimacy for any number of ruling authorities. It is simple for those in power to use Paul's "Let everyone be subject to the governing authorities; for there is no

---

[1] Matthew 5:17–19 (NRSV).
[2] Romans 13:1–10 (NRSV).

authority except from God" to mean that they are divinely ordained and anyone who might try to defy them is thus defying God's will. But when this passage is understood in its full context, we might recognize that the limit to one's respect for the legitimacy of the State is set by the commandment not to do wrong to a neighbor. Taking Jesus' words from Matthew 5 in conjunction with Paul's 13th chapter of Romans and its comments regarding subjection to political authority, the meaning behind the declaration that "love is the fulfillment of the law" takes on new significance.

Love is the radical embodiment of anarchy. That is, love is the radical embodiment of anarchy whereof the prefix, "an," refers not simply to absence, but the completion, fulfillment, and passing away of the law. Radical political theology—resisting theology—is a thinking that brings all established orders into question. Its relentless skepticism, insistent desire, and iconoclasm are also politically directed as anarchic resistance. Radical political theology is subjunctive political theology without sovereignty. It is theologically iconoclastic and apophatic, as I showed above. But it is also politically subversive. It is a religious atheism and a political anarchism. I demonstrate this more clearly in the next chapters.

Resisting Theology (Again)

This is a work of political theology. Carl Schmitt, the point of departure of my understanding of the field, describes a political theology that is both descriptive and normative. He uncovers and examines the ways in which theological concepts became secularized into modern political concepts, and he valorizes sovereignty. Schmitt's political theology is therefore quite specific in its parasitism on the modern State. Instead, this work has understood political theology differently, considering it a hybrid branch of political philosophy, philosophy of religion, and theology that investigates ways in which religious concepts, postures, and thinking underlie political, social, economic, and cultural discourses and institutions.

Further, religious community is only possible in God's absence. This means that the most appropriate places to look for religious community are the ones wherein nothing explicitly religious appears at first glance. And so, for similar reasons that the craftsperson described in Chap. 2 might be more theological in her work than a priest might, the secular gathering of friends or trade unionists might be more religious in their community than the groups inside any given sanctuary during a prayer service. The second half of this book's thesis is that acts, movements, and events of political resistance are the expressions of resisting theology *par excellence*. That is, when one considers ritual subjunctivity and social construction, religious practice as craft and craft as religious practice, and the experience of the death of God with its ensuing political imperative, it becomes both novel and *right* to theologize political resistance.

Schmitt described his work as a sociology of concepts.[3] This work is a transposition of concepts. It plays with terms and ideas, transposing them into different orders of thought to see what might register differently. Theology of resistance becomes possible through such play—a resisting theological experiment in transposition. So, religious practice becomes craft which becomes labor more generally, harkening back to "the work of ritual" in construction of a subjunctive, social reality. This is the transposition that allows us to begin thinking in terms of a theology of work.

The process of resisting theology in this work has been one of enacted subjunctivity all along. So here, in the second half of the book, I write about resistance *as if it is* a theological object. I am wagering that it is, but it need not be in order to undertake the work. Thinking of religion in terms of craft—of labor—opens us up to a new way of understanding capitalism, globalization, and neoliberalism as theologically relevant. This is not to say that they weren't theologically relevant before; only to suggest that they might be brought under the religious spotlight of subjunctivity differently than their more traditional religious contexts concerning such concepts as the Protestant work ethic, for instance. This project's early invocation of Marx has now taken on new significance. Marx's concern with religion was driven by his desire to liberate humanity from what oppressed it. But when religion is understood in terms of craft and of the *work* of ritual, Marx's concern with the eradication of alienation and oppression becomes a radically *theological* concern. Superficially, I might have been able to make this argument earlier, solely on the basis of Tillich's notion of religion as ultimate concern and the impossibility of being nonreligious. But it's more than that. Marx's concern with labor might subjunctively be considered a concern with religious practice—again, not on the simple level of translation where laborers become the Church, work becomes worship, the party becomes the body of priests, and so on, but in the very real sense of religion as the mode of construction of the world.

So below, I begin to rely more heavily on this principle of transposition. While the move from a discussion of political theology involving an

---

[3] Schmitt, *Political Theology*, 45–6.

anthropologist of ritual by way of craft and mysticism that takes the death of God as axiomatic might not immediately or intuitively arrive at a discussion of contemporary North American social movements, I argue to the contrary, that it is both entirely appropriate and natural. Musical performance is a good metaphor for this project's approach. The word "religion," as we might remember, has its roots in the Latin *religare*: to bind again. In the Middle Ages, there was a mark used in musical notation known as a "ligature." One of its most common uses within chanted song was to signify the performance of multiple notes with a single gesture. That is, in sung music, it tied multiple notes together into one sung syllable.[4] This project has sought to perform such religious ligatures through the demonstration of a variety of affinities across disciplinary and methodological lines.

So I repeat: resistance is theological activity. I've demonstrated this through a deployment of radical political theology. But there is also a way of understanding ritual as containing the seed of resistance already, before the performance of any transpositions. In Chap. 3, I discussed *The Milagro Beanfield War* as an example of one of the ways in which the multitude always already understands the emptiness of the sovereign. But it is also a resource for us in another way. Michel de Certeau writes of the same phenomenon—indigenous Latin Americans' manipulation and appropriation of imperialist-imposed social orders—when he writes:

> … the ambiguity that subverted from within the Spanish colonizers' "success" in imposing their own culture on the indigenous Indians is well known. Submissive, and even consenting to their subjection, the Indians nevertheless often made of the rituals, representations, and laws imposed on them something quite different from what their conquerors had in mind; they subverted them not by rejecting or altering the system they had no choice but to accept. They were other within the very colonization that outwardly assimilated them; their use of the dominant social order deflected its power, which they lacked the means to challenge; they escaped it without leaving it. The strength of their similar ambiguity creeps into our societies through the use made by the "common people" of the culture disseminated and imposed by "elites" producing the language.[5]

---

[4] For instance, when the word "alleluia" is chanted over a series of six notes, one note each for the first, second, and fourth syllables, but "lu" being stretched out over three notes.

[5] Certeau, xiii.

The oppressor unwittingly provides the very means of resistance against it. This line of thinking will come up again in a more sustained way in this chapter in my discussion of the theology of urban resistance. Rappaport's definition is that ritual is "the performance of more or less invariant sequences of formal acts and utterances not entirely encoded by the performers."[6] The component of ritual that ties it to tradition—that it is not entirely encoded by its performers—is also the very component that opens up the possibility of resistance. Ritual is never entirely mine. My stake in it is negotiable. And it is that distance—that lack of authenticity—that allows ritual performers to invest the ritual with new, unforeseen content, purpose, and meaning. This indigenous Latin American example is a link between Rappaport's notion of insincerity in ritual, the political properties of subjunctivity, resistance, and Merton's notion of celebration, which I discuss later.

Ritual has resistance built in. Building off of Rappaport's definition of ritual and reading it through Certeau, we must conclude that there is a peculiar way that ritual performance—by its very nature of not being entirely circumscribed by its performers, by its appropriation from some other who came before—is itself already 'an act of resistance.' This secondary production hidden in the process of the utilization of a given image or action is the resistance to a power dynamic—theological, political, or otherwise—already contained within the performance of that power dynamic. And this is all part of the very structure of ritual itself. As Seligman et al. explain, the resistance of ritual begins with a structural, ethical imperative:

> We are constituted on our boundaries, that is to say, constituted on a plane we do not totally control, one that is always also open to the other, to the stranger, to what is different and unknown and beyond the controlling power of the center. This is what makes boundaries dangerous. Rather than trying to eliminate boundaries or to make them into unbreachable walls—the two approaches that so typified the 20th century—ritual continually renegotiates boundaries, living with their instability and labile nature. Only by paying closer attention to the play of ritual—to its formal elements, even when those formal rhythms may overwhelm claims of content—can we find the way to negotiate the emergent demands of our contemporary world.[7]

---

[6] Rappaport, *Ritual and Religion*, 24.

[7] Seligman et al., 11. This line of thought continues, "By recognizing limits, ritual provides as well the vehicle for transcending them. In the beginning of the Jewish daily prayers, for example, the devotee proclaims: 'What are we? What is our life? What is our goodness? What

There are clear affinities here with both radical democracy and radical theology on the point of provisionality and renegotiation. Each of these maintains a relentless openness and suspicion. In Certeau's terms, subjunctivity is tactical, as opposed to strategic. For him, "The place of a tactic belongs to the other. A tactic insinuate itself into the other's place, fragmentarily, without taking it over in its entirety, without being able to keep it at a distance."[8] And ritual is not entirely encoded by its performers. Ritual is tactical.

It would have been simple, if uninteresting, to map Rappaport's theory of ritual onto Occupy Wall Street or the AIDS Coalition to Unleash Power's (ACT UP's) anarchist organizing principles and tactics—decision-making through consensus and the resulting virtually endless debate over mundane matters and minutiae as a satirical reflection of ritual and theology's tendencies toward all-encompassing *Summas*, the liturgical quality of the people's microphone, the evangelical tone of the rhetoric surrounding "the 99%," and so on. But instead, I have tended to be more focused on the abstract affinities, reading the entirety of this experiment through the lens of subjunctivity. Still, each of these resisting theological partners concern themselves with the subjunctive task of creating the world anew. But this is only necessary if the world is first viewed as broken or incomplete.[9] For Seligman et al., ritual always functions within the register of the tragic.

> ... the subjunctive world created by ritual is always doomed ultimately to fail—the ordered world of flawless repetition can never fully replace the broken world of experience. This is why the tension between the two is inherent

our righteousness? What our helpfulness? What our strength? What our might? ... Indeed all the heroes are as nothing before thee, the men of renown as though they never existed.' But then, immediately declares as well: 'However, we are thy people, thy people of the covenant, the children of Abraham thy friend to whom thou didst make a promise on Mount Moriah.' The first set of sentences circumscribes existence and its meaning, the last opens it up" (12).

[8] Certeau, xix. He also explains, "I call a 'strategy' the calculus of force-relationships which becomes possible when a subject of will and power (a proprietor, an enterprise, a city, a scientific institution) can be isolated from an 'environment.' A strategy assumes a place that can be circumscribed as proper (*propre*) and thus serve as the basis for generating relations with an exterior distinct from it (competitors, adversaries, 'clienteles,' 'targets,' or 'objects' of research). Political, economic, and scientific rationality has been constructed on this strategic model." Strategy thus implies an advantageous power differential and its application from above, while strategic operations always occur from below.

[9] Seligman et al. write on p. 31, "From the point of view of ritual, the world is fragmented and fractured. This is why the endless work of ritual is necessary, even if that work is always, ultimately, doomed."

and, ultimately, unbridgeable. Indeed, this tension is the driving force behind the performance of ritual: the endless work of ritual is necessary precisely because the ordered world of ritual is inevitably only temporary. The world always returns to its broken state, constantly requiring the repairs of ritual. ... Although the claims of ritual may be of an ordered, flawless system, the workings of ritual are always in the realm of the limited and the ultimately doomed.[10]

There are no big solutions; there are only tactics for dealing with what's in front of us. Ritual must remain constantly dynamic and in response to conditions as they develop. This is another point of contact between ritual and the secular where, for Talal Asad, "In brief, this world is 'secular' not because scientific knowledge has replaced religious belief (that is, because the 'real' has at last become apparent) but because, on the contrary, it must be lived in uncertainty, without fixed moorings even for the believer, a world in which the real and the imaginary mirror each other. In this world the politics of certainty is clearly impossible."[11] This is a world all the more deserving of ritual subjunctivity's ability to navigate—however provisionally—the uncertainties of everyday life. This is why theology of resistance is so important. And it is here that the tactics of ritual have taken on additional significance.

Remaining tactical requires a fundamental uncertainty about the world. The world often presents us with situations for which we have no ready-at-hand ritual.

> ... if one is constructing a subjunctive world of "as if" through ritual, then what happens when one confronts a situation (as one does all the time—it is, after all, a fractured world) where there is no clear ritual telling one what to do, or where there are conflicting ritual obligations? ... one of the goals of ritual is to train practitioners to be able to act as if there were a ritual telling them what to do.[12]

So it's subjunctive tactics all the way down, always bobbing and weaving in response to the fractures appearing in front and around. This is why, "One of our concerns with so much ritual theory ... is that it has been overly concerned with reading ritual according to a vision of system, of totality, and of harmony. Whether that totality is read as a functional

---

[10] Seligman et al., 30.
[11] Asad, 65.
[12] Seligman et al., 35.

system or a system of meanings, it is always ordered and, when idealized, is always seen as either creating or exemplifying a static, harmonious world." They continue:

> In contrast, we have argued here that ritual—particularly when it is effective—more often operates in the realm of the limited and thus the subjunctive. ... Ritual, therefore, means never-ending work. It is a recurrent, always imperfect, project of dealing with patterns of human behavior—patterns that are always at risk of shifting into dangerous directions—or of unleashing demons.[13]

The tactics of ritual must always take their position from below. No God's-eye view is possible here. This is why resistance from below without the possibility of a strategic perspective—the sub-jungere resistance of the polis, joining from below—is the political instantiation of the death of God. Its ritual thus works best through its very uncertainty—another world is possible, but no perfect world will ever come. This is why we conclude that, however counterintuitively or paradoxically, ritual works best in the absence of God.

Ritual becomes destructive when it shifts from tactics to a strategic position. This is why resistance is built in to the very foundations of religion. The world is always fractured and ritual subjunctivity is a tactical response to healing the world (*tikkun olam*). But the subjunctive must always remain positioned in response to that fracture: it resists the chaos and meaninglessness of that fracture. So we have a litany of resonances across this project: tactics, ritual's subjunctivity, and resistance. McKenzie Wark suggested that the genius of Occupy was to suggest that there could be a politics when all there is at the moment is a void at the center of American life.[14] Occupy, and ACT UP before it, quite literally did the work of healing that fracture, however provisionally.

So we've circled back to where we began, but in a new key. Notes have resonated throughout this project, sustaining affinities where they may not have been apparent at the outset, producing unexpected harmonies. In the final paragraphs of this section, I hope to demonstrate some of the affinities that have arisen out of the subjunctive gamble of this project. That is, the-

---

[13] Seligman et al., 42.
[14] McKenzie Wark, "How to Occupy an Abstraction," from the Verso Books blog, October 3, http://www.versobooks.com/blogs/728-mckenzie-wark-on-occupy-wall-street-how-to-occupy-an-abstraction.

ology of resistance is not a simple matter of superficial conflation, but the production of a subjunctive and interdisciplinary composite. We may read this project in a non-linear way—taking the medieval ligature as our inspiration—layering ideas on top of one another, hopefully allowing them to be heard differently than we heard them the first time around. The previous chapters have undertaken the work of sufficiently establishing the method and context for a more rigorous interdisciplinary enterprise. Now—as a kind intermission—we'll quickly note some significant gestures.

The first and most important such affinity is between radical theological method and our understanding of ritual subjunctivity—both of which emphasize action and performance over specific content. This is a shift in how both disciplinary traditions—social science of ritual and theology—have approached their studies. Regarding the former, Seligman et al. write, "Ritual, as we shall be arguing here, is best approached through what it does rather than through what it may mean, although a focus on meaning has characterized much of the social scientific literature on ritual in the past. While that literature's findings are many and significant, they do tend to blind us to certain core aspects of ritual that gain much from shifting the focus of study from meaning to doing."[15] Likewise, as we saw initially in Tillich, it is the doing of theology that concerns us here, rather than its aim or object. This is a note that resonates across the project, connecting the earliest sections with the latest.

Political collectivities are another example of a note of transposition and resonance. Schmitt argued that the theological underlies the political through the secularization of theological concepts into modern political concepts within the State. In the discussion of cities in the previous chapter, political theology became urban theology through reading the city, like Certeau, as a subject—a Leviathan.[16] This further resonated with radical theology's emphasis on going out into the city in God's absence and working there.[17] On that point, the world-construction work of ritual is implicit. So this project has been concerned with various forms of making. Subjunctivity is creative. Ritual works to create social solidarity.

> This is why Seligman et al., following Rappaport, understand "… ritual as a subjunctive—the creation of an order as if it were truly the case. Or, putting

---

[15] Seligman et al., 15.
[16] Certeau, 94–5.
[17] Thomas J. J. Altizer and William Hamilton. *Radical Theology and the Death of God* (Indianapolis and New York: Bobbs-Merrill Company, Inc., 1966), 44.

it in different words, the subjunctive creates an order that is self-consciously distinct from other possible social worlds. ... we emphasize the incongruity between the world of enacted ritual and the participants' experience of lived reality, and we thus focus on the work that the ritual accomplishes."[18]

This explains how we could come to suggest that craft is a form of religious practice. This theme got picked up again with the assertion that cities are produced, and yet again in arguing that resistance to neoliberalism is an expression of the desire to take control of one's labor, which is thus another expression of religious practice. The city is where humanity makes itself. "Heaven and Earth give life, but they are also fundamentally chaotic, without pattern. And so, therefore, is humanity. Only humans can give pattern and order to the world. In short, order is an artifice of humanity."[19] The city is what humanity makes with the tool of subjunctivity, through resistance, ritual, and craft. The city is thus a radical, political-theological object. I cover this is more detail below.

Another note of resonance throughout this project is risk. Radical democracy—or the anarchic multitude—is the political instantiation of the death of God. Radical democracy risks everything. It risks the entire established order for the possibility of a world that might be. As we saw in Chap. 2, Tillichian faith is only meaningful in proportion to its risks. So, radical theology risks theology itself. Tying back into our discussion of labor, work, and creativity, read alongside recent and contemporary North American social movements, we may now say that both anarchy and God create new worlds.

All of this has been done in the spirit of a performance experiment. We have arrived at the suggestion that music is an appropriate metaphor for considering the methodological activities employed throughout this project: something I'm calling a transposition of concepts. It has described and demonstrated an alternate lineage of political theology moving from an anthropology of ritual and its operative concept, subjunctivity, through apophaticism, craft, and radical theology, to arrive at a demonstration of resisting theology in a secular theological understanding of ACT UP, Occupy Wall Street, and #BlackLivesMatter. In the academy struggling with disciplinary boundaries, navel-gazing, and entrenched thinking—and in our contemporary world, rife with conflict, resistance, and religion, this kind of work is not only appropriate, but also necessary.

[18] Seligman et al., 20.
[19] Seligman et al., 18.

The following chapters look at ACT UP, Occupy Wall Street, and #BlackLivesMatter as expressions of resisting theology. So, in a sense, I am stacking the deck. In looking at Occupy Wall Street and its anarchist roots, for instance, I am arguing that resistance movements are politically subjunctive ("another world is possible!"), and also that religion is inherently subjunctive as well. If cities are a kind of material, enacted, lived subjunctivity (as opposed to an imaginative or cerebral subjunctivity) on a social or political scale, then resistance movements that happen within cities that rely on modeling life lived differently serve as hyperbolic cases, exemplary of the kind of resisting theological expression I have been working up to.

I am not looking for theological content in resistance movements, though it may often be found there. To do so would be akin to the ways in which one might map religious forms and concepts onto secular content as is popularly performed with sports: the game is the worship service, the fans are the congregation, nachos and beer are a sacramental meal, the crowd's chants are hymns, cheerleaders are the choir, and so on. I am not doing that. I'm also not attempting to colonize resistance in a supersessionist gesture to invoke a kind of natural theology unwittingly revealed in acts of resistance. Rather, I am exploring resistance movements and events through a radical theological lens—or, better yet, resisting theologically. What does this process reveal? Or more precisely, what does it produce? What new possibilities does it open up? This is initially a matter of emphasizing affinities between theology and resistance. But in theologizing resistance, radical theology's concern comes to the fore. Radical theology is skeptical of the very grounds of theology itself. My hypothesis is that this process might open us up to a reflexivity between theology and resistance. In a conscious rejection of disciplinary colonization, theologizing resistance might then help us, in turn, to resist theology—radicalizing politics may help to further radicalize theology.[20] As Bonhoeffer advocated living in the world as if there were no God (before God!), this process of theologizing resistance may allow us to resist theology for theology.

---

[20] I am inspired by Maia Ramnath for this line of thinking and I am following her lead in her use of anarchist analysis in understanding South Asian anti-colonial movements. See: Maia Ramnath, *Decolonizing Anarchism: An Antiauthoritarian History of India's Liberation Struggle* (Oakland, CA: AK Press/Institute for Anarchist Studies, 2011). The two fields she brings into tension are anarchist political philosophy and decolonial theory. In that text, she uses anarchy to understand anti-colonial activities and, in the process, attempts a decolonization of anarchy. This inspires the component of my project that not only theologizes resistance, but—in the vein of the radical theological tradition—resists theology as well.

Modernity, Politics, and Religion

Resistance is theological and theology resists. That is my thesis. At its core, this book is about the relationship between religion and politics, or more specifically, between the functions and methods of the theological and the operations of political resistance. Some clarity on these terms is in order. Throughout this book, I understand the theological as that which inspires and animates both the religious and the political. But it hasn't always been so. "Religion" and "politics" are fluid concepts. I argue that the modern European understanding of the relationship between religion and politics was based on the concept of sovereignty (not the theological) and the priority of Christendom over any particular State.

By "modernity," I am following Marshall Berman's schema referring to the era that followed the medieval period and began over the course of the long sixteenth century.[21] This is the time in the West that saw the invention of the printing press and the corresponding possibility of mass literacy, the Protestant Reformation, the Renaissance, the development of Enlightenment rationalism and the scientific revolution, the development of the State as a world force and its corresponding political liberalism, the European colonization of the Americas and the creation of the transatlantic race-based slave trade, the development of capitalism in its initial mercantilist phase, and the start of the Anthropocene.[22] This is also the period which, due to the confluence of factors including the Reformation and the development of the State, produced the so-called "Wars of Religion." According to William Cavanaugh:

> The "Wars of Religion" were not the events which necessitated the birth of the modern State; they were in fact themselves the birthpangs of the State. These wars were not simply a matter of conflict between "Protestantism"

---

[21] Marshall Berman, *All That Is Solid Melts into Air: The Experience of Modernity* (New York: Penguin, 1988), 16–7. While I follow Berman's analysis regarding the *foundations* of modernity, as will become clear, I do not share his conclusions about the status of modernity in recent decades. This is due largely to the fact that Berman's primary consideration is art, while mine is the relationship between religion and politics.

[22] The history here is complicated and non-linear. The modern concept of the *nation* did not emerge until the French Revolution. Only afterward did it spread unevenly and incompletely across the European continent. See Eugen Weber's *Peasants into Frenchmen* (Stanford, CA: Stanford UP, 1976), for instance, for an explanation of how France didn't become a nation until the end of the nineteenth century. I must give a nod to reviewer #1 for helping me flesh this out. I'm also following Lewis and Maslin's definition of the Anthropocene as starting in 1610 as they lay out in their article, "Defining the Anthropocene," (Simon L. Lewis and Mark A. Maslin. pp. 171–180, *Nature*. Vol. 519, March 12, 2015).

and "Catholicism," but were fought largely for the aggrandizement of the emerging State over the decaying remnants of the medieval ecclesial order. I do not wish merely to contend that political and economic factors played a central role in these wars, nor to make a facile reduction of religion to more mundane concerns. I will rather argue that to call these conflicts "Wars of Religion" is an anachronism, for what was at issue in these wars was the very creation of religion as a set of privately held beliefs without direct political relevance. The creation of religion was necessitated by the new State's need to secure absolute sovereignty over its subjects.[23]

When considering the relationship between religion and politics in the West, it is important to begin during the modern period in order to come to a historical understanding of that relationship and how it has developed over time. In other words, the concepts of religion and politics are not pure abstractions, floating free and disconnected from lived, historical experience.

The significance of modernity for understanding religion and politics is due in part to the period in which "religion" became a separate category of social life. Cavanaugh explains that, "In the medieval period the Church was the supreme common power; the civil authority, as John Figgis put it, was 'the police department of the Church.' The net result of the conflicts of the sixteenth and seventeenth centuries was to invert the dominance of the ecclesiastical over the civil authorities through the creation of the modern State."[24] Theologically, Cavanaugh argues, this newly developing relationship was advocated by none other than Martin Luther himself. Luther, writes Cavanaugh, understood "coercive force by its very nature [to be] secular, and so the Church could be understood only as a moral, and not a jurisdictional, body." Cavanaugh continues explaining:

> Every Christian, Luther maintained, is simultaneously subject to two kingdoms or two governances, the spiritual and the temporal. Coercive power is ordained by God but is given only to the secular powers in order that civil peace be maintained among sinners. Since coercive power is defined as secular, the Church is left with a purely suasive authority, that of preaching the Word of God. ... Because the Christian is saved by faith alone, the Church will in time become, strictly speaking, unnecessary for salvation, taking on the status of a *congregano fidelium*, a collection of the faithful for the purpose

---

[23] William Cavanaugh, "'A Fire Strong Enough to Consume the House:' The Wars of Religion and the Rise of the State," pp. 397–420 in *Modern Theology* 11:4 (October 1995), 398.
[24] Cavanaugh, 399.

of nourishing the faith. What is left to the Church is increasingly the purely interior government of the souls of its members; their bodies are handed over to the secular authorities.[25]

Cavanaugh spends the bulk of his article, "A Fire Strong Enough to Consume the House," detailing the various political figures involved in "the Wars of Religion" during this period and their political uses of theological distinctions. He argues that Charles V, the Holy Roman Emperor and belligerent against the Lutheran States in the first major War of Religion, was more concerned with consolidating Imperial authority than he was with theological differences.[26] The result of these birth pangs of the modern State was "the springboard for the development of the absolutist vision of sovereign power unchallenged within the state which would come to full fruition in seventeenth century France. ... The rise of a centralized bureaucratic state preceded these wars and was based on the fifteenth century assertion of civil dominance over the Church in France."[27]

Cavanaugh notes that the term *religio* appears very infrequently during the medieval period and when it does so, it is in reference to monastics. He clarifies, "*Religio* for St. Thomas is just one virtue which presupposes a context of ecclesial practices which are both communal and particular to the Christian Church."[28] The birth of the State with its assumption of many of the historical governing powers of the Church thus required a change in how religion is understood. According to Cavanaugh, this is a two-fold change. First, Cavanaugh argues that the discrete category we call "religion" was created as a necessary counterpart to the new political entity known as the State.

> What is at issue behind these wars is the creation of "religion" as a set of beliefs which is defined as personal conviction and which can exist separately from one's public loyalty to the State. The creation of religion, and thus the privatization of the Church, is correlative to the rise of the State. It is important therefore to see that the principal promoters of the wars in France and Germany were in fact not pastors and peasants, but kings and nobles with a stake in the outcome of the movement toward the centralized, hegemonic State.[29]

---

[25] Cavanaugh, 399.
[26] Cavanaugh, 400.
[27] Cavanaugh, 402.
[28] Cavanaugh, 404.
[29] Cavanaugh, 403.

Succinctly, Cavanaugh's argument is that "... the rise of the modern concept of religion is associated with the decline of the Church as the particular locus of the communal practice of *religio*. ... The second major shift in the meaning of the term religion, which takes shape through the late sixteenth and seventeenth centuries, is toward religion as a system of beliefs. Religion moves from a virtue to a set of propositions."[30] All of this occurs for the sake of power. It's sovereignty at stake.

> The dominance of the State over the Church in the sixteenth and seventeenth centuries allowed temporal rulers to direct doctrinal conflicts to secular ends. The new State required unchallenged authority within its borders, and so the domestication of the Church. Church leaders became acolytes of the State as the religion of the State replaced that of the Church, or more accurately, the very concept of religion as separable from the Church was invented.[31]

While Cavanaugh focuses on this historical development of the discrete categories of religion, Church, and State, I am more concerned here with the power that was in flux during that early modern transition, and which still reverberates today.

Sovereignty was the genesis of that power—coercive or suasive—that was at stake. While once unified, sovereignty bifurcated into two categories and spheres of life. Sovereignty became expressed privately through the category of religion and publicly through the State. Berman writes that

> to be modern ... is to experience personal and social life as a maelstrom, to find one's world and oneself in perpetual disintegration and renewal, trouble and anguish, ambiguity and contradiction: to be part of a universe in which all that is solid melts into air. To be a modernist is to make oneself somehow at home in the maelstrom, to make its rhythms one's own, to move within its currents in search of the forms of reality, of beauty, of freedom, of justice, that its fervid and perilous flow allows.[32]

---

[30] Cavanaugh, 404. He continues, "The concept of religion being born here is one of domesticated belief systems which are, insofar as it is possible, to be manipulated by the sovereign for the benefit of the State. Religion is no longer a matter of certain bodily practices within the Body of Christ, but is limited to the realm of the 'soul,' and the body is handed over to the State," 405.

[31] Cavanaugh, 408.

[32] Berman, Marshall (2009). *All That Is Solid Melts into Air: The Experience Of Modernity* (9th ed.). London, New York: Verso. pp. 345–346.

Table 4.1 Religion and politics at modernity's start

Animator	Category	Social sphere	Function	Product
Sovereignty	Religion (the sacred Church)	Private	Ordering/maintaining	Meaning-maintenance
	Politics (the secular State)	Public	Disordering/reordering	War, State-making

I argue, following Cavanaugh, that religion advanced as a way to maintain continuity in meaning in a tumultuous public world. Understanding modernity as perpetual disintegration and renewal, I take politics to be the principal force behind disintegration and religion the principal force behind renewal or maintenance during this period. Politics, the realm newly dominated by the State, was a disordering or reordering force in the world. Its process during modernity is a disordering one. It's the force of war and State-making. Religion, on the other hand, develops in modernity into a private affair, still based on and inspired by sovereign power, as a way of ordering and maintaining social life and maintaining a sense of meaning in a rapidly changing world (Table 4.1).

Politically, modernity ushered in the ubiquity and hegemony of the State. This was achieved largely through the growth of capitalism after the European invasion of the Americas and the institution of the transatlantic slave trade. I discuss this in much more detail in Chap. 7. For now, suffice it to say that, theologically, the modern period culminated in the disintegration of Christendom. Modernity made religion a private matter, while the public sphere was reserved for matters of the State. Disciplinarily, that means the end of theology as a discourse in control of its own terms.

Rather than conceiving of modernity as a proper stage in its own right, I understand modernity as the *transition* from a period of sovereignty as the animator of social life to our current period when sovereignty has dissolved into the market. "Modernity" is the name of that long dissolution. If modernity is the name of the transition of sovereignty being emptied into the market, then liberalism is the vehicle of this transition. At the start of modernity, Spinoza already saw that sovereignty was being displaced. In this way, Spinoza is the prophet of the theological. Not only Antonio Negri, but even the great enemy of Spinoza, Leo Strauss, could recognize Spinoza's contribution. "He was the first philosopher who was both a democrat and a liberal. He was the philosopher who founded liberal democracy, a specifically modern regime."[33] This insight of Spinoza foreshadows what Alexis de Tocqueville would witness in his travels in the United States in the nineteenth century: "The people reign in the American political world as the Deity does in the universe. They are the cause and the aim of all things; everything comes from them, and everything is absorbed in them."[34] It is clear that Spinoza foresaw the collapse in sovereign authority brought on by modernity through political liberalism, but it wasn't until a mature United States that the process was completed: sovereign God had been emptied into the body politic. Nietzsche, writing not long before Tocqueville, noticed the death of sovereignty in the moral realm and called it the death of God. He begins by searching, "Have you not heard of that madman who lit a lantern in the bright morning hours, ran to the market-place, and cried incessantly: 'I am looking for God! I am looking for God!'" It is not incidental that the madman began his search and made his proclamation in the marketplace rather than in the church, but God was nowhere to be found.[35]

In 1979, Jean-Francois Lyotard published *The Postmodern Condition: A Report on Knowledge* as a study of the recent changes in what he calls "the condition of knowledge."[36] Lyotard is concerned primarily with changes in knowledge during the postwar period—and the question of where legitimacy is to be found. He is also interested in the specialization of knowledge and study. But more than all that, Lyotard is concerned with justice.[37] Lyotard describes knowledge in postindustrial societies as undergoing a crisis of legitimacy. What might we believe? Why? Lyotard writes:

---

[33] Leo Strauss, *Spinoza's Critique of Religion*, trans. E. M. Sinclair (Chicago and London: University of Chicago Press, 1997), 16. Additionally, Negri writes in *Subversive Spinoza*, ed. Timothy S. Murphy (Manchester and New York: Manchester University Press, 2004), "Spinoza's *Political Treatise* is the work that founds, in theoretical terms, modern European democratic political thought," p. 9. Finally, see also Chap. 16 of Baruch Spinoza's *Theological-Political Treatise*, second edition trans. Samuel Shirley (Indianapolis and Cambridge: Hackett, 2001), 173–184.

[34] Alexis de Tocqueville, *Democracy in America*, ed. Richard D. Heffner (New York: Mentor Books, 1956), 57–8. Tocqueville's insight and its relevance to both radical and political theology are treated fully in Jeffrey W. Robbins's *Radical Democracy and Political Theology*.

[35] Friedrich Nietzsche, *The Gay Science*, trans. Walter Kaufmann (New York: Vintage, 1974), aphorism 125, pp. 181–82.

[36] Jean-Francois Lyotard, *The Postmodern Condition: A Report on Knowledge*, trans. Geoff Bennington and Brian Massumi (Minneapolis: University of Minnesota Press, 2002), xxiii.

[37] For instance, Lyotard ends his essay, "Answering the Question: What is Postmodernism?" on page 82 of *The Postmodern Condition*, (translated by Geoff Bennington and Brian Massumi, foreword by Fredric Jameson, Minneapolis: University of Minnesota Press, 2002)

> Simplifying to the extreme, I define *postmodern* as incredulity toward metanarratives. This incredulity is undoubtedly a product of progress in the sciences: but that progress in turn presupposes it. To the obsolescence of the metanarrative apparatus of legitimation corresponds, most notably, the crisis of metaphysical philosophy and of the university institution which in the past relied on it. The narrative function is losing its functors, its great hero, its great dangers, its great voyages, its great goal. It is being dispersed in clouds of narrative language elements–narrative, but also denotative, prescriptive, descriptive, and so on. Conveyed within each cloud are pragmatic valencies specific to its kind. Each of us lives at the intersection of many of these. However, we do not necessarily establish stable language combinations, and the properties of the ones we do establish are not necessarily communicable.[38]

The repercussions of that collapse in sovereign authority that had been foretold by Spinoza in the mid-seventeenth century were only coming to be understood fully in the twentieth century.

THEOLOGY TODAY

Charles Winquist, more than any other recent theologian, is concerned with the historical implications that the end of modernity has for theological thinking. Winquist is a theological thinker of desire without God. Following Tillich, Winquist insists upon theology as a mode of interrogation. "I especially want to think about theology as a way of thinking," he writes.[39] And he further insists upon being honest about thinking theologically after the death of God. Again, God's absence does not mean the absence of theology or of the sacred. "In what appears to be an oxymoronic formulation, the death of God is celebrated as a possibility for a new theological thinking."[40] Whether ironically or dialectically, it should be clear what is going on here: the death of God is not a contestation of a tradition, but an affirmation of it through its subversion. Death-of-God thought is borne of a sincere theological impulse. As Clayton Crockett explains, "... the death of God is the result of a genuine theological

---

by writing, "The answer is: let us wage a war on totality; let us be witnesses to the unrepresentable; let us activate the differences and save the honor of the name."

[38] Lyotard, xxiv.

[39] Charles E. Winquist, "Postmodern Secular Theology," in pp. 26–36 of *Secular Theology: American Radical Theological Thought*, ed. Clayton Crockett (London and New York: Routledge, 2001), 26.

[40] Winquist, 27.

yearning for God, not simply a cynical and self-serving pronouncement."[41] What death-of-God theology accomplishes is an injection of the subjunctive back into experience. The death of God makes theology newly possible again.

Winquist defines theology as the desire for a thinking that doesn't disappoint.[42] For Winquist, in practice, this shifts the focus of defining theology by its object which has historically been *theos*—God—to defining it by its method. This means that anything that expresses a desire for a thinking that doesn't disappoint is theological. Winquist bases his understanding of theology in part on his reading of Paul Tillich's theology of culture: "... faith is the state of being grasped by an ultimate concern, and God is the name for the content of the concern. Such a concept of religion has little in common with the description of religion as the belief in the existence of a highest being called God, and the theoretical and practical consequences of such a belief. Instead, we are pointing to an existential, not a theoretical, understanding of religion."[43]

I take this point from Winquist fully. Theology is the desire for thinking that doesn't disappoint. But following on the understanding of religion developed above wherein religion is a form of world-manufacture and meaning-production, this understanding of theology needs some more unpacking. Reading theology of desire and subjunctive religion together, I want to heuristically propose that religion is the living of an alternative. Religion is the application of the theological will to everyday life. Tillich, upon whom Winquist's definition of theology rests, explains that "faith is an existential risk, a risk in which the meaning and fulfillment of our lives is at stake."[44] So while desire may be the operative element within theological *thinking*, I want to supplement that when that desire element becomes expressed in social or political life, it takes a different form.

Theology is the desire for a new world which is why we can say that religion is the living of a world that may exist. But theology may be lived politically, too. Theology is the desire for a different world, while, after modernity, politics is the maintenance of the world as we find it. I am arguing here that resistance is the theological enacted politically. It is the

---

[41] Clayton Crockett, *Radical Political Theology: Religion and Politics After Liberalism* (New York: Columbia University Press, 2011), 14.
[42] See his *Desiring Theology* (Chicago: University of Chicago Press, 1995).
[43] Tillich, *Theology of Culture*, 40.
[44] Tillich, *Theology of Culture*, 20.

expression of the theological—of desire for an alternate, less disappointing world—within the political sphere. Theology is the impulse toward resistance brought into the political ordering of life. Resistance takes up the meaning-making function of religion within the sphere of the political. Resistance is the political act through which the desire for a world that does not disappoint becomes expressed. Resistance is the activity through which theology animates the political. Theology itself is thus insurrectionary. It moves in religion and in politics from below. Theology is the desire for a *thinking* that doesn't disappoint. Theology lived turns into something else: resistance. Resistance is the desire for a *living* that doesn't disappoint.

The religious is the disordering, reordering function of human society through the act of meaning-making. The political is the ordering function through the act of social maintenance. Pure order is totalitarianism. Pure disorder is entropy. So there is no such thing as religious or political purity other than death. Rather, they are both expressions—dynamic expressions—of the world that may be otherwise than it is. The religious disorders and reorders the way the world is while the political reinforces and bolsters it. The religious and the political are flip sides of the same subjunctive coin. The question is not the possibility of the world but the will to either keep it or remake it. Thus the religious—the desire to remake the world—becomes expressed politically as resistance. Resistance is an attempt at remaking the world (Table 4.2).

During the modern period, as we saw above in the discussion of Cavanaugh's article, "A Fire Strong Enough to Consume the House," religion moved from a virtue to a set of propositions. Here in this period at the end of modernity, after the death of God, those propositions have lost their force of authority. The world did not secularize according to plan, but God did indeed die. Religion is no longer an argument, nor a virtue. Religion floats free, untethered. Theology, as a form of thought,

Table 4.2 Heuristic proposal for religion and politics after modernity

Animator	Category	Social sphere	Function	Product
Theology (desire)	Religion (homeless)	Public/private	Disordering/reordering	Resistance
	Politics (the post-secular world)	Public/private	Ordering/maintaining	Meaning-making

expresses not the aim of virtue, nor the proposition of argument, but raw desire undergirding it all. The decline of the Church as the locus of the communal practice of *religio* that Cavanaugh describes results in the contemporary homelessness of theology.

By the late nineteenth century, the modern relationship between religion as a force of order and politics as a force of disorder began to invert. In the early part of the twentieth century, fascism grew by asserting the State as the solution to society's disintegration. This was also the time that the State-ification of the world became complete. There had been no true States in the sixteenth century. But by 1900, nearly the entire world had been divided up into States. In our contemporary situation, a century later, wherein the secularization thesis has failed rather spectacularly, where religiously motivated or at least religiously oriented revolutions are cropping up all over the world, and yet where God is nevertheless dead, theology's role is ever more clear and urgent. Theology after secularization and after the death of God is politicized theology. Crockett declares the charge:

> We now need a radical theological thinking that is at the same time radically political. Radical theology is here the freedom to think God without God, liberated from the weight of traditional formulations that constrain its creativity in dogmatics and sap its vitality in apologetics. Radical theology in the wake of the death of God is freed up to engage in constructive political thought and challenged to create a radical political theology, which is its urgent contemporary task. The political stakes of radical theology are enormous, because what is at stake is the world, which is all that is the case, including whether we can continue to have one.[45]

Radical theology is political theology. A radical theology that isn't political is neither radical nor theological. Radical theology—which emphasizes not only theology without God as an exercise but also the death of God as a foundational religious experience—demonstrates its political engagement time and again. So Crockett is somewhat misleading here. Yes: a radical theological thinking that is at the same time radically political is needed. But such a suggestion verges on tautology. Radical theological thinking *is already political.* Those implications have merely been ignored until now. And yet, one must insist upon keeping the theological and the political, radically, together. As Jeffrey W. Robbins explains, "What political theology

---

[45] Crockett, *Radical Political Theology*, 12.

brings is a sustained focus on the nature of sovereign power … democracy fundamentally alters the experience and understanding of sovereign power. In this way, it is not only the political instantiation of the death of God but also a theological affirmation of the political power particular to humanity."[46] It is humanity's political power to which I begin to turn next.

Tactics and Liberation

Resisting theology is tactical. Paul Tillich explained that "religion" is the term for the depth-dimension in human experience. And as Schmitt stated, "… today everything is theology, with the exception of what the theologians talk about …."[47] As a result, any sphere of human meaning may be examined theologically—especially those spheres that do not necessarily present themselves as religious. Theology has become tactical, inserting itself into pre-existing discourses. So, one might still speak theologically despite dominant cultural discourses today that do not include the theological. Rather, one tends to hear about science, economics, politics, or even of the secular or post-secular. We have come a long way since the days when theology sat at the pinnacle of the academy as its queen. This shift puts theology in a new position. Winquist, a secular theologian indebted to the death-of-God movement, Tillich's theology of culture, and postmodern deconstruction, explains that theology need not attempt to establish its disciplinary dominance again. After passing through the crucible of the modern development of the State, theology has become something new in the contemporary West. Of the conditions of possibility for theology, Winquist writes:

> First, theology cannot posture as the "queen" of the sciences. It has a marginal status in contemporary discourse and it needs to recognize that its strategic formulations are worked out in the margins and interstices of the dominant culture. Movements into the mainstream of the culture are tactical implementations and experimentations. Second, within theological thinking at the close of the twentieth century there are competing hypotheses but there are no dominant paradigms to internally define theology as a science. Even definitions of religion and theology are in dispute. There are

---

[46] Robbins, *Radical Democracy*, 190.
[47] Carl Schmitt in a letter to Armin Mohler on August 14, 1958. Schmitt cites Jacob Taubes as the originator of this idea. See: Jacob Taubes, *To Carl Schmitt: Letters and Reflections*, trans. Keith Tribe (New York: Columbia University Press, 2013), 26.

certainly no agreed-upon first principles for theological thinking. There are, instead, assemblages of ideas, epochal arrangements, and conflicting interpretations. Epistemic undecidability has unmoored the philosophical, linguistic, and social scientific foundations of theology, thus setting it adrift. Third, the dominant discourse of exchange is materialistic. That is, the economy is the dominant sector of society and shapes its primary values. This dominant discourse is vehicular, the vehicle for the exchange and establishment of power. Fourth, a text, even the text of a dominant discourse, is never a totality. There are spaces, even when there are not proper places, for thinking, speaking, and writing other than in the style of the dominant discourse. These spaces are the possibility for developing a minor literature within a major or dominant discourse.[48]

When the dominant culture is suspicious of religion and theology—terms which are in dispute—when idealism has been roundly shown wanting, and when all discourses remain unfinished and fractured, theology has become a kind of parasite of thinking, latching itself on to a variety of possible hosts.[49] Winquist is correct here, but fails to explicitly name the new dominant discourse: neoliberal capitalism. The economy, that materialistic discourse of exchange which shapes society's values, becomes the locus for resisting theology. Lest we be mistaken for lamenting this development, we should insist that theology's ability to insinuate itself into other discourses—and especially the discourse of the market—is precisely its power. This ability is in fact resisting theology's propensity and its potency.

Winquist is making the case for an insurrectionist thinking—one that operates from underneath or on the margins of dominant ways of thinking and speaking.[50] "There are always spaces, discursive and nondiscursive spaces, that, although they are not sanctioned or proper to a dominant discourse, can be inhabited by theological interrogations. I am suggesting

---

[48] Winquist, 128.

[49] John D. Caputo's argument that radical theology is parasitic upon confessional theology (see Chap. 4, "Theopoetics as the Insistence of a Radical Theology," *The Insistence of God*, Bloomington, IN: Indiana University Press, 2013) does not go nearly far enough. Radical theology is not parasitic upon confessional theology. All of theology is parasitic upon culture. Confessional theology is a naked emperor.

[50] Michael Loadenthal's *The Politics of Attack: Communiqués and Insurrectionary Violence* (Manchester: Manchester University Press, 2017) is a study in property destruction and street violence that studies a truly insurrectionary politics. While I engage with similar concepts in Chap. 7, I mean to distinguish that form of insurrectionary politics from what I am calling "insurrectionist thinking" at work here in Winquist.

that theology can insinuate itself into the dominant culture."[51] Theology has become displaced from intellectual centers of power. What this means is that honest theology has been compelled to become tactical in its movements. There are plenty of found resources here, precisely because the sovereignty of theology has been subverted. Theology's fall from power allowed it to begin working within other discourses. Again, writes Winquist:

> This is what I mean by the tactical use of theological strategies. These tactics are not new strategies. Tactics are the use value of strategies of resistance in a dominant secular culture. It is because theology does not have a proper place of its own in the dominant secular culture that it must value and affirm its identity as a marginal and interstitial [sic] reality. That is, theology inhabits the edges and cracks of the dominant culture. It is a nomad discipline wandering, wondering, and erring.[52]

Theology is no longer in the business of dwelling in its own dominant discourse. Instead, Winquist explains:

> The tactical use of theological strategies is not unlike what Michel de Certeau calls the tactics of consumption in the practice of everyday life.... Since theologians do not have a proper place in the dominant culture they, like other marginalized consumers, must rent their space. They must insinuate their differences into the dominant text. Theological strategies are efficacious to the extent that they can be tactically insinuated into existing textual practices. Tactics exploit the discursive and nondiscursive spacing in the dominant discourse. A minor literature is generated inside and alongside of the dominant discourse, metonymically pressuring its continual formation.[53]

In the essay from which I've drawn these quotations, Winquist is implying a secular theology of literature and language. His concern is with our inability to speak or write theologically in any way that makes sense in a culture that doesn't hold religion as its highest value. While this is a significant concern, it isn't exactly mine. Instead, I find Winquist's argument compelling for its willingness to transpose theological registers. I am arguing for a reading of theology's tactical insinuation not in literature, but political resistance.

---

[51] Winquist, 133.
[52] Winquist, 133.
[53] Winquist, 134.

In his discussion of the ways in which everyday activities resist oppressive conditions, Certeau describes an agonal context—a context within which the ordinary person finds herself in a place of someone else's making. Certeau distinguishes between strategies and tactics in part by their directionality and position. Strategies are imposed from above and require an established position. He writes, "… strategies are actions which, thanks to the establishment of a place of power (the property of a proper), elaborate theoretical places (systems and totalizing discourses) capable of articulating an ensemble of physical places in which forces are distributed. They combine these three types of places and seek to master each by means of the others."[54] Tactics, on the other hand, are the possibilities of action that the ordinary person might deploy within an existing context, as explained later. Certeau explains that, "a tactic is a calculated action determined by the absence of a proper locus."[55] A tactic is deliberate, but without its own proper place. Further, a tactic "… must play on and with a terrain imposed on it and organised by the law of a foreign power." That is, tactics are possible only within strategic places. Tactics are only every enacted on the other's terrain. This is why Certeau explains that "… a tactic is an art of the weak"[56] and "a tactic is determined by the absence of power just as a strategy is organised by the postulation of power."[57]

Following Certeau's lead, Winquist describes this shift in spatial terms vis-á-vis theology. That is, theology is no longer a landlord, but a renter. After the modern, when the position of religion has been supplanted by the neoliberal State, theology must embrace its propensity for the tactical, rather than the strategic. In terms of language, Winquist appropriates Deleuze and Guattari's terminology, describing theology as a "minor literature" that appears within a dominant discourse. "The need for a minor literature is to resist the repressive totalizing tendencies of the dominant discourse that seeks to stabilize itself in the midst of incompleteness."[58] Thus, we find theology resisting. Winquist's theology-as-a-minor-literature makes resistance theology's procedure. And resistance is not a house, but a vehicle.

Theology shares a deep affinity with resistance. But Winquist goes on to admit that theology's resistance is also *political* when he explains, with reference to Deleuze and Guattari, that "Minor literatures are political. They are

[54] Michel de Certeau, *Practice of Everyday Life*, 38.
[55] Certeau, 37.
[56] Certeau, 37.
[57] Certeau, 37.
[58] Winquist, 128.

pragmatically bound to tacts of deterritorialization and reterritorialization. They are pragmatically bound to new becomings that are also configurations of power and language ... They mark zones of intensity that risk the established order. They open spaces for forces to pressure the articulation of order in any representational economy."[59] The risk of the established order is the subjunctive expression of the religious within the political sphere. I wager that Winquist is correct when he writes that "theological thinking makes openings for rethinking self, community, and society."[60] Rethinking, transposed from the intellectual realm of theological thinking—the desire for a thinking that doesn't disappoint—becomes the act of resistance when lived in the political sphere. Enacted, the rethinking of self, community, and society is the living of an alternative to the world as it appears.

That which is theological is always already political whenever it becomes manifest in the world. Traditionally, the discipline of political theology investigates the theological that underlies the political. But things move in the other direction as well. Marcella Althaus-Reid argues that while theologians tend to position themselves as exploring and interpreting God's will, all theology already puts forward a political agenda.[61] Theology has a tendency to disguise political interests with references to the divine. Instead of a political theology, then, the dominant theological discourse is a theological politics. In any case, theology is always already performed in medias res. There is no pure, apolitical position from which to do theology. Theology is always political. The question is whether one's theology underlies a politics—that is, if politics grows out of theology—or whether one's theology is simply a vehicle for a pre-established political agenda. Politics and theology always implicate each other. They just may not admit it. Theology has often been able to ignore its own political implications and imperatives, the political interests it affirms, reproduces, and conceals. If we are always already politically postured—either by accepting the status quo, advocating neutrality (which also accepts the status quo), or by resisting the status quo—then our theology is always already politically charged.

Winquist writes that, "There is no sanctuary for theological reflection. The locus of a theology is the space of the other .... theology does not have a proper place of its own."[62] As discussed above, Winquist was explaining theology's dislocation from academic and intellectual positions

---

[59] Winquist, 135.
[60] Winquist, 137.
[61] Marcella Althaus-Reid, *From Feminist Theology to Indecent Theology* (London: SCM Press, 2004).
[62] Winquist, 127–9.

of dominance in a secular culture. But when we read Winquist in a different context, through Althaus-Reid, we notice that the discourse of theology, with its colonial genealogy, occurs in a colonized place. The place of the other is the place of those oppressed by an alliance of politics with theology itself. Althaus-Reid goes further still in explaining a kind of double theological colonization. Althaus-Reid's theological tradition is liberation theology. Liberation theology did not only emerge out of a weapon of oppression in Latin America. It also became an object of consumption for North Atlantic academics. This is what prompts Althaus-Reid to ask, "How did Liberation Theology become commodified in the North Atlantic market, and how did the selling of theological books and fashion become the death of a theology originally done with courage and risk? In this, there is almost a process of 're-colonizing' Liberation Theology by converting it into an exotic product for the North Atlantic academic market."[63] Theology's relationship with economics is thus deepened in liberation theology. Not only does liberation theology reproduce certain economies—certain inter-human relations—it has become an object of consumption and exploitation itself.

On the other hand, the kind of political theology I am advancing in this project—the kind of theology that, after Winquist, is conscious that it has no place of its own—is a hermeneutic of suspicion. Its critical approach goes to the end. As a result, a critical theology produces religious community without God. Radical and relentless critique is not antithetical to the production of social solidarity. Winquist elaborates on this idea when he writes, "We want to be able to talk about life in the critical wake of the hermeneutics of suspicion .... This speaking requires ongoing radical criticism and interrogation of all conceptual formulations. Radical criticism is, in this perspective, an ethical formulation and a possibility for meaningful community."[64]

Liberation thought should not, however, be abandoned entirely. Althaus-Reid argues that the challenge of liberation theology is to abandon its problematic ideological background, lest it reproduce alienation, patriarchy, and capitalist structures of society.

> [This challenge] will take us to reconsider the whole basis of our theological enterprise of liberation, but this time the liberation of theology would be costlier than ... during the 1970s. It could be a liberation which may kill theology, or at least empty theology of ideological methodologies and

---

[63] Althaus-Reid, 105.
[64] Winquist, 143.

therefore transform its message deeply. A kenosis of theology. Who knows, but perhaps we are only going to know if theology is more than ideology when and if this kenosis happens.[65]

Any honest theology is a threat to itself. Like the physician whose healing work would ultimately render the need for a physician obsolete since health requires no doctor, the goal of the theologian should always be to put theology out of business. Honest theology—to use Philip Goodchild's words, theology that is "a critical engagement with the actual fundamental forces and structures that shape our lives, rather than simply a reflection upon past traditions"[66] and "Theology, concerned with the ultimate criteria of life, is the most fundamental and radical inquiry"[67]—is charged with resisting theology.

Theology is an imperative. Theology must recognize its homelessness and its dependence upon other, secular discourses. As the depth-dimension of life (Tillich), the desire for a thinking that doesn't disappoint (Winquist), and a liberated and tactical enterprise emptied of ideology (Althaus-Reid), theology becomes free to engage with what is politically liberating, regardless of its explicitly religious or non-religious content. Theology is a thinking that resists the here and now and it is thought through other discourses not of its own kind or making. It is simultaneously empty of its own content and open to creating an alternate, meaningful future. Theology is the desire for a *thinking* that doesn't disappoint. Theology lived turns into something else: resistance. Resistance is the desire for a *living* that doesn't disappoint. This is what I mean when I say that the theology I am advancing is a methodological theology. Secular political theology is subjunctive. Put politically, theology must *resist* itself. Put theologically, theology must *risk* itself. Theology's imperative is to resist. Resistance is theological activity. This is what I mean when I use the term *resisting theology*.

Democracy, or Anarchy

Resistance is theological activity. Radical democracy—or better, anarchy—is an expression of resistance writ large. Robbins claims that, "Politics as democracy consists in the belief that this world could be otherwise."[68]

---

[65] Althaus-Reid, 72.
[66] Philip Goodchild, interview for Rorotoko, November 30, 2009, http://rorotoko.com/interview/20091130_goodchiled_philip_on_theology_of_money/?page=1.
[67] Philip Goodchild, *Theology of Money* (Durham & London: Duke University Press, 2009), 4.
[68] Robbins, *Radical Democracy*, 63.

So democracy is religious. With this as the case, subjunctivity gets opened up beyond resistance alone to radical democracy and forms of anarchist activity as well. But why is it that democracy must be radical?

> ... by conflating popular sovereignty with a representative system of government, modern liberal philosophy effectively restores or maintains the theopolitical rule of the one. In this way, the revolutionary impact of modern democracy is contained and curtailed. Rather than following the logic of democracy to its true ideal of self-governance by the rule of all by all, which would mean the dispersal and diffusion of power, the sovereignty of the people kept the logic of sovereign power inherited from the theology of the indivisible divine intact. While radical democratic theory accomplishes the conceptual shift from the people as one to the multitude as many, a democratic political theology might serve as its critical and necessary supplement by drawing on alternative theological sources, specifically theologies of the weakness of God as opposed to those traditionally oriented around divine power. Or ... a democratic political theology reveals democracy as the political instantiation of the death of God.[69]

To quibble some, one might say that radical democracy is the political instantiation of the death of God and therefore as a mode of radical, political-theological expression, anarchy goes slightly further, no longer attempting to ride on the back of inoffensiveness. Anarchy is the political instantiation of the death of God and the mode of subjunctive community-creation.

It may be instructive at this juncture to linger on this relationship between radical democracy and anarchy a bit more. As Robbins explains through his reading of Jacques Rancière, "democracy is not simply a form of politics but the very *principle of politics*. It is not antigovernmental but government otherwise."[70] Radical democracy—democracy at its root—is a principle. But what might grow from that root? The danger, of course, is that it has become relatively simple to graft different varieties of plants onto all manner of root-stock. For contrast, Maia Ramnath explains anarchy this way:

> ... the word anarchism implies a set of assumptions and principles, a recurrent tendency or orientation—with the stress on movement in a direction, not a perfected condition—toward more dispersed and less concentrated power;

---

[69] Robbins, *Radical Democracy*, 5–6.
[70] Robbins, *Radical Democracy*, 62. In this passage, Robbins is summarizing and commenting upon Jacques Rancière's work on radical democracy.

less top-down hierarchy and more self-determination through bottom-up participation; liberty and equality seen as directly rather than inversely proportional; the nurturance of individuality and diversity within a matrix of interconnectivity, mutuality, and accountability; and an expansive recognition of the various forms that power relations can take, and correspondingly, the various dimensions of emancipation. This tendency, when it becomes conscious, motivates people *to oppose or subvert* the structures that generate and sustain inequity, unfreedom, and injustice, and *to promote or prefigure* the structures that generate and sustain equity, freedom, and justice.[71]

So while democracy is the very principle of politics, anarchy is the political expression that most self-consciously exhibits that principle. Radical democracy *is* anarchy.[72]

Robbins does, in a way, go all the way to the end when he admits that, "Structurally anarchic, radical democracy undoes the present, known forms of corporatist governance, leaving the future uncertain, like a throw of the dice in which all our presumed entitlements are at risk. This is a far cry from Pascal's wager, because here we stand to lose everything. The world turned upside down. The world made anew. Democracy as if for the first time."[73] Anarchy is here shown as the highest form of Tillichian faith. "The risk of faith is based on the fact that the unconditional element can become a matter of ultimate concern only if it appears in a concrete embodiment."[74] The political instantiation of the death of God in anarchist resistance is subjunctivity *par excellence*, combining subjunctive expressions of ritual, the establishment of social bonds, and meaning-making. It is an example wherein radical religion and political resistance become impossible to disentangle.

And here is the rub: the principle of politics is democracy; the principles of anarchist tactics are simultaneously resistance and prefiguring emancipation. Ramnath again:

---

[71] Ramnath, *Decolonizing Anarchism*, 7. My emphasis.

[72] I am well aware of the historical tradition of political anarchism that includes such luminaries as William Godwin, Peter Kropotkin, Pierre-Joseph Proudhon, Mikhail Bakunin, Emma Goldman, and others. While I am deeply informed by that tradition, I do not mean to suggest that what I am calling "anarchy" here is identical with that. I am using the term, following Ramnath, in a more abstract sense. I am certainly interested in how that abstraction is worked out in practice as I detail in the chapters to follow, but I am less concerned with a lineage of thought than with the workings of a subjunctive concept.

[73] Robbins, *Radical Democracy*, 72.

[74] Paul Tillich, *Theology of Culture*, ed. Robert C. Kimball (New York: Oxford University Press, 1959), 28.

Resistance is by definition a negative project, aimed at the removal of that which obstructs equity and emancipation. Such a goal may be held in common—even if for different reasons—among many who share nothing else. The positive counterpart is the prefigurative project of creating the conditions that generate equity and emancipation. Many anarchists emphasize this as a distinguishing feature of their praxis; here limitless variation is possible among divergent visions of an idealized future.[75]

So, according to Ramnath, while resistance might at first glance appear to be simply negative, especially in its anarchistic expressions, resistance has the potential and the power to produce conditions conducive to a myriad of possible futures. In other words, resistance's negativity is also its creativity. This was already evident in the Ramnath's earlier quote in the description of anarchism through the use of the verbs "to oppose or subvert injustice" as well as "to promote or prefigure justice." Further, this was also already apparent in Marx who "… situated himself equidistant between the old materialism and idealism; more precisely, he presented his position as the dialectical transcendence of both. Of the first he retained the affirmation of the objectivity of the external world; of the second he kept the transforming capacity of human nature. For Marx, to know was something indissolubly linked to the transformation of the world through work."[76] Look back in critique; look forward in creativity. Resistance is work and the human capacity for imagination has practical consequences.

Resistance shares an affinity with subjunctivity as described by Roy A. Rappaport in his discussion on the possibilities created by grammar. He explains that subjunctivity moves in two directions, writing:

It may be suggested that the transcendence of the concrete and the emergence of grammar were mutually causal, but, be this as it may, when discourse can escape from the concrete as well as the present, and when it is empowered by grammar, it finally becomes free to search for such worlds parallel to the actual as those of "the might have been," "the should be," "the could be," "the never will," "the may always be." It can, then, explore the realms of the desirable, the moral, the proper, the possible, the fortuitous, the imaginary, the general, *and their negatives*, the undesirable, the immoral, the impossible. To "explore" these worlds is not simply to discover

---

[75] Ramnath, *Decolonizing Anarchism*, 15–6.
[76] Gustavo Gutiérrez, *A Theology of Liberation*, trans. Sister Caridad Inda and John Eagleson (Maryknoll, NY: Orbis Books, 1988), 19.

what is there. It is to create what is there. Language does not merely facilitate the communication of what is conceived but expands, eventually by magnitudes, what can be conceived.⁷⁷

Subjunctivity is a double movement. The world might be otherwise, but it also might not be. Subjunctivity allows the thinking of both what the world *might be changed into* and what it *should be changed from*. There is clearly an affinity with anarchic resistance here, as I have shown through my reading of Ramnath. Resistance's negativity toward what exists is also and already a creative gesture toward what may come. The tactic of anarchy is resistance, while its principle is becoming. It is not just about rejecting antiauthoritarianism; it is also about the creation of new worlds.

The subjunctive brings together God and the desire to know God. That is, if "the most compelling definition of God is," as Peter Canning argues, "the power to exist" which in turn "is immediately frustrating to the theological desire to know God,"⁷⁸ then the subjunctive might offer us a way out. Anarchy and God create new worlds. The subjunctive provides both God with *posse* and humanity with desire. The subjunctive is both *posse*—possibility or power (to exist), potency—and the desire for alternatives—for that which might be. And so the subjunctive undergirds God, theology, religion, politics, and resistance.

THE CITY

The city is the source of the political. Politics, as such, derives from the *polis*—the city itself—and is impossible without it. In "The Gods of Politics in Early Greek Cities," Marcel Detienne investigates the relationship between the gods and the ancient Greek *polis*.⁷⁹ He argues that the gods either recede from the city or were never included in the first place, thus

---

⁷⁷ Roy A. Rappaport, *Ritual and Religion in the Making of Humanity*, 5. My emphasis. See section "Manufacturing the World" in Chap. 2 for my initial discussion of this point.

⁷⁸ Peter Canning, "God Is of (Possibility)" in *Secular Theology: American Radical Theological Thought*, ed. Clayton Crockett (London and New York: Routledge, 2001), 233.

⁷⁹ Marcel Detienne, "The Gods of Politics in Early Greek Cities," trans. Janet Lloyd, in *Political Theologies: Public Religions in a Post-secular World*, eds. Hent de Vries and Lawrence E. Sullivan (New York: Fordham University Press, 2006), 91–101. He writes, "... we thus find a society ... in which a certain idea of the city, *Hestia* [the goddess of the hearth, architecture, and the right ordering of the domestic sphere], is formed by a group that, for its part, comes to believe that the sovereignty of this new unit, the city, resides in itself," p. 100.

opening a political space for human affairs. So right away, there is an intimate relationship between the gods, their absence or withdrawal, the city, and the political sphere. This bears out etymologically, too. "Political" is derived directly from the Latin *politicus* and its Greek cognate, *politikos*, each meaning, "pertaining to citizens, civic, civil, political" with connotations of pertaining to the State and its administration and to public life.[80] In turn, the root for *politikos* is *polites*, "citizen," from *polis*, "city." *Polis*, in turn, refers to "city, one's city; the State, citizens."[81] So the city creates the civil and the political citizen. And all of this happens with a particular stance toward the gods' lack of dominion over political affairs. The city founds politics in the absence of the gods.

But what is the city and what does is have to do with political theology? Certeau argues that, "the city" is an operational concept. He writes:

> The "city" founded by utopian and urbanistic discourse is defined by the possibility of [...] the creation of a *universal* and anonymous *subject* which is the city itself: it gradually becomes possible to attribute to it, as to its political model, Hobbes' State, all the functions and predicates that were previously scattered and assigned to many different real subjects—groups, associations, or individuals. "The city," like a proper name, thus provides a way of conceiving and constructing space on the basis of a finite number of stable, isolatable, and interconnected properties. [...] This is the way in which the Concept-city functions; a place of transformations and appropriations, the object of various kinds of interference but also a subject that is constantly enriched by new attributes, it is simultaneously the machinery and the hero of modernity.[82]

The operational concept of the city is subjunctive in its reorganizations of the functions of the State. Reading through Certeau, it is possible to transpose political theology into an urban register. Political theology's investigation of the ways in which religious concepts, postures, and thinking underlie political, social, economic, and cultural discourses and institutions may here be extended to the city itself. That is, the city becomes an object of theological investigation—political theology becomes urban theology.

---

[80] *The Oxford English Dictionary*, second edition, prepared by J. A. Simpson and E. S. C. Weiner, Volume XII: Poise-Quelt (Oxford: Clarendon Press, 1991), *politic*, 31–32; *political*, 32–34.

[81] OED, Volume XII, 29, 32.

[82] Certeau, 94–5.

Cities are produced. They're made by our labor. Obviously, all human spaces are produced and, within urban life, this is particularly evident and difficult to ignore. Streetscapes change before our eyes, sometimes overnight. We remake the city and we do so in our image. It reflects who we would make ourselves to be. Insofar as the city is a product that we receive, we also *make things of it*. We consume the city, but our consumption is also productive. Certeau writes that consumption "… is devious, it is dispersed, but it insinuates itself everywhere, silently and almost invisibly, because it does not manifest itself through its own products, but rather through its *ways of using* the products imposed by a dominant economic order."[83] We are both the makers and consumers of cities, which is to say that we, makers, make the city. Inhabiting cities that we may not have made ourselves nevertheless makes us makers.

The city is the source of the political. But the city is also religious. Regardless of explicit theological content, as my reading of Certeau and Thomas Merton later will demonstrate, the city is a theological concept and cities are theological objects. This is why it's important to focus on urban forms of resistance. David Harvey quotes urban sociologist Robert Park's *On Social Control and Collective Behavior*, writing that the city is "… man's most successful attempt to remake the world he lives in more after his heart's desire. But, if the city is the world which man created, it is the world in which he is henceforth condemned to live. Thus, indirectly, and without any clear sense of the nature of his task, in making the city man has remade himself."[84] Harvey continues in his own words:

> If Park is correct, then the question of what kind of city we want cannot be divorced from the question of what kind of people we want to be, what kinds of social relations we seek, what relations to nature we cherish, what style of life we desire, what aesthetic values we hold. The right to the city is, therefore, far more than a right of individual or group access to the resources that the city embodies: it is a right to change and reinvent the city more after our hearts' desire. It is, moreover, a collective rather than an individual right, since reinventing the city inevitably depends upon the exercise of a collective power over the processes of urbanization.[85]

---

[83] Certeau, xii–xiii.
[84] Harvey, "The Right to the City," 23 and *Rebel Cities*, 3–4.
[85] David Harvey, *Rebel Cities*, 4.

The city is an exemplary site of human subjunctivity. And the city is much more than a neutral collection of streets, parks, and buildings; it is a materialized manifestation of who we are creating ourselves to be. So the Occupy Movement's creation of tent cities within existing urban spaces is a kind of self-referential world creation focused on the way human relationships *might be*.

"The city is a huge monastery," wrote Erasmus.[86] Certeau writes that, "The desire to see the city preceded the means of satisfying it. Medieval and Renaissance painters represented the city as seen in a perspective that no eye had yet enjoyed. The fiction already made the medieval spectator into a celestial eye. It created gods. Have things changed since technical procedures have organized an 'all-seeing power'? The totalizing eye imagined by the painters of earlier times lives on in our achievements."[87] Skyscrapers possess a divine mandate. The city is a *theological object*.

Again, one might ask: what is a city? For Thomas Merton, "A city is something you do with space."[88] The city is an operational concept and a city is something you do with space. The distinction here is between the material and the concept. The concept of the city operates while cities *themselves* are produced and performed. For this reason, one can say both—the city is an operator and cities are the products of operations. They both are the stages of activities and those activities' media. The city is not neutral; it *does things*. The city might oppress or uplift. "The quality of a city depends on whether these spaces are 'inhabited' or just 'occupied.' The character of the city is set by the way the rooms are lived in. The way the buildings are lived in. And what goes on in the streets."[89]

---

[86] As quoted in Certeau, 93.

[87] Certeau, 92. Commonly, Certeau's chapter, "Walking in the City," to which much of our discussion here refers, is read as a response to Michel Foucault's chapter from *Discipline and Punish* on panopticism. This is quite appropriate as Certeau was writing with Foucault in mind as one of his principal interlocutors. The "all-seeing eye" that looks down on a city from atop a skyscraper resonates explicitly with Foucault's understanding of Bentham's penitentiary. My interest in Certeau's "Walking in the City" is less for its engagement with Foucault's understanding of surveillance and more for its use of reading cities like texts and listening to urban actions like speech. In short, I find Certeau's methodological synesthesia useful for my purposes here in performing a theology of resistance. Still, the common understanding of Certeau's essay should not go unremarked. We should not forget that Bentham designed the viewing position in the panopticon to remain potentially empty, dispersing the function of surveillance out among the inmates themselves. This is the view of a god who isn't there.

[88] Merton, "Celebration," 46.

[89] Merton, "Celebration," 46.

For Merton, the question of the quality of a city is a matter of activity or passivity—that is, it's not about what the city is, but what we do with it and how we live in it. For Merton, the difference is between occupation and inhabitation. He asks and answers, "*Can the street become an inhabited space? Yes, when it becomes a space for celebration.*"[90] In terms more befitting this project, the street ceases being an oppressive, alienated space when its occupants realize their subjunctive participation in the city. In practical terms, this realization is one of ownership and stewardship. That is, it is a realization that the streets are ours to use and to care for. Merton marks the problematic:

> A street where there are thousands of people in this condition [passive, oppressed occupants, not inhabitants] is an alienated street. It is a street in a foreign country: yet all the people on it may be natives .... Such a street is always somebody else's street. But whose? The owner is never there. So the building belongs to the landlord? But who is he? Maybe he is a business.[91] So the street belongs to a fiction. [...] Somebody says the street belongs to the city. It is everybody's public street. All right. Is it? You can move around in it under certain conditions. But the conditions are such that you do not feel it is *your* street, because you are not safe, you are not wanted, you are not noticed, you are not liked, and in the end you may just not be allowed.[92]

Impersonal streets owned by fictions produce alienation by curtailing subjunctivity. This is bad theology. Bad cities are cities that restrict their occupants, causing a sense of restrained subjunctivity. The city has the potential to be an opiate.

One of the principal concerns of radical theology is freedom. And following Marx, Freud, and Niebuhr, one of the jobs of religion is to liberate. Richard Rubenstein—the Jewish, reluctant member of the American death-of-God movement in the 1960s—once wrote that, "For Tillich and Altizer, human freedom is the issue that compels humanity to will the death of the theistic God ...."[93] In this sense, Altizer finds God's

---

[90] Merton, "Celebration," 52.

[91] This brings to mind Mitt Romney's infamous comments at the Iowa State Fair in August, 2011: "Corporations are people, my friend. Of course they are. Everything corporations earn ultimately goes to people."

[92] Merton, "Celebration," 47–8.

[93] Richard L. Rubenstein, *After Auschwitz* (Baltimore and London: Johns Hopkins University Press, Second Edition, 1966 and 1992), 248.

death to be positive, optimistic turn in the course of history. Altizer wills God's death for the sake of humanity. Thus, humanity's social and political emancipation is a movement *within* religion, but *without* God. The city is the site of this activity. Merton describes the challenge: "To acquire inhabitants, the street will have to be changed. Something must *happen* to the street. Something must be *done to it*."[94] Tillich's existential understanding of religion is at work here. The people occupying the street must turn it into a site of subjunctive activity. The city becomes a place of love and life when its occupants change it. The alternative is submission and submission to the owner-fiction and alienation is opposed to subjunctivity.

> Instead of submitting to the street, they must change it.
> Instead of being formally and impersonally put in their place by the street, they must transform the street and make it over so that it is livable.
> *The street can be inhabited if the people on it begin to make their life credible by changing their environment.*
> *Living is more than submission: it is creation.*
> *To live is to create one's own world as a scene of personal happiness.*[95]

Living is creation. So life itself is subjunctive. Later, Merton continues, "He who celebrates is not powerless. He becomes a creator because he is a lover."[96] Love is subjunctive, celebratory power.

Cities lend themselves to celebration by their structures. Celebration happens in community. Again, writes Merton:

> But celebration is not for the alone.
> To pull down the blind and empty the bottle and lie on the floor in a stupor: this may help you forget the street for a while, but it is a surrender. It is the crowning submission, the acceptance of powerlessness, willingness to admit you are a nothing. The alienated city isolates men from one another in despair, lovelessness, defeat. It is crowded with people who are not present to each other: it is like a desert, although it is full of people.
> Celebration is not noise. It is not a spinning head. It is not just individual kicks.

---

[94] Merton, "Celebration," 48.
[95] Merton, "Celebration," 49.
[96] Merton, "Celebration," 52.

> It is the creation of a common identity, a common consciousness.
> Celebration is everybody making joy.
> Not as a duty (you can't manufacture joy out of the duty to have fun).
> Celebration is when we let joy make itself out of our love.[97]

Merton is describing the ritual subjunctive creation of the social here. He continues,

> Celebration is crazy: the craziness of not submitting even though "they," "the others," the ones who make life impossible, seem to have all the power. Celebration is the beginning of confidence, therefore of power.
> When we laugh at them, when we celebrate, when we make our lives beautiful, when we give one another joy by loving, by sharing, then we manifest a power they cannot touch. We can be the artisans of a joy they never imagined.
> We can build a fire of happiness in this city that will put them to shame.[98]

As Merton shows, the urban community that we might produce has the potential to shame our oppressors through its joy and celebration and by virtue of being incomprehensible, as explained earlier. Thus, subjunctive celebration is resistance. It appears mad. Urban celebratory resistance's ability to create communion against all odds—the making of the common—coupled with the inability of the powers that be to understand it make it both appear mad and elicit a sense of shame from those who attempt to prevent it. Resistance is joy-craft—it is theological activity.

Celebration has pleasant connotations. That's all well and good. But it's not the only form of resistance to the alienation of the corporate-controlled city. For Merton, the street belongs to a fiction. Everything is someone else's. The landlord owns the place in which we live. The furniture in it came from a catalog. We escape in media-provided entertainment and corporate-sponsored relaxation. It all seems to come from someone or somewhere else. But the *way* we live, our practices, and our work—those belong to no one else. Again, even our consumption is a making or re-making. The street belongs to a fiction, but our living on it is our own. What is the city? For Harvey:

---

[97] Merton, "Celebration," 52–3.
[98] Merton, "Celebration," 53.

The term "city" has an iconic and symbolic history that is deeply embedded in the pursuit of political meanings. The city of God, the city on a hill, the relationship between city and citizenship—the city as an object of utopian desire, as a distinctive place of belonging within a perpetually shifting spatio-temporal order—all give it a political meaning that mobilizes a crucial political imaginary .... there are already multiple practices within the urban that themselves are full to overflowing with alternative possibilities.[99]

Based on this reading of Merton and Harvey together, one will conclude that the city is theological, civic, utopian, and subjunctive. But how might one think of this overflow of alternative possibilities within this theo-political frame?

For Certeau, the ordinary citizens of a city live "below the thresholds at which visibility begins."[100] He continues explaining that walking is, "an elementary form of this experience of the city" and inherent components of this experience are the walkers themselves, "*Wandersmänner*, whose bodies follow the thicks and thins of an urban 'text' they write without being able to read it."[101] Yes, this text might be transcribed as a map—the route I take from my home to the subway stop, to work, and then to the grocer, for instance. These trajectories can be traced "on city maps in such a way as to transcribe their paths ... But these thick or thin curves only refer, like words, to the absence of what has passed by."[102] The pedestrian act itself of riding a bicycle, of getting a cup of coffee at a cafe, of pausing to pet a dog, to speak with an acquaintance, or to read flyer on a wall are examples of expressing one's own agency giving force and meaning—however temporary—to possibilities and alternatives. These acts are expressions of the subjunctive.

> ... the walker transforms each spatial signifier into something else. And if on the one hand he actualizes only a few of the possibilities fixed by the constructed order (he goes only here and not there), on the other he increases the number of possibilities (for example, by creating shortcuts and detours) and prohibitions (for example, he forbids himself to take paths generally considered accessible or even obligatory). He thus makes a selection.[103]

---

[99] Harvey, *Rebel Cities*, xvi–xvii.
[100] Certeau, 93.
[101] Certeau, 93.
[102] Certeau, 97.
[103] Certeau, 98.

These little resistances are our practice. They aren't imposed by anyone else, though the conditions within which they operate might be given. The city is an operational concept and through it, we produce the possibilities of resistance.

I must insist on this tension: our actions are our own; we might only celebrate together. City subjunctivity is thus democratic: it is the expression of the multitude, at once multiple and collective. Jacques Rancière illuminates the ritual nature of democracy and its relationship to both resistance and celebration:

> [Democracy] is not based on any nature of things or guaranteed by any institutional form. It is not borne along by any historical necessity and does not bear any. It is only entrusted to the constancy of its specific acts. This can provoke fear, and so hatred, among those who are used to exercising the magisterium of thought. But among those who know how to share with anybody and everybody the equal power of intelligence, it can conversely inspire courage, and hence joy.[104]

Cities are thus the sites of our rituals, labor, communities, celebrations, and resistances—together. In this way, they provide the conditions for both our theological and our political activities. Resisting theology thus answers the charge laid out by Jeffrey W. Robbins for a theology that "… insists upon the immanence of our common life together and the generative power that comes from our modes of cooperation. … [and valorizes] the City of Man as our home, [grapples] with the nature of sovereign power as it has become radically transformed by its divestment and diffusion, [and affirms] humanity's own creative capacities and political potency."[105]

---

[104] Jacques Rancière, *Hatred of Democracy*, trans. Steve Corcoran (London: Verso, 2006), 97.
[105] Jeffrey W. Robbins, *Radical Democracy and Political Theology* (New York: Columbia University Press, 2011), 191.

CHAPTER 5

Act Up

THE AIDS COALITION TO UNLEASH POWER

The AIDS Coalition to Unleash Power (ACT UP) was a theological movement.[1]

That is a controversial claim. It may not be immediately apparent why a New York-based, anarchically structured organization of gay activists and artists living with HIV and their allies operating most successfully in the late 1980s and early 1990s, engaging in various forms of direct action with the principal goal of forcing the US government and pharmaceutical companies to invest in the research and development of drugs to treat AIDS and cure HIV is theologically relevant. Theology as the most fundamental and radical inquiry into the ultimate criteria of life makes theology an imperative. It is for these reasons that ACT UP represented people that we should take as our theological measure. Or, at least, we might consider that ACT UP should reorient how we conceive of our own concerns. This in itself is theological activity. I make the case in the pages that follow that ACT UP's actions were theological in nature, despite the secularity of the group, due to the subjunctivity of its activities and statements. ACT UP

---

[1] I would like to thank Alan Jay Richard for his generosity in reading an early version of this chapter and providing invaluable feedback. His insights and reflections have immensely improved my argument and challenged the way I think about its subjects. I am especially grateful to Jan Powers, Pam Monn, and Grady Crittendon for presenting me with opportunities to fight back and to witness meaning-making in action.

© The Author(s) 2019
J. E. Miller, *Resisting Theology, Furious Hope*,
Radical Theologies and Philosophies,
https://doi.org/10.1007/978-3-030-17391-3_5

poetically produced and clarified meaning in the face of absurdity, expressed utopian desire, and haunted the American public consciousness. These acts of political resistance are expressive of theology's imperative.

"ACT UP is a diverse, non-partisan group united in anger and committed to direct action to end the AIDS crisis. We advise and inform. We demonstrate. WE ARE NOT SILENT," reads ACT UP's statement of purpose.² A more accurate and succinct description of the group would be difficult to find or make. ACT UP was formed in 1987 as the AIDS epidemic was plaguing major US cities like New York, Philadelphia, Chicago, and San Francisco. It was borne of frustration with the lack of developments in HIV and AIDS treatments. Pharmaceutical companies, the federal government, and research institutions lacked the sense of urgency that a plague requires. What treatments were available were prohibitively expensive. The collective negligence of government, business, and research was killing people. ACT UP was not only fed up and angry, but also thoughtful and creative. Benjamin Shepard, a member almost from its inception, explains that, "The group offered an outlet for an otherwise horrendous situation. Sometimes it was through humor, style, and camp; sometimes it was through direct action. The group recognized the subversive effectiveness of a joke, as well as the sentiment that many were tired of spending their days mourning lost friends, possibilities, and sexual communities. 'Don't mourn, organize'."³ One of ACT UP's founders, Eric Sawyer, continues, "We realized early in our ACT UP experience the importance of street theater, witty chants, slick graphics, and sound bites. Often the coverage we received was limited to fifteen seconds on the television news. Reporters seldom covered our issues accurately. We learned that witty chants and slick graphics were a better way to make sure that the media reported the facts correctly."⁴ Sawyer then continues by providing an example:

> [W]e were pushing for the development of housing for homeless people living with AIDS. We collected old furniture, loaded it into my pickup truck, and placed the furniture in the middle of the street in front of the New York

---

²ACT UP's statement of purpose, http://actupny.org.
³Shepard, 13.
⁴Eric Sawyer, "An ACT UP Founder 'Acts Up' for Africa's Access to AIDS," 88–102 in From ACT UP to the WTO: Urban Protest and Community Building in the Era of Globalization, eds. Benjamin Shepard and Ronald Hayduk (Verso: London and New York, 2002), 90.

City housing commissioner's office. We hung a big banner between two streetlights that read, "Squatters Camp for Homeless People with AIDS." Then we sat on the furniture while rush-hour traffic tried to drive around us, until we were arrested. The police had to cart our old furniture away in garbage trucks and tow my old pickup truck to the police vehicle pound; the demonstration kept city employees busy for more than an hour. This gave reporters time to ask sufficient questions to understand the dangers of homelessness for people with AIDS and to communicate these dangers to the public. The next month the housing commissioner announced that the city was budgeting $25 million dollars for new AIDS housing programs.[5]

From the very beginning, ACT UP wielded a mastery of direct action through its remarkable ability to create scenes, images, slogans, and chants that commanded attention from the media and the public. For the purposes of this essay, I restrict my analysis primarily to a particularly striking, poetic response to the trauma of the epidemic in the form of protest. The political funeral, which ACT UP borrowed from the anti-apartheid movement in South Africa, was a potent media spectacle and also a profoundly meaningful and affective expression of a community in mourning. Sawyer recalls that, "we carried the ashes of people who had died of AIDS, or the actual bodies of the dead, to the feet of those who contributed to their deaths through inaction or inappropriate action."[6] David Wojnarowicz, a prominent early member of the group, explained political funerals this way:

> I imagine what it would be like if friends had a demonstration each time a lover or a friend or a stranger died of AIDS. I imagine what it would be like if, each time a lover, friend or stranger died of this disease, their friends, lovers or neighbors would take the dead body and drive with it in a car a hundred miles an hour to Washington D.C. and blast through the gates of the White House and come to a screeching halt before the entrance and dump their lifeless form on the front steps.[7]

In the sections that follow, I perform a secular political-theological reading of ACT UP by examining its responses to the crisis of meaning that the AIDS epidemic created, the role and function of desire—as a personal, political, and theological category—in ACT UP's activities, and the role that haunting plays in political funerals.

[5] Sawyer, 90–1.
[6] Sawyer, 92.
[7] David Wojnarowicz, http://actupny.org/diva/polfunsyn.html.

Subjunctivity: Crisis of Meaning

Paula A. Treichler's *How to Have Theory in an Epidemic: Cultural Chronicles of AIDS* is a cultural study of the beginning of the AIDS epidemic. In it, Treichler makes the case that HIV/AIDS should be viewed not simply as a virus and its effects, but also as a cultural construction.[8] Treichler continues to explain that at the end of the 1980s, the dominant medical wisdom of the twentieth century was being unraveled by the AIDS epidemic. While previously, it may have made sense to emphasize that, "AIDS represented an 'epidemic of infectious disease and nothing more,'" the moral and social issues at work with this epidemic could not be contained by such a tidy encapsulation. Treichler thus argues that, "the AIDS epidemic has produced a parallel epidemic of meanings, definitions, and attributions. This [is a] semantic epidemic, which I have come to call an epidemic of signification."[9] AIDS caused a traumatic rupture in American culture. It was terrifying and not only new, but something that the discourses of medicine and science, public health, politics, religion, and culture did not know how to engage or explain. AIDS was intimate, but unknown. AIDS didn't make sense. But it didn't produce that meaninglessness—it shined a spotlight on it. AIDS forced us to give something up against our will, opening up a void. Again, Treichler writes:

> In multiple, fragmentary, and often contradictory ways, we struggle to achieve some sort of understanding of AIDS, a reality that is frightening, widely publicized, yet finally neither directly nor fully knowable. AIDS is no different in this respect from other linguistic constructions that, in the commonsense view of language, are thought to transmit preexisting ideas and represent real-world entities yet in fact do neither. The nature of the relation between language and reality is highly problematic; and AIDS is not merely an invented label, provided to us by science and scientific naming practices, for a clear-cut disease entity caused by a virus. Rather, the very nature of AIDS is constructed through language and in particular through the discourses of medicine and science; this construction is "true" or "real" only in certain specific ways—for example, insofar as it successfully guides research or facilitates clinical control over the illness. The name AIDS in part constructs the disease and helps make it intelligible. We cannot therefore look

---

[8] She writes, "The AIDS epidemic is cultural and linguistic as well as biological and biomedical." Paula A. Treichler, How to Have Theory in an Epidemic: Cultural Chronicles of AIDS (Durham and London: Duke University Press, 1999), 1.

[9] Treichler, 1.

"through" language to determine what AIDS "really" is. Rather, we must explore the site where such determinations really occur and intervene at the point where meaning is created: in language. [...] Of course, AIDS is a real disease syndrome, damaging and killing real human beings. Because of this, it is tempting—perhaps in some instances imperative—to view science and medicine as providing a discourse about AIDS closer to its "reality" than what we can provide ourselves. Yet, with its genuine potential for global devastation, the AIDS epidemic is simultaneously an epidemic of transmissible lethal disease and an epidemic of meanings or signification. Both epidemics are equally crucial for us to understand, for, try as we may to treat AIDS as "an infectious disease" and nothing more, meanings continue to multiply wildly and at an extraordinary rate. This epidemic of meanings is readily apparent in the chaotic assemblage of understandings of AIDS that by now exists. The mere enumeration of some of the ways AIDS has been characterized suggests its enormous power to generate meanings.[10]

This is a description of the theological problem at its core. The world is inherently meaningless; it's a lump of stuff. Language itself cannot solve the problem of its own legitimacy; Treichler was wrong on that point. Language can propose meaning, but only take us as far as an argument. As the epidemic of meanings during the early years of the AIDS crisis demonstrates, language may signify truth or falsehood. Not every statement is true, believable, or found to be authoritative. Language may open us up to the possibility of meaning, but it is our actions—how we perform—that may provide that meaning with legitimacy. Treichler either missteps in the end or isn't clear. The disease hasn't had the power to generate meanings; the language of AIDS as developed, deployed, and performed by its poets has that power. But this is not a simple or clean process.

The AIDS epidemic forced society to reckon with this meaninglessness. But, as Clifford Geertz has taught, we cannot live in a world we do not understand. In shining a spotlight on the meaninglessness of things, AIDS insisted that meaning be produced. This is the sense in which AIDS was an epidemic of signification. The meaninglessness illuminated by AIDS produced a glut of possible meanings. One possibility—maybe the dominant cultural narrative—was that biology itself had vindicated the opponents of the licentiousness of the 1960s and gender and sexuality liberation movements. This "sense" of AIDS wasn't just something that the religious right embraced (AIDS as a punishment from God). It was widely embraced

[10] Treichler, 11–2.

within the conservative movement in general, even among atheist Ayn Randers. More widely, it was embraced by ordinary people who weren't particularly religious. Even gay AIDS activists like Michael Callen, who explicitly rejected the "punishment from God" nonsense, nevertheless associated AIDS not with a virus but with a "lifestyle" that involved, crucially, receptive anal sex.[11] The "traumatic rupture" of AIDS among queers was precisely its destruction of the narrative of gay liberation and the imposition of the narrative of the "unnatural lifestyle" that this movement had opposed. In other words, all the sense-making around AIDS in the early days of the epidemic had to be overcome in order for ACT UP to carry forward any liberatory hope. Of AIDS was made a sad sense. Rendering AIDS senseless—which in fact it was, as is the world—was an effortful act, not something that happened automatically.

There is a double movement here. On the one hand, the world is inherently meaningless already—it's absurd. But on the other, we live in a meaningful world. It is subjunctive action which produces the meaning, but only upon the possibility created by absurdity. The old world must either fall apart or be destroyed before the new one may be built on the rubble. One could neither reduce AIDS to a disease of signification nor find a way out of its stigmatizing significance except by going through that stigmatizing significance and reinscribing it otherwise. Doing so involves rigorous, close, and intentional attention to senselessness. Only then and out of that comes the inevitable reinscription of sense. This is a way in which theology is a transgressive reinscribing: it renders senseless the so-called common sense by drawing attention to the senselessness that this sense produces, but in doing so it shapes a new sense. The AIDS epidemic and its accompanying epidemic of signification led to a resisting theology that made a new world.

ACT UP functioned as the religious authority creating the liturgy—the people's work—that made sense of AIDS. In the words of Charles E. Morris III, "ACT UP materially transformed with bodies and words and graphics the definition and meanings and visibilities of AIDS, development of and access to its treatment and prevention, its politics and politicization. If SILENCE = DEATH, as its brilliant mantra exhorted, then, even as activists succumbed, ACT UP = LIVING."[12] In so doing,

---

[11] Richard Berkowitz and Michael Callen, *How to Have Sex in an Epidemic: One Approach*, with medical and scientific consultation from Joseph Sonnabend, M.D. (New York: Tower Press, N.Y.C., 1983).

[12] Charles E. Morris III, "ACT UP 25: HIV/AIDS, Archival Queers, and Mnemonic World Making," *Quarterly Journal of Speech* (Vol. 98, No. 1, February 2012, pp. 49–53), 50.

ACT UP's subjunctive practices created a world in which AIDS was placed, found meaning, and pointed toward a future yet to dawn. "In many significant senses," writes Morris, "we are here because of ACT UP."[13] ACT UP created the once-future in which we now live by performing a meaningful and alternative reality to the one in which so many were dying.

Subjunctivity: Poetry

For Mark Lewis Taylor, poetry is political. And when it enters into an agonistic fray, it becomes or reveals the theological latent within the political. But this is a peculiar sense of what poetry might be. It is both open and practiced, according to Taylor. It isn't just words. Poetry that fully expresses the theological is the practice of an art-force that interconnects the individual artistic act through solidarity to a network of others who also have "borne the weight of the world."[14] It is this weightedness as expressed through poetic action that Taylor argues is the theological latent within the political. One might say then that this sense of poetry-as-theological-practice is resistance. Taylor prefers the term "agonistic" to "resistance," but it strikes me as an unfortunate vestigial example of an intellectual elitism and a reluctance to move from the discourse of high theory to the discourse of those very heroes of *The Theological and the Political* that concern Taylor throughout: poets, prisoners, the tortured, and the defiant.

Nevertheless, Taylor describes the activities of poet-resisters this way:

> [T]heir weighing-in is a practice. The prodigious art-force that is the fullest expression of the theological is not only an individual creative performance, as necessary and impressive and as cunning and brilliant a display of individual resilience though it may be. As a practice of weighing-in, the creators of these art-full forms take on their force through the ways humans organize actions with and through them ... we will know that the individual's resilient art-force has its force as linked in practical activity, to other persons, structures, and practices.[15]

Mark Lowe Fisher's corpse was carried in an open casket procession in the pouring rain from Judson Memorial Church for almost 40 blocks to 43rd

---
[13] Morris, 50.
[14] Taylor, 165.
[15] Taylor, 164–5.

Street in front of the New York City Republican Headquarters on the day before Election Day in November 1992.[16] Before he died, he explained his desire for a political funeral in a document entitled "Bury Me Furiously." In it, he explains,

> I have decided that when I die I want my fellow AIDS activists to execute my wishes for my political funeral. I suspect—I know—my funeral will shock people when it happens. We Americans are terrified of death. Death takes place behind closed doors and is removed from reality, from the living. I want to show the reality of my death, to display my body in public; I want the public to bear witness. We are not just spiraling statistics; we are people who have lives, who have purpose, who have lovers, friends and families. And we are dying of a disease maintained by a degree of criminal neglect so enormous that it amounts to genocide. I want my death to be as strong a statement as my life continues to be. I want my own funeral to be fierce and defiant, to make the public statement that my death from AIDS is a form of political assassination. We are taking this action out of love and rage.[17]

Fisher's funeral is forceful in the way its defiance, love, and rage are linked, through ACT UP, to the public. Following Taylor, we may say that ACT UP's political funerals were acts of interconnected art-force. Political funerals are poetic acts that express the theological within the political. Fisher's pallbearers carried the weight of the world on their shoulders that day.

Subjunctivity: Desire

Winquist's definition of theology as the desire for a thinking that doesn't disappoint is relevant here.[18] For Winquist, theology is a desire, but desire is also both religion's method and object. He bases this formulation in part upon Paul Tillich's assertion that religion is the depth-dimension of life.[19] Winquist explains his desiring theology this way:

---

[16] See Joy Episalla's interview with Sarah Schulman from December 6, 2003, for the ACT UP Oral History Project. Episalla—a close friend of Fisher as well as Tim Bailey—described Fisher's political funeral on pp. 39–41 of the transcript of the interview. http://www.actuporalhistory.org/interviews/images/episalla.pdf.

[17] Mark Lowe Fisher, "Bury Me Furiously." http://actupny.org/diva/polfunsyn.html.

[18] Charles E. Winquist, *Desiring Theology* (Chicago and London: University of Chicago Press, 1995).

[19] Tillich writes, "Religion is the dimension of depth in all [functions of man's spiritual life] .... What does the metaphor depth mean? It means that the religious aspect points to that which is ultimate, infinite, unconditional in man's spiritual life. Religion, in the largest and

> I have equated the desire for a thinking which does not disappoint with a desire to think theologically ... to seek depth today is to desire a complex association of meanings that are weighted with a sense of being real and important. This is a desire to know an "other" in and of language that can be valued in the forming of personal and communal identity. This is a desire to think the singularities of experience that can exfoliate themselves in the production of new meaning. What remains of Tillich's formulation of depth is the desire for a thinking that resists the trivialization of ultimate questions. There is in this formulation a secular mandate for theology even in the context of the transitoriness, contingency, and dissimulations of postmodern thinking.[20]

There are many resonances in this short passage with the discussion unfolding on these pages including the weightedness, the sense of reality and importance, the formation of personal and communal identity by making the private public, the production of new meaning, and the notion of a secular mandate for theology. Each of these resonates with the way I've been using the term "subjunctivity" that runs throughout this project. All of this is to say that, if theology is desire, there is a queer desire at work in ACT UP.

This queer desire is part of what makes ACT UP worthy of theological interpretation. That desire is closely related to José Esteban Muñoz's key operative concept: queer futurity. Queerness, in Muñoz's sense, is "a temporal arrangement in which the past is a field of possibility in which subjects can act in the present in the service of a new futurity."[21] Further, "The time of the past helps mount a critique of the space of the present.

---

most basic sense of the word, is ultimate concern. And ultimate concern is manifest in all creative functions of the human spirit. It is manifest in the moral sphere as the unconditional seriousness of the moral demand. Therefore, if someone rejects religion in the name of the moral function of the human spirit, he rejects religion in the name of religion. Ultimate concern is manifest in the realm of knowledge as the passionate longing for ultimate reality. Therefore, if anyone rejects religion in the name of the cognitive function of the human spirit, he rejects religion in the name of religion. Ultimate concern is manifest in the aesthetic function of the human spirit as the infinite desire to express ultimate meaning. Therefore, if anyone rejects religion in the name of the aesthetic function of the human spirit, he rejects religion in the name of religion. You cannot reject religion with ultimate seriousness, because ultimate seriousness, or the state of being ultimately concerned, is itself religion. Religion is the substance, the ground, and the depth of man's spiritual life. This is the religious aspect of the human spirit." Paul Tillich, *Theology of Culture*, ed. Robert C. Kimball (New York: Oxford University Press, 1959), 7–8.

[20] Winquist, ix–x.

[21] José Esteban Muñoz, *Cruising Utopia: The Then and There of Queer Futurity* (New York and London: New York University Press, 2009), 16.

This is not revisionary history or metahistory; it is a critical deployment of the past for the purpose of engaging the present and imagining the future."[22] It is worth quoting the opening passage of Muñoz's *Cruising Utopia: The Then and There of Queer Futurity* at length:

> Queerness is not yet here. Queerness is an ideality. Put another way, we are not yet queer. We may never touch queerness, but we can feel it as the warm illumination of a horizon imbued with potentiality. We have never been queer, yet queerness exists for us as an ideality that can be distilled from the past and used to imagine a future. The future is queerness's domain. Queerness is a structuring and educated mode of desiring that allows us to see and feel beyond the quagmire of the present. The here and now is a prison house. We must strive, in the face of the here and now's totalizing rendering of reality, to think and feel a then and there. Some will say that all we have are the pleasures of this moment, but we must never settle for that minimal transport; we must dream and enact new and better pleasures, other ways of being in the world, and ultimately new worlds. Queerness is a longing that propels us onward, beyond romances of the negative and toiling in the present. Queerness is that thing that lets us feel that this world is not enough, that indeed something is missing … Queerness is also a performative because it is not simply a being but a doing for and toward the future. Queerness is essentially about the rejection of a here and now and an insistence on potentiality or concrete possibility for another world.[23]

Muñoz's concept of queer futurity is particularly useful for understanding ACT UP's political funerals. Rather than emphasizing the present or the closure of the future as many queer theorists have done,[24] Muñoz instead points to queer performativity's openness to alternate realities and alternate futures which are generated, in part, by reflecting on the past.[25] Similar to the double movement in the meaning-making response to the

---

[22] Muñoz, 116.

[23] Muñoz, 1.

[24] The two most notable examples are Leo Bersani, "Is the Rectum a Grave?" *AIDS: Cultural Analysis/Cultural Activism*, eds. Douglas Crimp and Leo Bersani (Cambridge, MA: MIT Press, 1988) and Lee Edelman, *No Future: Queer Theory and the Death Drive* (Durham, NC: Duke University Press, 2004).

[25] This is what has led historians examining what today's activists might learn from ACT UP to argue that, "In reflecting on ACT UP's 25th anniversary, we need a 'critical nostalgia' regarding not just what histories we tell but how this very telling structures the rules of engagement between queer leftist generations. Such considerations complement Muñoz's 'critically utopian' desire for a relationality that animates queer futurity." Pascal Emmer,

absurdity illuminated by the epidemic, political funerals also enact a kind of double movement. They have functioned as ritualized reflections upon what had been and what was lost for the purpose of energizing and mobilizing present actors to produce an alternate future that might never come. Muñoz's concept of queerness is embodied desire for what might be other than the here and now. Queerness is subjunctive. The points of contact with Winquist should be clear. "Queerness as utopian formation is a formation based on an economy of desire and desiring. This desire is always directed at that thing that is not yet here, objects and moments that burn with anticipation and promise."[26] Queerness's subjunctive desire means that we may begin to see queerness as theological.

I have been making the controversial claim that ACT UP was a theological movement. Religion is the thing that makes sense of a meaningless world. During the epidemic of signification that accompanied the plague of AIDS in the 1980s, ACT UP's demonstrations began to ritually generate meaningful public experiences and language. It did so, in part, through political funerals. These funerals simultaneously looked backward to what had been lost, and also forward toward the future. Tim Bailey was an ACT UP member who, according to his epitaph, died in 1993, "of AIDS complications: government neglect, greed, and indifference." This is ACT UP's eulogy for Bailey given at his political funeral in Washington, DC:

> He was a friend, a lover, a brother, and a son. He was also an AIDS activist––a hero in the fight against the epidemic. We're giving him a hero's funeral. When he was alive, Tim told us he wanted his body thrown over the White House gates. Because he was enraged by the government's lethargy—outright inhumanity—in confronting the AIDS crisis. Because he wanted his death to help more Americans understand that while the government drags its heels, real people are dying. We told him we couldn't throw his body over the gates. Not because we didn't share his fury. But because we loved him too much to treat his mortal remains that way. During his last days he said, "All right. Do something formal and aesthetic in front of the White House. I won't be there anyway. It'll be for you." This procession, then, is for us. Not just those of us who knew and cared for Tim. For all of us; for everybody. Because we're all living with AIDS. Every man, woman, and child.[27]

"Talkin' 'Bout Meta-Generation: ACT UP History and Queer Futurity," *Quarterly Journal of Speech* (Vol. 98, No. 1, February 2012, pp. 89–96), 93.
[26] Muñoz, 26.
[27] Tim Bailey's political funeral, held on July 1, 1993, in Washington, DC. http://actupny.org/divatv/netcasts/tim_bailey.html. Also, see the same interview with Joy Episalla as mentioned in note #33 above. Episalla was Bailey's healthcare proxy and describes his political

Bailey's political funeral was a performance that generated new meaning within the traumatic experience of a community's loss of a beloved friend who died too young under infuriating circumstances. But rituals such as funerals are not only undertaken for their explicit purposes—to mourn the dead, to celebrate the life of the deceased. Political funerals also serve to reinforce or create social solidarity and to generate new meaning through the act of publicly shaming—in a most dramatic fashion—those in positions of power and responsibility. Bailey's political funeral was an act of mourning of the life lost and a celebration of his heroism. It emphasized both the past and the present. But in invoking Bailey's own words that the event not be for him, but for the living, the funeral ironically pointed to the future. It was a performative act of queer futurity. Muñoz recognizes the potential pitfalls here. In emphasizing the future, one temptation—a classic theological problem—is to deny or ignore the present and, consequently, to use the future as an empty escape. But for Muñoz, an overemphasis on the present to the neglect of the future is potentially just as dangerous. "The way to deal with the asymmetries and violent frenzies that mark the present is not to forget the future," Muñoz explains. "The here and now is simply not enough. Queerness should and could be about a desire for another way of being in both the world and time, a desire that resists mandates to accept that which is not enough."[28] We emphasize the subjunctive: queerness might be other than it is, desiring of a world that might be enough. This is why queerness needs theology. Or better, this is why queerness—which itself is not yet—is already theological. Queerness is a desiring theology, and as such needs to heed theology's secular mandate. That is, queerness requires theological desire expressed politically as resistance.

Ghosts

ACT UP haunts us. It's an assembly of ghosts. This is most explicit in its political funerals and die-ins where human bodies, whether dead or alive, became specters.[29] According to Mark L. Taylor, "The specter is haunting

---

funeral on pp. 55–59 of the transcript of the interview. http://www.actuporalhistory.org/interviews/images/episalla.pdf.

[28] Muñoz, 96.

[29] ACT UP's most notable die-in occurred during the "Stop the Church" action. On December 10, 1989, almost 5000 people associated with ACT UP gathered outside St. Patrick's Cathedral in New York City to protest the Roman Catholic Archdiocese's public

congealed into a portentous promise or threat, one that carries and suggests an accountability, a demand upon the present to remember, often to effect a liberation for the effaced ones."[30] ACT UP activists used their deaths—biological or metaphorical—as political and moral statements meant to jar us into action. There is a danger when emphasizing the spectral nature of this kind of political action. According to Muñoz, "One of the things one risks when one talks of ghosts is the charge of ignoring the living, the real, and the material."[31] This sentiment is echoed by David Wojnarowicz: "I worry that friends will slowly become professional pallbearers, waiting for each death, of their lovers, friends and neighbors, and polishing their funeral speeches; perfecting their rituals of death rather than a relatively simple ritual of life such as screaming in the streets."[32] Wojnarowicz died in 1992 of government neglect. His body was carried through the East Village on July 29. ACT UP resists falling into the trap of neglecting the living. Die-ins and political funerals haunt the living for the living. Screaming in the streets is a ritual of life. The streets are for celebration. It is worth repeating the words from Tim Bailey's eulogy: "This procession, then, is for us. Not just those of us who knew and cared for Tim. For all of us; for everybody. Because we're all living with AIDS. Every man, woman, and child."[33]

Shortly after its inception in 1987, ACT UP created a Treatment and Data Committee (T&D) to research the science behind potential HIV/AIDS treatments. At the T&D group's first meeting, Iris Long, a PhD in chemistry, explained a clinical trial carried out on HIV-positive patients by the National Institute of Allergy and Infectious Disease (NIAID). She was able to effectively communicate the complexity of the science, research, and process. The T&D group would then review the medical information and report back to the rest of ACT UP.[34]

---

stand against AIDS education and condom distribution and its opposition to abortion. A few dozen people entered the cathedral and interrupted mass, chanting "stop killing us!" Others fell to the floor and remained limp, miming death, and were removed on stretchers like corpses. One hundred and eleven people were arrested. See Peter Lewis Allen, *The Wages of Sin: Sex and Disease, Past and Present* (Chicago: University of Chicago Press, 2000), 143. Also the ACT UP archives at http://www.actupny.org/YELL/stopchurch99.html and http://www.actupny.org/documents/cron-89.html.

[30] Taylor, 34.
[31] Muñoz, 41.
[32] David Wojnarowicz, http://actupny.org/reports/reportashes.html.
[33] Tim Bailey's political funeral. Emphasis added.
[34] *How to Survive a Plague.* Directed by David France. Public Square Films, 2012. DVD.

Echoing the logic of liberation theology's self-educating base communities, ACT UP consciously identified its need to learn about the science and business of drug development if it wanted to be able to advocate for better and cheaper HIV/AIDS treatment development. This self-education process helped the organization to contextualize a number of protests that were aimed at drug companies, the NIH, and the FDA who had been sluggish in getting drugs to market. One of the most powerful scenes in the ACT UP documentary, How to Survive a Plague, is when a small group of ACT UP members, including Bob Rafsky,[35] enter the offices of Daiichi Pharmaceuticals on October 29, 1992, and handcuff themselves to each other through PVC tubes. They're protesting Daiichi's slow development of an anti-Kaposi's sarcoma drug. A researcher walks into the room occupied by the activists and Rafsky calls out to him. "See this dark mark on my forehead? That's Kaposi's sarcoma. It's going to spread. It's going to kill me. Are you coming to my funeral? Because you're the man fucking responsible. You are my murderer, in your shirt and tie!"[36] Rafsky died four months later on February 20, 1993.

Only ghosts may address their own killers. Further, the activists participating in political funerals and die-ins not only haunt us by addressing our accountability and demanding our remembrance, but by virtue of their queerness. For instance, Muñoz argues that haunting is an especially useful concept for queer theory. "The double ontology of ghosts and ghostliness, the manner in which ghosts exist inside and out and traverse categorical distinctions, seems especially useful for a queer criticism that attempts to understand communal mourning, group psychologies, and the need for a politics that 'carries' our dead with us into battles for the present and future."[37] The ritualization and politicization of queer death simultaneously stand outside of easy conceptual boxes while also weighing on public witnesses. It is precisely this queerness of both content and form that opens up the possibility of alternate realities. The queer art-force of the political

---

[35] Rafsky gained notoriety in March of 1992 when he heckled then-presidential candidate Bill Clinton by interrupting him in the middle of his stump speech to say, "This is the center of the epidemic. What are you doing about it?" When Clinton asked Rafsky to calm down, Rafsky responded, "I can't calm down. I'm dying of AIDS while you're dying of ambition." "Robert Rafsky, Writer and Activist in AIDS Fight, Dies," February 23, 1993. The Washington Post as found at http://www.actupny.org/divatv/netcasts/rafsky_reads.html.

[36] Bob Rafsky speaking at a protest at the offices of Daiichi Pharmaceuticals as seen in the documentary film, *How to Survive a Plague.*

[37] Muñoz, 46.

funeral is thus poetic in its form and subjunctively theological in its content. Or, in the words of Muñoz, "our remembrances and their ritualized tellings—through film, video, performance, writing, and visual culture—[have] world-making potentialities."[38] David Wojnarowicz explains that the world-making potentiality of the ritualized telling is in the way it makes public what had been private.

> To make the private into something public is an action that has terrific repercussions in the reinvented world. The government has the job of maintaining the day-to-day illusion of the ONE-TRIBE NATION. Each public disclosure of a private reality becomes something of a magnet that can attract others with a similar frame of reference; thus each public disclosure of a fragment of private reality serves as a dismantling tool against the illusion of a ONE-TRIBE NATION; it lifts the curtains for a brief peek and reveals the probable existence of literally millions of tribes. The term "general public" disintegrates. What happens next is the possibility of an X-ray of Civilization, an examination of its foundations. To turn our private grief for the loss of friends, family, lovers and strangers into something public would serve as another powerful dismantling tool.[39]

The private reality made public is thus an act of resistance with the potential to not only dismantle our problematic conceptual illusions, but to rebuild the world in a new and more meaningful way. Winquist writes that, "What is special about theology as a discursive practice is that its extreme formulations are intensive uses of language that can and often do transgress the repressive totalizations of dominant discourse."[40] ACT UP's political funerals are thus theological acts of resistance.

Theopoetic Utopianism

Putting ACT UP with Muñoz's concept of queer futurity into a conversation with Taylor's theopoetics and Winquist's desiring theology may not only appear queer, but possibly offensive. Doing a secular theology with non-theological material is a risk. But there is justification for appropriating Muñoz for this political-theological project. At the end of *Cruising Utopia* Muñoz offers his book "as a resource for the political imagination"

---
[38] Muñoz, 35.
[39] David Wojnarowicz, http://www.actupny.org/diva/synWoj.html.
[40] Winquist, x.

and "something of a flight plan for a collective political becoming."[41] Additionally, it is in the spirit of queering both the theological with the political and the political with the theological through the mechanism of resistance that I think this kind of project is not only warranted, but necessary. The world might be otherwise than it is if we were more open to its possibilities. Within the context of the AIDS epidemic, Muñoz proposes that, "queer politics, in my understanding, needs a real dose of utopianism. Utopia ... permits us to conceptualize new worlds and realities that are not irrevocably constrained by the HIV/AIDS pandemic and institutionalized homophobia. More important, utopia offers us a critique of the present, of what is, by casting a picture of what can and perhaps will be."[42]

I am arguing that the use of the subjunctive mood in that final sentence is not coincidental. Subjunctivity—living and thinking as if the world were otherwise than it is—makes alternate worlds possible. I have been articulating an odd thing: a secular, political theology of a queer activist organization that put its faith in the possibility of turning AIDS into a chronic illness, rather than a death sentence. Perhaps I have been articulating it as if it were a thing to be articulated. Perhaps a secular political theology of ACT UP is not something that exists, but something that might. "I have insisted that there has always been something queer about utopia and utopian thinkers," writes Muñoz.[43] What he has been calling "utopian," Mark Lewis Taylor might call "the theological." It is that within the political that haunts it, pointing out toward alternatives. The utopian, then, is theopoetical. Further,

> Because the theological traces and theorizes ways that persons and groups who are traditionally rendered subordinate under the concentrated weight of the world are able, nevertheless, to haunt, unsettle, and perhaps dissolve the structures of those systems of knowledge and power, the theological also haunts the Theology whose effects often participate in the world's weight as concentrated.[44]

The art-force of the theological haunts us and also haunts the discipline of theology. So, ACT UP embodies and performs a secular, subjunctive political theology. But additionally, we may now propose that theology is embodied by that which is queer. What we might learn from ACT UP is that there is both a queerness and a resistance to theology itself.

---

[41] Muñoz, 189.
[42] Muñoz, 35.
[43] Muñoz, 169–70.
[44] Taylor, 62.

CHAPTER 6

Occupy Wall Street

Seasons

Mohammed Bouazizi set himself on fire on December 17, 2010.[1] He was a grocer responding to the specific concern of years of harassment by the police in Sidi Bouzid, Tunisia. It was a small, albeit dramatic action. Bouazizi ignited a wave of protests that would ultimately end the autocratic rule of President Zine el-Abidine Ben Ali, force him into exile, and dissolve the Tunisian parliament. Then, from January 25 until February 11, 2011, hundreds of thousands of Egyptian people occupied Cairo's Tahrir Square

---

[1] The timeline of the events leading up to Occupy Wall Street and the first two months of its encampment here described are largely taken from my own notes taken at the time and clarified by http://www.occupytogether.org/aboutoccupy/. I performed further fact checking and gained clarification by consulting Adbusters, NPR, Mother Jones, and Slate. See: "#OCCUPYWALLSTREET," on the Adbusters website, July 13, 2011. https://www.adbusters.org/blogs/adbusters-blog/occupywallstreet.html; Bill Chappell, "Occupy Wall Street: From A Blog Post To A Movement," on the NPR website, October 20, 2011, http://www.npr.org/2011/10/20/141530025/occupy-wall-street-from-a-blog-post-to-a-movement; James West, "365 Days of Occupy Wall Street— an Anniversary Timeline," on Mother Jones's website, September 17, 2012, http://www.motherjones.com/mojo/2012/09/occupy-wall-street-anniversary-timeline; David Weigel and Lauren Hepler, "Everything You Need To Know About Occupy Wall Street Entry 3: A Timeline of the Movement, from February to Today," on Slate.com, November 18, 2011, http://www.slate.com/articles/news_and_politics/politics/features/2011/occupy_wall_street/what_is_ows_a_complete_timeline.html.

© The Author(s) 2019
J. E. Miller, *Resisting Theology, Furious Hope*,
Radical Theologies and Philosophies,
https://doi.org/10.1007/978-3-030-17391-3_6

in protest of President Hosni Mubarak's dictatorship. Mubarak's regime fell, and the combined actions of Bouazizi and the Tahrir Square protests inspired democratic uprisings in Lebanon, Yemen, Oman, Bahrain, Syria, Libya, and Morocco, as well as preemptive pacification and reform measures by government officials in Algeria, Jordan, Saudi Arabia, and Kuwait. Collectively, these protests, revolutions, and reforms have come to be known as the Arab Spring.

On the other side of the Atlantic, beginning on February 17, 2011, hundreds of thousands of public and union employees and their supporters occupied the Wisconsin State Capitol building in Madison. Governor Scott Walker's budget was not only austere, but it threatened the collective bargaining rights of unions in the state. Similar protests broke out in Columbus, Ohio. Austerity also became the object of protest in 58 Spanish cities beginning on May 15, 2011. In Madrid, the 15-M movement demanded a more significant role in political decision-making and occupied the central square, Puerta del Sol. Underscoring their indignation, the protest was organized through participatory democratic tactics. It only made sense that protests demanding more democracy would be democratic. For weeks, the 15-M Movement, as it became known due to its start date, focused the public's attention on the ways in which politics as usual corporate influence on decision-making and policy had ruined Spain's economy. Then, on May 25, tens of thousands of people began gathering in Athens, Greece, after austerity announcements were made by the government there. In exchange for a €110 bailout, the government had agreed to dramatically cut public spending and to raise taxes. Echoing the 15-M Movement (which was composed of what the press called *indignados*, or angry ones), the *aganaktismenoi* (indignants) struggled against State repression, tear gas, and police violence.

On July 13, 2011, Adbusters—a Canadian magazine without corporate sponsorship and a "global network of culture jammers and creatives working to change the way information flows, the way corporations wield power, and the way meaning is produced in our society"[2]—issued a call to "occupy Wall Street" on September 17. The communique was accompanied by a now famous image of a ballet dancer, arabesque, atop the Wall Street charging bull. Inspired by the Arab Spring, the Wisconsin State House takeover, and the *acampadas* of 15-M, Adbusters called out to "you 90,000

---

[2] Adbusters, https://www.adbusters.org.

redeemers, rebels and radicals out there," asking and encouraging, "Are you ready for a Tahrir moment? On Sept 17, flood into lower Manhattan, set up tents, kitchens, peaceful barricades, and occupy Wall Street."[3] The invitation went on to quote the activist, Raimundo Viejo from Pompeu Fabra University in Barcelona, who said, "The antiglobalization movement was the first step on the road. Back then our model was to attack the system like a pack of wolves. There was an alpha male, a wolf who led the pack, and those who followed behind. Now the model has evolved. Today we are one big swarm of people."[4]

This initial call thus indicated one of the important components of what would become the Occupy movement: the anarchic, participatory democracy of the multitude. Jeffrey W. Robbins explains the revelatory—one might even say, religious—qualities of radical democracy:

> ...democracy is not simply a form of politics but the very *principle of politics*. It is not antigovernmental but government otherwise. Though rejecting the necessity of the rule of one, it is not entirely without rule, only this rule has no foundation other than that of the shifting sands of a whimsical people of impropriety. As such, it is not that democracy creates the trouble; rather, it merely reveals it. Democracy is an unveiling, a stripping away of the pretense of the authority to govern and to rule, of the special right of the highly born and well connected.[5]

Occupy Wall Street would indeed go on to govern itself otherwise and as a multitude, revealing something of the real power of subjunctivity in the process.

Adbusters' call was heeded by thousands. On September 17, 2011, New York City's financial district indeed flooded with occupiers protesting inequality and the corporate influence on political process. According to Stephanie McMillan, conditions in 2011 contributing to inspiring the occupation included a wide variety of issues ranging from the political and economic to the environmental and technological. Sadly, there was something to inspire almost anyone:

---

[3] Adbusters, "#OCCUPYWALLSTREET." July 13, 2011. https://www.adbusters.org/blogs/adbusters-blog/occupywallstreet.html.
[4] Adbusters, "#OCCUPYWALLSTREET."
[5] Robbins, *Radical Democracy,* 62. In this passage, Robbins is summarizing and commenting upon Jacques Rancière's work on radical democracy.

More than 54% of the U.S. Discretionary budget was spent on imperialist aggression.
6 million Americans had lost their homes.
A million people annually faced bankruptcy due to medical bills.
100,000 in the U.S. Died annually by being denied decent medical care.
Real joblessness spiraled to over 20%.
Average college tuition in the U.S. Had risen by 900% since 1978.
The average college graduate was $25,000 in debt.
No 2010 income taxes were paid by corporations that made huge profits or took huge bailouts and subsidies, such as Citicorp, Exxon/Mobil, Bank of America, Wells Fargo, Boeing, Verizon, News Corporation, Merck, and Pfizer.
78% of the world's old growth forests were gone.
94% of the large fish in the oceans were gone.
Phytoplankton, the tiny plants that produce half of the oxygen we breathe, had declined by 40% since 1950.
200 species per day became extinct.
Industries produced 400 million tons of hazardous waste each year.
The water in 89% of U.S. Cities tested had been found to contain the carcinogen hexavalent chromium.
The Earth's average temperature had risen by 1.4 degrees F since 1920.
There were 56 million active Twitter users.
600 million people visited Facebook each month.[6]

Thousands of people flooded lower Manhattan. The police blocked the occupiers from Wall Street itself, then One Chase Manhattan Plaza. Eventually, a group of a few dozen occupiers gathered at Zuccotti Park, just north of the Stock Exchange. Symbolically, and with reference to Tahrir Square, they renamed it Liberty Square. The group's numbers swelled. There were hundreds of people staying every night through the middle of November. This model ultimately become adopted by people in more than 500 cities. On September 29, using anarchist organizing and decision-making techniques that emphasize consensus, the New York General Assembly—the democratic, decision-making mechanism of Occupy Wall Street—approved a Declaration of the Occupation that asserts "the feeling of mass injustice" that has been inspiring protest movements around the world. The Declaration details many of the ways that the global capitalism system causes suffering and harm.[7]

[6] Stephanie McMillan, *The Beginning of the American Fall: A Comics Journalist Inside the Occupy Wall Street Movement* (New York: Seven Stories Press, 2012), 4–5.
[7] NYC General Assembly, "Declaration of the Occupation of New York City." September 29, 2011. http://www.nycga.net/resources/documents/declaration/.

The initial General Assemblies and the various groups that fed into them garnered consensus on the problem: global capitalism. There were a myriad of concerns being put forward: economic exploitation, monopolization of medical care, housing, and education turning each into creators of crippling debt, imperialism and the global US military presence, ecocide (especially through extraction of energy resources), political repression, and oppression through institutions like prisons.[8] But, at bottom, Occupy Wall Street agreed that all of these particular problems have capitalism at their root. As such, advocating specific solutions doesn't make very much sense. Instead, Occupy decided to insist that the only demand it was willing to make was the occupation itself—all other demands remained provisional and under discussion.[9] In the words of the New York General Assembly, "We are not merely a protest movement. What we communicate is not just outrage, but a full-on call to action. Further, we do not have one or two simple demands (though many demand them of us). We are a movement which does call for accountability, however—accountability to ourselves and to our country."[10]

If the problem is a system, the solution must be centered around a *process*. Slavoj Žižek said of the burgeoning movement that, "This is precisely what the protesters are underlining—that global capitalism undermines democracy."[11] Global capitalism is the problem; participatory democracy is the only reasonable response. Žižek explains:

> Given their international character, large-scale economic processes cannot be controlled by democratic mechanisms, which are by definition limited to Nation-States. For that reason, people increasingly experience democratic institutions as failing in terms of expressing their vital interests. Beneath the profusion of (often confused) statements, the OWS movement thus harbors two basic insights: (1) the contemporary popular discontent is with capitalism *as a system*—the problem is the system as such, not any particular corrupt form of it; (2) the contemporary form of representative multi-party democracy is incapable of dealing with capitalist excesses; in other words, that democracy has to be reinvented.[12]

---

[8] Stephanie McMillan, *The Beginning of the American Fall: A Comics Journalist Inside the Occupy Wall Street Movement* (New York: Seven Stories Press, 2012), 79.
[9] See Nathan Schneider, "Occupy Wall Street: FAQ" on The Nation's website. September 29, 2011. http://www.thenation.com/article/163719/occupy-wall-street-faq.
[10] NYC General Assembly, "Occupy Wall Street FAQ." http://www.nycga.net/resources/faq/.
[11] Slavoj Žižek, *The Year of Dreaming Dangerously* (London: Verso, 2012), 86.
[12] Žižek, *Year of Dreaming*, 87.

The structural principles of Occupy Wall Street, based in anarchist organizing tactics—that is, Occupy's method—became its goal. Occupy didn't make demands because its purpose was to live differently.[13] Again, writes Žižek: "Their basic message is: the taboo has been broken, we do not live in the best possible world; we are allowed, obliged even, to think about the alternatives."[14] The solution was to live together conscious of the subjunctive nature of community.

After a police crackdown in mid-October, more than 900 cities around the world rallied in an international day of solidarity with Occupy Wall Street. More occupations sprung up around the United States. But in other cities, municipal governments and local police responded more harshly than they had in New York. 53 people were arrested in Atlanta, Georgia. Riot police were deployed in Oakland, California, using tear gas and flash grenades, and firing rubber bullets at the occupiers. There, 24 year-old Iraq War veteran, Scott Olsen, who had served two tours had his skull fractured by such tactics.[15] Occupations all over the country were being met by violent police repression and had to find ways to resist eviction from their various occupied sites. By November 2, Occupy Oakland joined with local unions and called for a general strike. Teachers and students did not go to school. Thousands of occupiers marched to the Port of Oakland—the fifth largest port in the US—and shut it down. "During the rest of the first half of November, police abruptly shut down more than a dozen camps across the country. The mayors of 18 cities coordinated their raids in consultation with the Department of Homeland Security, the FBI, and other federal agencies."[16]

New York did not escape the crackdown. On November 15, only hours after the Portland and Oakland encampments had been raided, the NYPD and officers from the Counter-Terrorism Bureau entered Liberty Square

---

[13] This is, of course, somewhat of an overstatement. There were plenty of proximal, small, achievable demands that were issued over the course of the occupation. But as Nathan Schneider explains, "When the time comes to fight and win something, demand it. Why not? But when there are just a few hundred people precariously holding to a park, still only beginning to organize, still starting, still trying to shake off the habits of powerlessness, what they can offer and offer one another matters so much more than what they might demand." Nathan Schneider, *Thank You Anarchy: Notes from the Occupy Apocalypse* (Berkeley, LA, and London: University of California Press, 2013), 59.
[14] Žižek, *Year of Dreaming*, 77.
[15] McMillan, 80.
[16] McMillan, 82.

at about 1:00 a.m. The raid was one of many federally coordinated raids around the country. The police wore riot gear, used pepper spray and sound cannons, and swept through the encampment destroying and throwing occupiers' belongings into dumpsters. The park was cleared. Routes into lower Manhattan were shut down. More than 200 occupiers were arrested. The activist networks that Occupy Wall Street created would mobilize for other actions—such as an attempt to occupy a park owned by Trinity Church in December and in response to Hurricane Sandy in October, 2012—but the occupation of Freedom Plaza had ended two months after it began.

Spirit

Occupy is the Holy Spirit, according to Žižek. This is certainly a striking claim coming from an atheist at a secular gathering of political dissidents. In the manuscript for his speech at Occupy Wall Street, he wrote, "They will tell us we are un-American. But when conservative fundamentalists tell you that America is a Christian nation, remember what Christianity is: the Holy Spirit, the free egalitarian community of believers united by love …We here are the Holy Spirit, while on Wall Street they are pagans worshipping false idols."[17] Occupy, of course, has had no explicit theology. It was secular in the sense that it was generally egalitarian and advocated theological neutrality. It was open to those who are theologically motivated as well as those who aren't. This is a fairly superficial understanding of the relationship between Occupy, religion, and the secular which I hope might be challenged by Žižek's comment that Occupy is the Holy Spirit. Resistance happens because of a subjunctive perspective that resisters have toward the world: that it doesn't have to be the way it is. At least one significant component of the shared ground between a radical democratic movement like Occupy and religion is the subjunctive. As such, it is appropriate to theologize political resistance.

Margaret Thatcher's program advocated that, "economics are the method, but the object is to change the soul."[18] Or, ironically, "*Social econ-*

---

[17] The manuscript of Žižek's speech may be found at http://www.versobooks.com/blogs/736 which also contains links to videos of the event. The transcript of his speech as it was actually delivered may be found at http://criticallegalthinking.com/2011/10/11/zizek-in-wall-street-transcript/.

[18] Quoted in David Harvey, *Spaces of Global Capitalism* (London: Verso, 2006), 17.

omy is for Marx the *economy of salvation*," according to Jacob Taubes.[19] Hegel—who is, of course, foundational for both Žižek and Harvey principally through Marx—identifies "the spirit, not with the logical principle ordering the world of forms, but with the principle that realizes the history of salvation."[20] If one might on the one hand connect history with economics and politics and on the other connect spirit with religion, then political resistance becomes an attempt at realizing spirit. Resistance becomes theological. Occupy—a resistance movement with neoliberal economic policies and expressions as its most consistent focus—might very well be our soul's redemption. Such an assertion, taken in conjunction with Žižek's Holy Spirit, might provoke us into thinking a bit more deeply about the relationship between religion and Occupy.

According to the Adbusters website, "#OCCUPYWALLSTREET [OWS] is a leaderless people powered movement for democracy that began in America on September 17 [2011] with an encampment in the financial district of New York City. Inspired by the Egyptian Tahrir Square uprising and the Spanish *acampadas*, [OWS] vow[s] to end the monied corruption of our democracy."[21] Simply by virtue of its presence, Occupy pushed these issues up the media agenda and towards the front of the public consciousness. Occupy Wall Street's very existence suggests that things might be different. Furthermore, the anarchic nature of Occupy's organization and its refusal to issue a list of concrete demands are exemplary of ironic and liberal democracy. John Rawls might have to be prodded some on this, but I'd like to suggest that Occupy was even more exemplary of public reason than the Supreme Court. Occupy was, to use Agamben's phrase, "a potentiality that has as its object potentiality itself, a *potentia potentiae*."[22] Occupy's absence of demands was precisely its power and its potential. It matters because it remains subjunctive and silent.

It's worth pointing out that this lack of demands was both a theoretical concern as well as a practical or functional one. The structure of the General Assembly and its consensus decision-making process made approving specific demands nearly impossible. So that even when constituencies

[19] Jacob Taubes, *Occidental Eschatology*, trans. David Ratmoko (Stanford: Stanford Press, 2009), 184.

[20] Taubes, 93. Taubes is comparing Jaochim of Fiore and Hegel in their respective dialectical understandings of the relationship between spirit and history with this sentence.

[21] Adbusters. "Occupy Wall Street." http://www.adbusters.org/campaigns/occupy wallstreet.

[22] Giorgio Agamben, *The Coming Community*, trans. Michael Hardt (Minneapolis and London: University of Minnesota Press 1993), 36.

within the GA had demands, the organizing structure of the GA resisted their adoption. There was a Demands Working Group, for instance, but it was not able to pass anything through the GA. Further, individual working groups had provisional, and local demands that applied to their particular projects all the time. This was not the same thing, however, as Occupy Wall Street having a list of concrete demands.

Occupy took accurate stock of the situation in the United States at the time. We no longer have real political discourse here. Overlapping consensus has been rendered impotent. Fourteen million Americans are out of work and millions more are underemployed. Wages have fallen after 30 years of stagnation. Massive, growing income inequality is the rule. The 1% remains unchecked in power and completely unaccountable.[23] It only benefits. It never loses. Berkeley Professor and former Labor Secretary Robert Reich has said that, "The 400 richest people in the United States have more wealth than the bottom 150 million put together."[24] Oxfam released a report that the 85 richest people in the world share a combined wealth equaling that of the poorest 3.5 billion people—fully half of the world's population.[25] This isn't about laziness. Productivity has risen. Big business profits have risen. CEO bonuses continue to follow suit. However, worker salaries have declined. There are 4 unemployed people for every open job. In academia, this ratio is closer to 40:1. The problems have been system-wide. Žižek identifies it this way: "…'capitalism' is now clearly re-emerging as the name of *the* problem. The first lesson to be learned is not to blame individuals and their attitudes. The problem is not individual corruption or greed, but the system that encourages you to be corrupt. The solution is not 'Main Street, not Wall Street,' but to change the system in which Main Street is dependent on Wall Street."[26]

---

[23] Alex Pareene, "A New Declaration of Independence: 10 Ideas for Taking America Back from the 1%." AlterNet.org. October 31, 2011. http://www.alternet.org/story/152912/a_new_declaration_of_independence%3A_10_ideas_for_taking_america_back_from_the_1?akid=7799.250815.H41J8L&rd=1&t=8.

[24] See "How income Inequality hurts America," by Steve Hargreaves, *CNN Money*, September 25, 2013, http://money.cnn.com/2013/09/25/news/economy/income-inequality/. See also *PolitiFact Wisconsin*, March 10, 2011, http://www.politifact.com/wisconsin/statements/2011/mar/10/michael-moore/michael-moore-says-400-americans-have-more-wealth-/.

[25] Graeme Wearden, "Oxfam: 85 Richest People as Wealthy as Poorest Half of the World," *The Guardian*, January 20, 2014, http://www.theguardian.com/business/2014/jan/20/oxfam-85-richest-people-half-of-the-world.

[26] Žižek, *Year of Dreaming*, 77–78.

Occupy's refusal to issue a list of concrete demands was paramount in expressing its understanding of this problem. When the system is broken, asking for specific components of it to be fixed is ridiculous. If your problem is with the people in power, asking those people to fix themselves would be markedly unreasonable. It was, therefore, simply not appropriate for Occupy to make concrete demands. And this was precisely why the opponents of the movement were so insistent that Occupy was pointless until it would make demands. It was indeed most certainly pointless from the perspective of the powers that be. When you play by the rules only to lose because the game is rigged, it does not make sense to ask for better rules. Play a different game.[27] In the words of Žižek,

> [The occupiers] are dismissed as dreamers, but the true dreamers are those who think things can go on indefinitely the way they are, just with some cosmetic changes. [The occupiers] are not dreamers; they are awakening from a dream that is turning into a nightmare. They are not destroying anything, but reacting to how the system is gradually destroying itself. We all know the classic scene from cartoons: the cat reaches a precipice but goes on walking; it starts to fall only when it looks down and notices the abyss. The protesters are just reminding those in power to look down. ... What one should resist at this stage is precisely such a quick translation of the energy of the protest into a set of concrete pragmatic demands. Yes, the protests did create a vacuum—a vacuum in the field of hegemonic ideology, and time is needed to fill this vacuum in a proper way, as it is a pregnant vacuum, an opening for the truly new.[28]

---

[27] Marla Daniels, the wife of police lieutenant Cedric Daniels on the HBO series, *The Wire*, put it slightly differently:

Marla Daniels:	You can't lose if you don't play.
Cedric Daniels:	I always heard it that you can't win if you don't play.
M:	The department puts you on a case it doesn't want. You're given people that are useless or untrustworthy.
C:	Correct.
M:	If you push too hard and any shit hits the fan, you'll be blamed for it.
C:	Correct.
M:	If you don't push hard enough, and there's no arrest, you'll be blamed for that, too.
C:	Correct.
M:	The game is rigged. But you cannot lose if you do not play.

From "The Detail," *The Wire*, written by David Simon and directed by Clark Johnson (HBO, originally aired on June 9, 2002).

[28] Slavoj Žižek, "Occupy First. Demands Come Later." The Guardian website, October 26, 2011. http://www.guardian.co.uk/commentisfree/2011/oct/26/occupy-protesters-bill-clinton.

So this is the fundamental difference between the Tea Party and Occupy: the former seeks to fill a void—or to replace one substance with another; the latter sought absence. Occupy dreamed while the Tea Party reminisced. Occupy refused any particular contract and instead insisted upon maintaining a contract-in-question. The Tea Party still has faith in the free market. Occupy was much more realistic. It had very little to no nostalgia. The Tea Party deployed the Constitution immediately. It looks backward. *Take our country back.* Occupy rarely invoked the Constitution—the founding—because Occupy was present. Evidence for this may be found in these two movements' respective uses of the visual and performing arts. The arts have no noticeable role in the Tea Party, but they meant almost everything to Occupy. The people's microphone, zombie parades, the mock trial of Goldman Sachs by Chris Hedges and Cornel West, dancing is not a crime, the thoroughly orange man—Occupy was composed of performers, activists, artists, students, laborers, and intellectuals. It had a sense of humor. It refused to take itself too seriously.

The people's microphone was a remarkable expression of Occupy's anarchic subjunctivity. It was an ingenious method developed to circumvent the police ban on amplification at the Occupy sites. A speaker would say a short phrase and anyone within ear-shot would repeat that phrase *en masse*: thus, the people became both microphone and amplifier. Elaine Scarry explains that, "Through his ability to project words and sounds out into his environment, a human being inhabits, humanizes, and makes his own a space much larger than that occupied by his body alone."[29] As Derrida makes abundantly clear in his *Signature Event Context*, repetition is always difference. The people's microphone was no monologue. It was not rhetoric or discourse. It was emphasis of difference and consent—of harmony—through the transformation of the mode of communication from that of unidirectional dictation to that of collaborative participation. It was speech absent a speaker.

Occupy was an ironic movement. It was one that refused to posit its own, new metanarrative. Or to put it in Richard Rorty's terminology, the dissenters had an aversion to creating yet another final vocabulary. For Rorty, an ironist is one who "has radical and continuing doubts about the

---

[29] Elaine Scarry, *The Body in Pain: The Making and Unmaking of the World* (Oxford and New York: Oxford University Press, 1985), 49. In that text, Scarry examines torture, the tortured person, their body, and the inexpressibility of pain. This particular quote is reference to the tortured person screaming out in pain.

final vocabulary she currently uses," "her present vocabulary can neither underwrite nor dissolve these doubts," and "she does not think that her vocabulary is closer to reality than others."[30] So this pervasive critique of Occupy—that it was all protest and no program—sounds remarkably metaphysical (that is, conservative, not ironic—humorless) by comparison. Whether liberal or conservative, the critics of Occupy tended to be metaphysicians desperately pleading for some kind of program that might resolve the tension and reform the current system. This is common sense. Douglas Rushkoff wrote for CNN that,

> As the product of the decentralized networked-era culture, [Occupy] is less about victory than sustainability. It is not about one-pointedness, but inclusion and groping toward consensus. It is not like a book; it is like the Internet. [It is] a way of life that spreads through contagion, creates as many questions as it answers, aims to force a reconsideration of the way the nation does business and offers hope to those of us who previously felt alone in our belief that the current economic system is broken. But unlike a traditional protest, which identifies the enemy and fights for a particular solution, [Occupy] just sits there talking with itself, debating its own worth, recognizing its internal inconsistencies and then continuing on as if this were some sort of new normal. It models a new collectivism, picking up on the sustainable protest village of the movement's Egyptian counterparts, with food, first aid, and a library.[31]

It is not clear if Rushkoff is familiar with Rorty's work. But his description makes it clear that Occupy had radical and continuing doubts about itself. This was manifest in its silence; its refusal to issue a list of concrete demands. Rorty writes,

> The view I am offering says that there is moral progress, and that this progress is indeed in the direction of greater human solidarity. But that solidarity is not thought of as a recognition of a core self, the human essence, in all human beings. Rather, it is thought of as the ability to see more and more traditional differences (of tribe, religion, race, customs, and the like) as

---

[30] Richard Rorty, *Contingency, Irony, and Solidarity* (Cambridge and New York: Cambridge University Press, 1989), 73.

[31] Douglas Rushkoff, "Think Occupy Wall St. Is a Phase? You Don't Get It" on CNN opinions website, October 5, 2011. http://www.cnn.com/2011/10/05/opinion/rushkoff-occupy-wall-street/index.html.

unimportant when compared with similarities with respect to pain and humiliation—the ability to think of people wildly different from ourselves as included in the range of 'us.'[32]

Occupy's irony thus looks remarkably democratic in its expression. That is, the rhetoric surrounding the 99%, to take one example, sought to enlarge the realm of inclusion for the sake of solidarity without any attempt at solidifying that solidarity into a program. It was a solidarity with an absence at its center. Appropriating Levinas, Occupy was "…a bond that [was] established between the same and the other without constituting a totality."[33] It was multitudinous; at once both multiple and collective.

Occupy's irony exemplified radical democracy. Everyone had a voice for oneself and each other. The people's mic made that link abundantly clear. For anyone to be heard, many had to speak. There was no corporate personhood at Occupy. No one spoke louder than anyone else and it was only *together* that any*one* might be heard. This was discourse without totality. And it might be that it remained liberal-irony-made-public because it remained local. Irony seems to exist in indirect proportion to the size of the community. The larger the group, the more difficult it is to maintain a sense of humor. Irony works better in networks than corporations. Corporations cannot laugh.

One might even say that not only was Occupy ironic, but it was also auto-deconstructing (in Derrida's sense). Derrida discusses the relationship between his deconstructive method and resistance to totality this way, "What disrupts the totality is the condition for the relation to the other. The privilege granted to unity, to totality, to organic ensembles, to community as a homogenized whole—this is a danger for responsibility, for decision, for ethics, for politics. That is why I insisted on what prevents unity from closing upon itself, from being closed up."[34] Derrida prefers democracy to any other political scheme because it is auto-deconstructive. Even in our markedly undemocratic republic, every few years we get the chance to self-reflect and change or vow to remain the same—though it

---

[32] Rorty, 192.

[33] Emmanuel Levinas, *Totality and Infinity: An Essay on Exteriority*, trans. Alphonso Lingus (Pittsburgh, PA: Duquesne University Press, 1961), 40. This was Levinas's definition of religion. Though he'd likely be surprised at the prospect, Žižek seems to be in full agreement with Levinas here: Occupy was the Holy Spirit.

[34] Jacques Derrida, *Deconstruction in a Nutshell: A Conversation with Jacques Derrida*, ed. and with a commentary by John D. Caputo (New York: Fordham University Press, 1997), 13.

remains within remarkably strict constraints, we decide. But how to remain deconstructive as the rule rather than the exception?

The horizontal structure of Occupy—as expressed most deliberately in its general assembly, spokes councils, and working groups—was profoundly important.[35] This was truly about consensus; *feeling together*.[36] Their meetings were laborious and consensus-seeking. They kept minutes and took votes. The spokespeople rotated. They were always only provisional. They did their best to remain polite. They were articulate. They were humble, self-critical, and determined to question. This self-reflection was irony in practice. And it was critique in community, too. *Critique together*. The etymological roots here are fascinating. "Critique" has its roots in the Greek *kritikos*, a critic is one who is "able to make judgments," which in turn comes from *krinein*, "to separate, decide, or judge." This separation has its roots in *krei* meaning "to sieve, discriminate, distinguish."[37] This essential decision-making function of political consensus thus has its roots in differentiation. Affirming alternatives is central to consensus. So what may appear on the face of it to be a consensus within politics in the US is deceptive because it is based upon agreement not to consider real alternatives to the usual. Consensus based upon similarity is a sham. And this is why politics-as-usual maintains the illusion of disagreement. Without it, the *appearance* of consent would vanish.

To criticize Occupy for a lack of solutions would be funny if the most recent US Congress had not been the least productive Congress in US history. Occupy was all means with no end, while politics-as-usual is all ends with no means; no overlap; no consensus. From *The Nation's* list of frequently asked questions about Occupy Wall Street:

> The General Assembly has become the de facto decision-making body for the occupation at Liberty Plaza... the General Assembly is a horizontal, autonomous, leaderless, modified-consensus-based system with roots in anarchist thought ... Working toward consensus is really hard, frustrating

---

[35] See New York City General Assembly's Spokes Council Proposal, http://www.nycga.net/spokes-council/ for a detailed description of Occupy's organization.

[36] *The Oxford English Dictionary*, second edition, prepared by J. A. Simpson and E. S. C. Weiner, Volume III: Cham-Creeky (Oxford: Clarendon Press, 1991), 760. Incidentally, another interpretation holds that we might think of consent in terms of harmony. When we consent, we sing together. This fits nicely with my transposition of concepts.

[37] *The Oxford English Dictionary*, second edition, prepared by J. A. Simpson and E. S. C. Weiner, Volume IV: Creel-Duzepere (Oxford: Clarendon Press, 1991), 29–32 and http://www.etymonline.com/index.php?term=critic and http://www.etymonline.com/index.php?term=crisis.

and slow. But the occupiers are taking their time. When they finally get to consensus on some issue, often after days and days of trying, the feeling is quite incredible. A mighty cheer fills the plaza. It's hard to describe the experience of being among hundreds of passionate, rebellious, creative people who are all in agreement about something. Fortunately, though, they don't need to come to consensus about everything. Working alongside the General Assembly are an ever-growing number of committees and working groups—from Food and Media to Direct Action and Sanitation. Anyone is welcome to join one, and they each do their own thing, working in tacit coordination with the General Assembly as a whole. In the end, the hope is that every individual is empowered to make decisions and act as her or himself, for the good of the group.[38]

This was resistance against the totality of an imposed consent through speech and silence. It was about the refusal to engage in a dialogue with the totality. Any dialogue with a totality immediately becomes a monologue; unidirectional. Occupy was careful to control its own language. This is again why, Agamben writes, full political and economic critique of capitalism is not simply concerned with productive activity, "but also and principally toward the alienation of language itself, of the very linguistic and communicative nature of humans...."[39] Taking control of language is a political and economic activity—maybe even especially in its rejection of particular politics and economics.

So the structure of Occupy became internally focused, rather than concerned with reform of the greater system outside. To put it in religious terms, Occupy was communion. But let us not forget that the Last Supper preceded the cross. Communion was followed by abandonment and then violence. Communion and emptiness are intimately linked. So what of potential upheaval? Žižek writes:

> Are the protesters violent? True, their very language may appear violent (occupation, and so on), but they are violent only in the sense in which Mahatma Gandhi was violent. They are violent because they want to put a stop to the way things are—but what is this violence compared with the violence needed to sustain the smooth functioning of the global capitalist system?[40]

[38] Nathan Schneider, "Occupy Wall Street: FAQ" on The Nation's website, September 29, 2011. http://www.thenation.com/article/163719/occupy-wall-street-faq.
[39] Agamben, 80.
[40] Žižek, "Occupy First."

This is Rawls's second principle of justice in action.[41] Occupy might be disruptive, but certainly less disruptive than the status quo. Žižek continues:

> What one should always bear in mind is that any debate here and now necessarily remains a debate on enemy's turf; time is needed to deploy the new content. All we say now can be taken from us—everything except our silence. This silence, this rejection of dialogue, of all forms of clinching, is our 'terror,' ominous and threatening as it should be.[42]

Threatening, yes. But hopeful. Full of potentiality. Hannah Arendt writes that, "the miracle that saves the world, the realm of human affairs, from its normal, 'natural' ruin is ultimately the fact of natality."[43] Birth—beginning—potential—the natal—the subjunctive. This is the fissure in the totality. Arendt continues, "Only the full experience of this capacity can bestow upon human affairs faith and hope."[44] This is similar to Derrida's notion of a deconstructive politics which opens up hegemony. John D. Caputo explains it this way, "Preparing for the incoming of the other, which is what constitutes a radical democracy—that is what deconstruction is."[45] And later, "What Derrida advocates, in a nutshell, is 'democracy,' which is supposed to be a very generous 'receptacle' for every difference imaginable."[46] Occupy Wall Street demonstrated this dual reception and natality for us. It did so silently, without demands. Occupy was politically apophatic. That is, the event itself expressed apophasis.

---

[41] Rawls argues that inequalities should be arranged such that they are to be of the greatest benefit to the least-advantaged members of society and that offices and positions must be open to everyone under conditions of fair equality of opportunity. John Rawls, *A Theory of Justice* (Cambridge MA and Oxford: Harvard University Press, 1971) 303.

[42] Žižek, "Occupy First."

[43] Hannah Arendt, *The Human Condition*, intro. Margaret Canovan (Chicago and London: University of Chicago Press, 1958 and 1998), 247.

[44] Arendt, 247.

[45] Caputo and Derrida, 44.

[46] Caputo and Derrida, 107. Caputo further explains on 122–3, "Democracy calls for hospitality to the Other, but the Other is the shore we cannot reach, the One we do not know. Democracy–the old name that for now stands for something new, a porous, permeable, open-ended affirmation of the other–is the best name we have for what is to come. ... Democracy is internally disturbed and continually haunted by the deepest demagogic corruption of democracy, by a crowd-pleasing, hate-mongering, reactionary politics that appeals to the basest and most violent instincts of the *demos*. Democracy is the name for what is to come, for the unforeseeable future, for the promise of the unforeseeable."

Silence

Certeau argues that it is both possible and fruitful to use language as a metaphor for understanding a variety of human activities. Specifically, he interprets urban life as though reading a text or listening to speech. He explains,

> The act of walking is to the urban system what the speech act is to language or to the statement uttered. At the most elementary level, it has a triple "enunciative" function: it is a process of *appropriation* of the topographical system on the part of the pedestrian ... it is a spatial acting out of the place ... and it implies *relations* among differentiated positions, that is, among pragmatic "contracts" in the form of movements.... It thus seems possible to give a preliminary definition of walking as a space of enunciation.[47]

But what of occupation, rather than walking? Jean-Luc Nancy wrote that, "Words do not 'come out' of the throat (nor from the 'mind' 'in' the head): they are formed in the mouth's articulation. This is why speech—including silence—is not a means of communication, but communication itself, an exposure..."[48] In light of Occupy's refusal to issue a list of concrete demands, occupation is a physical, embodied manifestation of such a communicative silence. And its silence is a revelation.

Looking through Certeau's lens of reading cities like text or acting in cities like speaking, one might hear occupation as a kind of silence. It expresses Certeau's three enunciative functions of language described above. First, occupation is a topographical appropriation through the pedestrian's claim over a space ("Whose streets? Our streets!"). Second, it is a spatial acting out, but through a refusal to walk rather than walking itself, and through that very topographical appropriation. And finally, occupation is a relation among differentiated positions—both internally and with positions outside of the occupation itself. If language is a metaphor for being in the city, Occupy was the absence or inverse of this triple enunciative function. It did not speak. It did not make demands. And yet it nevertheless remained a topographical appropriation, a spatial acting out, and a relation among differentiated opinions. As atheism is a theological position; silence is a form of speech; occupation is an/ambulation. Speech, of course, has deep theological importance. Once again, one

---

[47] Certeau, 97–8.
[48] Jean-Luc Nancy. *The Inoperative Community*, ed. Peter Connor, foreword by Christopher Fynsk, (Minneapolis and London: University of Minnesota Press, 1991), 30–31.

should be reminded of God's role in creation. In the beginning was the word and the word was God. God spoke creation into being. The city and language are both theological; this is a point of contact for understanding Occupy theologically. Occupation occurred in Erasmus's monastery and utilizes apophatic theological tactics, despite its inherent secularity. And this is why it could not speak. Monks take vows of silence.

Inverting the traditional Marxist proclamation, Jeffrey W. Robbins has said that, "The business of religion, to use that unfortunate turn of phrase, is to change the world. The theo-political implication of radical democracy is that we cannot wait for a God to save us. If [radical] democracy indeed is the political instantiation of the death of God, then this is a task that is ours alone."[49] Furthermore, Robbins defines radical democracy as "an open system" that is a "fundamental reconsideration of *who decides*."[50] Following Antonio Negri contra Carl Schmitt, Robbins's notion of radical democracy is political power generated by and held in common. "Through people's cooperation new power is created."[51] A religious interpretation of Occupy in the spirit of changing the world after the death of God seems warranted. What might theology have to say about one of the most important social (and secular) movements in the US of recent memory? This is why the Occupy movement is served well by an application of radical theology—the legacy of the death-of-God—for its understanding.

Today, resistance against totality—exemplified by occupation of a void in politics—is a matter of remaining silent. Gianni Vattimo has spoken of the need to subtract oneself from the game of power and, "Having many communities working—not necessarily together in the sense of a coordinated effort—but simply working against."[52] This kind of oppositional posture is another apophatic tactic. Following Vattimo, it is an exercise in subtraction. Politics-as-usual today has appropriated political speech such that breaching that totality is only possible through a refusal to engage in dialogue with it. But this isn't just a negative silence. Robbins argues that, "the political crisis that we face today is that no one or no-thing decides. The people have been rendered the object of market forces. The market, while banking on the power of the State to establish policies in its favor,

---

[49] Alan Jay Richard, "The Theo-politics of Radical Democracy: An Interview with Jeffrey W. Robbins (Part 2)," January 9, 2012. http://www.politicaltheology.com/blog/?p=1488.

[50] Robbins, *Radical Democracy*, 72.

[51] Robbins, *Radical Democracy*, 73.

[52] Gianni Vattimo, "A Prayer for Silence," *After the Death of God*, ed. Jeffrey W. Robbins (New York: Columbia University Press, 2007), 113.

nevertheless follows its own self-annihilating logic where only the few stand to benefit but none hold the power to control."[53]

Echoing Žižek's description of Occupy as creating a "vacuum in the field of hegemonic ideology,"[54] McKenzie Wark has suggested, "...the genius of the occupation is simply to suggest that there *could be* a politics, one in which people meet and propose and negotiate. This suggestion points to the great absence at the center of American life: a whole nation, even an empire, with no politics."[55] Radical theology's focus on working in God's absence—the absence of the sovereign—might provide us with a way of understanding Occupy's ability to create something new out of that political void: subjunctive politics. Occupy's creation of tent cities within existing urban spaces was a kind of self-referential world-creation focused on the way human relationships *might be*. It was the *work* of religion—anarchist craft.

Religion is too often constituted as withdrawal. And in some of its more stilted forms, that's absolutely true. The danger of the religious subjunctive is that its focus on possibility may turn fatalistic or escapist. One would be wise to remember that radical theology is political theology citing Hamilton as I did in the discussion in Chaps. 4 and 5. But one may not have noticed at the time that radical theology is *urban* political theology. Here is Hamilton again: "In order to overcome the death of the father in our lives, the death of God [...] we must give our devotion to the *polis*, to the city, politics, and our neighbor. Waiting for God, expecting the transcendent and the marvelous, searching for a means of enjoying them, we go out into the world and the city and, working, wait there."[56] Altizer and Hamilton were describing the secular-theological underpinnings of what would eventually become manifest in the counter-cultural revolution of the 1960s after the dominance of conservatism in the 1940s and 50s. At least on the surface, our time shares much in common with that time.

---

[53] Robbins, *Radical Democracy*, 74.

[54] Žižek wrote, "What should be resisted at this stage is any hasty translation of the energy of the protest into a set of concrete demands. The protests have created a vacuum—a vacuum in the field of hegemonic ideology, and time is needed to fill this space in a positive fashion," *The Year of Dreaming Dangerously*, 82.

[55] McKenzie Wark, "How To Occupy an Abstraction," from the Verso Books blog, October 3, http://www.versobooks.com/blogs/728-mckenzie-wark-on-occupy-wall-street-how-to-occupy-an-abstraction.

[56] Thomas J. J. Altizer and William Hamilton. *Radical Theology and the Death of God* (Indianapolis and New York: Bobbs-Merrill Company, Inc., 1966), 44.

The Arab Spring and Occupy Wall Street are evidence that the spirit of May 1968 has come around again. So, in a way, I am making a Nietzschean suggestion. We have returned. But repetition is, of course, always also difference. The Students for a Democratic Society (SDS) fractured at its 1969 convention largely over issues surrounding unity. That is, it had gotten too big and too internally multiplicitous to be able to remain cohered around a single program. In a sense, Occupy had been able to resist this type of fracture not by avoiding multiplicity, but by avoiding a specific program; by avoiding unity. Occupy maintained within itself an absence of teleological content. We have returned to a time of upheaval and social action, but with a rather significant difference. The apophatic makes an odd rallying cry.

Earlier, I invoked Richard Rubenstein's commentary on Tillich and Altizer that human freedom is the issue that compels humanity to will the death of the theistic God. This is absolutely accurate and important, but it is only half of the picture. Not only must *humanity* will the death of God for the sake of its freedom, but *God wills God's own death*. The death of God is built into the structure of who God is in the first place. It's worth revisiting that toward the end of his life, Dietrich Bonhoeffer recognized this double will—latent within God and an imperative for humanity—when he wrote that,

> we cannot be honest unless we recognize that we have to live in the world *etsi deus non daretur* [even as if there were no God]. And this is just what we ought to recognize—before God! God himself compels us to recognize it. So our coming of age leads us to a true recognition of our situation before God. God would have us know that we must live as men who manage our lives without him. The God who is with us is the God who forsakes us (Mark 15:34). The God who lets us live in the world without the working hypothesis of God is the God before whom we stand continually. Before God and with God we live without God. God lets himself be pushed out of the world and onto the cross. He is weak and powerless in the world, and that is precisely the way, the only way, in which he is with us and helps us.[57]

On the one hand, theological maturity requires living in the world, abandoned by God. But on the other hand, it is *God* who would have us know that one must live without God. This is *God willing God's own death*. Or,

---

[57] Dietrich Bonhoeffer, *Letters and Papers from Prison*, ed. Eberhard Bethge (New York: Touchstone, 1997), 360.

in Žižek's terms, "In the standard form of atheism, God dies for men who stop believing in him; in Christianity, God dies *for himself.* ... [this is the] separation of God not only from the world, but *from himself* also..."[58] God's death is built into the very foundations of who God is. So Žižek was on to something when he identified Occupy as a member of the Trinity, but he got the wrong one. Maybe it's as occupier George Schmidt says: Occupy was not the sovereign God or the Spirit, but rather Christ, who came to die.[59]

Likewise here, in Occupy's refusal to cohere around a program, Occupy was willing its own death. If Occupy is a particular case of the political instantiation of the death of God, then it should come as no surprise that Occupy not only is the result of God's death (that God's spirit is poured out, kenotically, into the community), but also that the structure and history of Occupy mirrors that of God, too. That is, if Occupy is the political instantiation of the death of God, then Occupy necessarily had built into itself an auto-kenotic mechanism—in this case, its avoidance of unification around a program. So, while the death of God is not just a case of humanity willing that death, but also of an internal dynamic already *within God*, then here is an example of the same thing happening to Occupy: the case of Occupy willing its own death.

The death-of-God movement had its pinnacle in the 1960s. So did the secularization thesis. In the same way that after the Iranian Revolution, the Moral Majority, the collapse of the USSR, the rise of an evangelical Congress, 9/11, and the Arab Spring, thinkers have been re-considering and revisiting how 'the secular' is thought, I'd like to suggest a similar approach to radical theology. This is not a nostalgic, but rather a timely way of interpreting current events. Altizer and Hamilton repeatedly

---

[58] Slavoj Žižek, "Dialectical Clarity Versus the Misty Conceit of Paradox" in *The Monstrosity of Christ: Paradox or Dialectic*, co-authored with John Milbank, ed. Creston Davis (Cambridge, MA and London. MIT Press, 2009), 237. It is on this point that Hegel is more radical than Nietzsche. At the opening of "The Death of God" in chapter 32, I quoted Nietzsche's famous aphorism of the madman to the effect that, "we have killed God" followed by Hegel's assertion that, "God sacrifices himself." These two thinkers seem to disagree as to whether the death of God is divine patricide or suicide. Altizer might very well say that it's both. It might very well be that Mohammed Bouazizi self-immolation was a kind of death-of-God passion play—a spectacular suicide for the sake of the world in which the world is nevertheless complicit.

[59] I am indebted to my friend and colleague, the Reverend George Schmidt for this insight. Other, much more significant figures than I have not given Schmidt credit for his ideas in their published work. While I cannot undo that injustice, I can refuse to perpetuate it.

insisted upon the timeliness—the modernity—of their thinking. The death-of-God is modern, they told us. Altizer's thinking is self-consciously modern in its reliance upon Hegelian methodology. But modernity, and the ways in which one understands it, has changed, too. Michael Hardt and Antonio Negri redefine modernity as a power relation, rather than a project or a process.

> When we understand modernity as a power relation, however, completing modernity is merely continuing the same, reproducing domination. More modernity or a more complete modernity is not an answer to our problems. On the contrary! For the first indications of an alternative, we should instead investigate the forces of antimodernity, that is, resistances internal to modern domination.[60]

In this invocation of antimodernity or altermodernity as internal to modernity itself, Hardt and Negri have out-dialecticized Altizer and Hamilton. Earlier, I showed that Certeau's city is simultaneously the machinery and the hero of modernity and also that cities have been at the center of many contemporary resistance movements against neoliberalism. Putting these together, one might then say that resistance to modernity, or altermodernity itself is mostly clear as an urban phenomenon. These resistances internal to modern domination tend to be *urban* resistances that create bonds of social solidarity.

So what happens to radical theology and its affirmation of modernity when modernity is no longer conceived of as progress, but a way of domination and resistance? How might radical theology reconceive itself in light of such a damning critique of the holy modern? One possible solution might be in a secular-theological understanding of *kenosis*. When radical theology focuses on the emptiness of God, rather than maintaining some kind of distinction between transcendence and immanence (that God emptied Godself into the immanent, laying transcendence bare), one might instead conceive of a God emptied from sovereignty into the multitude–a God-become-poor. Once again, one is reminded of Robbins's sovereignty from below through cooperation.

Resistance to such modern dualisms happens most effectively through deployment of the subjunctive. Occupy insisted upon remaining provisional in everything it did, ever asserting new alternatives. David Harvey's comments on the Zapatista rebellion are important here and they apply aptly to Occupy, too. He writes,

[60] Michael Hardt and Antonio Negri, *Commonwealth*, (Cambridge, MA: Harvard, 2009), 71.

The effect of all these movements has been to shift the terrain of political organization away from traditional political parties and labor organizing into a less focused political dynamic of social action across the whole spectrum of civil society. But what [the Zapatista rebellion] lost in focus it gained in terms of relevance. It drew its strengths from embeddedness in the nitty-gritty of daily life and struggle, but in so doing often found it hard to extract itself from the local and the particular to understand the macro-politics of what neo-liberal accumulation by dispossession was and is all about.[61]

So if one continues to take dialectical thinking seriously—as Altizer would have it, no doubt—Occupy's insistence on remaining local, particular, and relevant, 'without clear focus,' has the danger of losing sight of macro-politics. Except, unlike a rural, peasant movement, Occupy had the city and all her resources at its disposal. Occupy had people like David Harvey, David Graeber, Matt Taibbi, Cornel West, and a host of others to remind it to remain dialectical in its work. The particular and the universal cannot so easily be divorced within the kind of occupied, urban space that allows Occupy to thrive.

As we saw above, Occupy is the Holy Spirit (or Christ). Occupy's refusal to issue a list of demands demonstrates Occupy's affinities with apophatic mysticism. This resonates with Qushayri's point that mystics prefer silence, knowing the dangers of words.[62] And yet, while refusing to issue demands to the world outside Zuccotti Park, Occupy did speak to itself, using the people's microphone. But we understand the people's microphone less in regard to what it said than to the way it did it. That is, we understand the people's mic as a ritual procedure, producing social cohesion, not entirely dependent upon what it was used to say. "The meaning of ritual is the meaning produced through the ritual action itself. That is one reason that so many rituals include nondiscursive media like music or masks, and even language may be used in ways that defy discursive interpretation."[63] The people's mic —as well as the performance events that happened throughout the occupation like the zombie parades and the mock trial of Goldman Sachs —was a ritual instrument of and for communion.

Apophaticism resonates elsewhere as well. Looking through Certeau's lens of reading cities like text or acting in cities like speaking, we heard

---

[61] Harvey, *Spaces of Global Capitalism*, 63.
[62] Al-Qushayri, Principles of Sufism, trans. B. R. von Schlegell (Oneonta, NY: Mizan Press, 1990), 49.
[63] Seligman, et al. 26.

occupation as a kind of silence. Combined with radical theology's insistence upon the absence of God and the political implications that thinkers like Bonhoeffer drew from that, occupation's silence is enacted political theology. This, in turn, connects to Wark's argument that there is a political void at the center of American life. In both cases, the people are charged with filling the void themselves, directly.

There is an ideological-technical component at work here with Occupy's relationship to the city. Writing in the mid-twentieth century, Harvey explains,

> The suburbanization of the United States was not merely a matter of new infrastructures. As in Second Empire Paris, it entailed a radical transformation in lifestyles, bringing new products from housing to refrigerators and air conditioners, as well as two cars in the driveway and an enormous increase in the consumption of oil. It also altered the political landscape, as subsidized home-ownership for the middle classes changed the focus of community action towards the defence of property values and individualized identities, turning the suburban vote towards conservative republicanism. Debt-encumbered homeowners, it was argued, were less likely to go on strike.[64]

So the role of the city is paramount for resistance to economic oppression. If suburbanization was an ideological change that led, in part, to the mess we're in today, the shift back to cities may be part of the solution. Erasmus's city-as-a-huge-monastery is the location where living differently happens. It is the site of the subjunctive. And it is at least the possible site of the sovereignty of the multitude. In the words of David Graeber, "Sovereignty does ultimately belong to the people, at least in theory. You gave the bank the right to make up money that is then lent to you. We collectively create this stuff, and so *we could do it differently*."[65] Occupy was a resisting sovereignty—a subjunctivity.

This potentiality in the Occupy movement is its theology—specifically, a resisting theology, a political theology of the death of God, a theology wherein the people do not stand waiting for a God to save them. This is its excess—what makes it larger than itself. There is no need for God here—only the love of the *polis*—the love

---

[64] Harvey, "The Right to the City," *New Left Review*. Issue 53: September/October 2008, 27.
[65] David Graeber, as quoted by Drake Bennett in "David Graeber, the Anti-Leader of Occupy Wall Street," October 26, 2011. http://www.businessweek.com/printer/magazine/david-graeber-the-antileader-of-occupy-wall-street-10262011.html. Emphasis mine.

of the other—and the reliance upon the world. Occupy provides opportunity for true democratic cooperation. It did this through its silence and its lack of a rigid structure. It was slippery. It seeped through the cracks in American hegemony out into its own, new space. It was neither "with us" nor "against us." The friend/enemy distinction falls apart here. Occupy has no place in the State—and that is what makes Occupy politics *par excellence*. Again, Robbins reminds us that, "…democracy is not simply a form of politics but the very *principle of politics*."[66] Such a politics is also necessarily theological in its insistence upon recreating the world *as it might be*, and in the absence of God. Occupy is enacted, lived, resisting theology.

---

[66] Robbins, *Radical Democracy*, 62.

CHAPTER 7

#BlackLivesMatter

Impropriety, Resistance

Marcella Althaus-Reid famously asks at the beginning of her *Indecent Theology* whether or not a woman should keep her pants on in the streets.[1] She suggests that "writing theology without underwear may be punishable by law," but that a theologian who deconstructs "a moral order which is based on a heterosexual construction of reality, which organizes not only categories of approved social and divine interactions but of economic ones too" is a theologian who would "remove her underwear to write theology with feminist honesty."[2] Such a theologian, Althaus-Reid explains, would be a liberation theologian, but an indecent one. Althaus-Reid views liberation theology as a dynamic force and method. "Liberation Theology needs to be understood as a continuing process of recontextualisation, a permanent exercise of serious doubting in theology."[3]

What I am attempting to construct or perform here is not a liberation theology *per se*, but a resisting theology, which is certainly indecent, though in a different register than Althaus-Reid's feminist, sexual one. It is scandalous, in Fanon's sense. A resisting theology deconstructs a moral order which is based on a capitalist construction of reality, which organizes

---

[1] Marcella Althaus-Reid, *Indecent Theology: Theological Perversions in Sex, Gender, and Politics* (New York: Routledge, 2000), 1.

[2] Althaus-Reid, 2.

[3] Althaus-Reid, 5.

not only categories of approved social and divine interactions but of economic ones too. So it is economically and politically indecent. Such a capitalist ordering is inherently racist in nature. My question isn't whether a theologian should keep her pants on in the street. It's whether a theologian should smash windows. Rather than indecent, maybe it would be more appropriate to refer to this theology as improper.

The twin development of capitalism as a world system and trans-Atlantic slavery should by now be obvious. David Graeber argues that while the idea that ancient slavery is a primitive form of capitalism is relatively common, its reverse is rarely considered. That is, "One could, of course, take the exact same evidence to make the argument precisely the other way around, and argue that modern capitalism is really just a form of slavery, but it never seems to occur to contemporary authors to do this."[4] I'm not sure if Graeber is keeping his references to "contemporary authors" confined to anthropology and political economy, but there are plenty of thinkers who make this and similar cases. He may have missed these examples that view capitalism as a form of slavery because he neglected the third component of the equation: colonialism. The three must be taken together.

Kwame Ture and Charles V. Hamilton write in *Black Power: The Politics of Liberation* that "…black people in this country form a colony, and it is not in the interest of the colonial powers to liberate them. Black people are legal citizens of the United States with, for the most part, the same *legal* rights as other citizens."[5] In a very different context, Anatole France once quipped that "In its majesty equality, the law forbids rich and poor alike to sleep under bridges, beg in the streets and steal loaves of bread."[6] The law may be equal, but that does not mean that it applies evenly to all people. Ture and Hamilton continue, stating that Black people "…stand as colo-

---

[4] David Graeber, "Turning Modes of Production Inside Out: Or, Why Capitalism is a Transformation of Slavery," pp. 61–85 in *Critique of Anthropology* (March 2006, vol. 26, no. 1.), 61.

[5] Kwame Ture and Charles V. Hamilton, *Black Power: The Politics of Liberation* (New York: Vintage Books, 1992), 5. See also Malcolm X as quoted in *On the Side of My People: A Religious Life of Malcolm X,* by Louis A. DeCaro, Jr. (New York: NYU Press, 1997), 121: "The United States government did not need to look to 'foreign instigation' to see why America is hated abroad, but should look right here in America where the Gestapo tactics of the white police who patrol Negro neighborhoods are similar to those used by 'occupation forces' when the conquering armies take over and enter into 'occupied territories.'"

[6] Originally Anatole France, *Le Lys Rouge* (1894), but quoted by Walter Benjamin, "Critique of Violence," *Reflections: Essays, Aphorisms, Autobiographical Writings,* trans. Edmund Jephcott (New York: Schocken Books, 1986), 296.

nial subjects in relation to the white society. Thus institutional racism has another name: colonialism."[7] The point bears repeating: colonialism and racism are names for the same situation. And further, "The economic relationship of America's black communities to the larger society also reflects their colonial status. The political power exercised over those communities goes hand in glove with the economic deprivation experienced by the black citizens."[8] It is within this context—the close marriage of capitalism, colonialism, and racism—that we should understand the Black Lives Matter movement and the acts of resistance that accompany or run parallel to it. This includes what is typically called a riot, though I refer to such activity as uprising or rebellion. Without understanding racism, colonialism, and capitalism as inherently wed, one cannot understand the role that property destruction plays in the movement for Black lives. At the heart of this chapter is a relatively simple argument: property destruction is colonial iconoclasm. It's not just that the theologian should smash windows. It's that window smashers are already doing theology.

Property Destruction

First and foremost, the shock of the rebellion's act of destroying property forces a polarizing moral, political, economic, and even theological decision. Whose side are you on: property or life?[9] The rebellion is not random, senseless, or adolescent. Property destruction insists on a sophisticated questioning of the relation between objects and persons. This is the fundamental distinction between property destruction and sports riot. When (mostly white) college students pour out of dorms and bars to celebrate their team's win by setting fires and breaking street signs, they are no more performing an act of property destruction than is a child who breaks their toys. The students who sports riot are playing. Conversely, (Black) property destruction is a threat (to whiteness) and is treated as such by police. So while it may be tempting to refer to both forms of street action as

---

[7] Ture and Hamilton, 5.
[8] Ture and Hamilton, 16.
[9] Amaryah Armstrong writes, "…given that those who are descendants of people who were property, those dispossessed who through policing are made out to be property for the state, it would seem in the looting and property destruction is a critique of private property as the invention that produces public property, which is black flesh" "On Ferguson and Property," Women in Theology blog, November 24, 2014. https://womenintheology.org/2014/11/26/on-ferguson-and-property/.

childish, Amaryah Armstrong makes clear that "until we can come to terms with the fact that our faith in capitalist divisions of property, labor, and flesh, is faith in what keeps black lives expendable we will continue reading these disruptions to property as senseless."[10] This question is particularly pertinent because of the way in which liberal politics confuses the value of life and the value of property through the idea that property is an extension of the body.

John Locke, in Chap. 5, "Of Property," of the *Second Treatise of Government*, develops his labor theory of property. He argues that individuals own their bodies and the labor they produce with them. By extension, they come to own property through investing their spirit in the land through their labor.[11] This was a revolutionary and radically democratic sentiment in the seventeenth century due to its clear criticism of feudalism. Property was to be made first by effort, not inheritance. It's not surprising then that Alexander Hamilton, James Madison, Thomas Jefferson, and other founders of the US used much of Locke's philosophy as the basis for the Constitution. The law is built upon individual and property rights. But after the modern ascendency of liberalism and capitalism and their transformation of the world, a new irony develops. The making of property and its maintenance through personal rights in turn produced a new elite. Following Graeber, this elite class is dependent upon the abstraction of both labor and value through the institution of slavery—the very denial of humanity. Capitalism developed in such a way that it requires slavery. And "in America, property is racial. It always has been. … For 300 years, the very idea of a black person's freedom was a direct threat to white men's property."[12] This is why Raven Rakia writes,

---

[10] Armstrong.

[11] Locke writes, "Though the earth, and all inferior creatures, be common to all men, yet every man has a property in his own person: this no body has any right to but himself. The labour of his body, and the work of his hands, we may say, are properly his. Whatsoever then he removes out of the state that nature hath provided, and left it in, he hath mixed his labour with, and joined to it something that is his own, and thereby makes it his property. It being by him removed from the common state nature hath placed it in, it hath by this labour something annexed to it, that excludes the common right of other men: for this labour being the unquestionable property of the labourer, no man but he can have a right to what that is once joined to, at least where there is enough, and as good, left in common for others." John Locke, *Second Treatise of Government*, ed. C. B. Macpherson (Indianapolis and Cambridge: Hackett, 1980), 19.

[12] Raven Rakia, "Black Riot," in *The New Inquiry*, issue 45, November 14, 2013. http://thenewinquiry.com/essays/blackriot/.

With the destruction of property, violence can turn from an aspect of self-defense to a useful offensive tactic. Nothing gets the attention of the elite like taking away or destroying what they value above all else: property...When property is destroyed by black protesters, it must always be understood in the context of the historical racialization of property. When the same system that refuses to protect black children comes out to protect windows, what is valued over black people in America becomes very clear.[13]

Whose side are you on?

Due to the relationship between capitalism, colonialism, and racism, the destruction of property—which is always already racialized—is a gesture toward the dismantling of the colonial order. As Rakia argued above, during slavery Black freedom was a threat to white property. But we might follow Graeber's lead and take this evidence and make the argument the other way around. Black freedom was a threat to property because property destruction is evidence of black freedom. That is, the value of Black lives is inversely related to the valuing of property. The anti-colonial act is always one that asserts the value of life against the value of stuff.

Frantz Fanon tells us that "...decolonization is always a violent event."[14] But not only that, "Decolonization, which sets out to change the order of the world, is clearly an agenda for total disorder."[15] Every disordering is also the possibility of a new ordering. Each destruction is also the possibility for a new creation. This is why "decolonization is truly the creation of [a] new [humanity]. But such a creation cannot be attributed to a supernatural power: The 'thing' colonized becomes a man through the very process of liberation."[16] Decoloniality is destructive of capitalist ordering and valuing, but preparative of something new. In being destructive of property, one need not be antagonistic toward every world—merely the capitalist, colonialist, racist one. Fanon writes,

> I embrace the world! I am the world! The white man has never understood this magical substitution. The white man wants the world; he wants it for himself. He discovers he is the predestined master of the world. He enslaves it. His relationship with the world is one of appropriation. But there are

---

[13] Rakia.
[14] Frantz Fanon, *The Wretched of the Earth*, trans Richard Philcox (New York: Grove Press, 2005), 1.
[15] Fanon, *Wretched*, 2.
[16] Fanon, *Wretched*, 2.

values that can be served only with my sauce. As a magician I stole from the white man a "certain world," lost to him and his kind. When that happened the white man must have felt an aftershock he was unable to identify, being unused to such reactions. The reason was that above the objective world of plantations and banana and rubber trees, I had subtly established the real world. The essence of the world was my property. Between the world and me there was a relation of coexistence. I had rediscovered the primordial One. My "speaking hands" tore at the hysterical throat of the world. The white man had the uncomfortable feeling that I was slipping away and taking something with me. He searched my pockets, probed the least delineated of my convolutions. There was nothing new. Obviously I must have a secret.[17]

An indecent theological proposal: death is white—the color of bones. White is the color of the valley of the dead in Ezekiel 37 which comes to life when, Ezekiel prophesies to them: "I will cause breath to enter you, and you shall live. I will lay sinews on you, and will cause flesh to come upon you, and cover you with skin, and put breath in you, and you shall live."[18] Eric Garner couldn't breathe. White is the color of death. Black is the color of creation—the darkness that covered the face of the deep, while a wind from God swept over the face of the waters. This is the time of creation, of the feminine, of the ocean that produces identity, of the mother of God, the womb. Darkness creates, even as it destroys—it is life. White only kills—it is death.

This kind of resisting theology is an operation (not a discovery)—it acts, does things, forms and shapes them—it is both creative and destructive in its work. Or rather, it is destructive and creative. It does not uncover truth, but produces it. And in so doing, resisting theology makes claims that are both political and theological. In Genesis, humanity created in the image of the Creator. *Poiesis* is the divine faculty. Operating as individuals, poets, musicians, artists, surgeons and inventors exercise this faculty. These are the figures who, when in trouble, get accused of "playing God." But *poiesis* is as much a social act as it is an individual one. Prophets, revolutionaries, visionaries, advocates of the oppressed—in their dismantling of oppression flex this faculty as well—both destructive and creative. Social creation is the destruction of the established order. Institutions are maintainers. Institutional racism and its other names—capitalism, colo-

---

[17] Fanon, *Black Skin*, 107.
[18] Ezekiel 37:5–6, NRSV.

nialism—are the structures being targeted by the property destruction of the movement for Black lives. To be creative of the alternative to the colonial matrix of power requires destroying that which exists and oppresses. It is for this reason that "fuck the police" is a theological statement while torching police cruisers and smashing windows are theological acts. Property destruction is life. Breaking windows lets the wind in.[19]

For a thinker like Thomas J. J. Altizer, we may argue that the property destroyer is acting in a prophetic role. The "prophet's word of hope [is] only meaningful and real on the basis of its accompanying word of judgment and doom" and "We can even formulate the rule that power, the comprehensiveness and the immediacy of the prophetic affirmation are exactly equivalent to the depth, the extensiveness, and the parallel immediacy of its corresponding negation. Where there is no No, there is no Yes; for in prophecy the Yes and No are inseparable..."[20] In property-destruction, the No-saying is obvious, but the affirmation may not be. James Cone affirms this double movement of no- and yes-saying, and clarifies the Yes when he writes that,

> The violence in the cities, which appears to contradict Christian love, is nothing but the black man's attempt to say Yes to his being as defined by God in a world that would make his *being into* nonbeing. If the riots are the black man's courage to say Yes to himself as a creature of God, and if in affirming self he affirms Yes to the neighbor, then violence may be the black man's expression, sometimes the only possible expression, of Christian love to the white oppressor. From the perspective of a Christian theologian seeking to take seriously the black man's condition in America, what other view is possible?[21]

Property destruction is a decolonial affirmation. It is a double movement; a loving destruction.

Another Christian thinker once said that "a riot is the language of the unheard."[22] But this is a reduction of an act to language. And it concedes

---

[19] "Spirit," in the Greek of the New Testament, is *pneuma* which would typically connote moving air or breath. The Hebrew Spirit that moved across the face of the deep was *ruach*. The linguistic connections between life, spirit, breath, and air and strong.

[20] Thomas J. J. Altizer, "Radical Theology and Political Revolution," pp. 5–10 in *Criterion* 7 (Spring 1968), 7.

[21] James Cone, *Black Theology and Black Power* (Maryknoll, NY: Orbis Books, 1997), 55.

[22] Martin Luther King, Jr., "The Other America," speech at Grosse Pointe High School, March 14, 1968. http://www.gphistorical.org/mlk/mlkspeech/.

the terms of the colonial situation to the oppressors. This is a typical liberal argument based on what it views as the nature of social movements—that in the end, they are communicative. They protest. But many social movements are more than just PR and marketing. They not only propose, but also materially build alternatives to the world as we find it. Part of the work of building new worlds is clearing space for them. A people's uprising is an act, not a statement.

> As soon as we presume that the riot is a language, we take the claims of the former group as a set of truths already agreed upon. We exclude all aspects but discourse. This would have been perplexing to the rioters of the eighteenth century, for whom the need to secure bread, to get rid of bosses and their armed lackeys, was why they left their cottages in the first place. A riot is more or less by definition the moment when the presumptions of a functioning and just democratic state—one in which citizens might petition for the redress of grievances—start to collapse. A riot is a riot because, at least in part, it is not simply a message.[23]

The meaning of an act is not exhausted by what it says. Actions are not encompassed by their symbolic meaning. The performance is something that cannot be reduced to language. When a man stands with his fiancé in front of an altar and says 'I do,' he may not mean it, but too bad. The act was performed and something new was created. This is why a different Martin Luther King, Jr. reference is more useful.

In 1967, he addressed the American Psychological Association at its Annual Convention. Mainstream psychology at the time emphasized the psychologically healthy person's ability to adjust to society. In his speech, King advocated that social science consider the creation of a new organization devoted to the study of "creative maladjustment," for one should never become well-adjusted to injustice. In that context, King speaks of property destruction this way:

> The rioters are not seeking to seize territory or to attain control of institutions. They [riots] are mainly intended to shock the white community.... The looting which is their principal feature serves many functions. It enables the most enraged and deprived Negro to take hold of consumer goods with the ease the white man does by using his purse. Often the Negro does not

---

[23] Joshua Clover, "Propaganda, Deed," in *The Nation*, December 9, 2014. http://www.thenation.com/article/propaganda-deed/.

even want what he takes; he wants the experience of taking. But most of all, alienated from society and knowing that this society cherishes property above people, he is shocking it by abusing property rights. ... Let us say boldly that if the violations of law by the white man in the slums over the years were calculated and compared with the lawbreaking of a few days of riots, the hardened criminal would be the white man.[24]

[24] Martin Luther King, Jr., "The Role of the Behavioral Scientist in the Civil Rights Movement," in *Journal of Social Issues* (Vol. 24, No. 1, 1968). There were 159 riots in American cities during the summer and fall of 1967. King did not advocate for rioting, but neither did he denounce it. Instead, he recognized property destruction for what it is. It's worth quoting him here at length.
This bloodlust interpretation ignores one of the most striking features of the city riots. Violent they certainly were. But the violence, to a startling degree, was focused against property rather than against people. There were very few cases of injury to persons, and the vast majority of the rioters were not involved at all in attacking people. The much publicized "death toll" that marked the riots, and the many injuries, were overwhelmingly inflicted on the rioters by the military. It is clear that the riots were exacerbated by police action that was designed to injure or even to kill people. As for the snipers, no account of the riots claims that more than one or two dozen people were involved in sniping. From the facts, and unmistakable pattern emerges: a handful of Negroes used gunfire substantially to intimidate, not to kill; and all of the other participants had a different target—property.
I am aware that there are many who wince at a distinction between property and persons—who hold both sacrosanct. My views are not so rigid. A life is sacred. Property is intended to serve life, and no matter how much we surround it with rights and respect, it has no personal being. It is part of the earth man walks on; it is not man.
The focus on property in the 1967 riots is not accidental. It has a message; it is saying something.
If hostility to whites were ever going to dominate a Negro's attitude and reach murderous proportions, surely it would be during a riot. But this rare opportunity for bloodletting was sublimated into arson, or turned into a kind of stormy carnival of free-merchandise distribution. Why did the rioters avoid personal attacks? The explanation cannot be fear of retribution, because the physical risks incurred in the attacks on property were no less than for personal assaults. The military forces were treating acts of petty larceny as equal to murder. Far more rioters took chances with their own lives, in their attacks on property, than threatened the life of anyone else. Why were they so violent with property then? Because property represents the white power structure, which they were attacking and trying to destroy. A curious proof of the symbolic aspect of the looting for some who took part in it is the fact that, after the riots, police received hundreds of calls from Negroes trying to return merchandise they had taken. Those people wanted the experience of taking, of redressing the power imbalance that property represents. Possession, afterward, was secondary.
A deeper level of hostility came out in arson, which was far more dangerous than the looting. But it, too, was a demonstration and a warning. It was designed to express the depth of anger in the community.
Martin Luther King, Jr. *Testament of Hope: The Essential Writings and Speeches of Martin Luther King, Jr.* ed. James Washington (New York: HarperCollins, 1986), 648–650.

Uprising expresses the desire for the experience of freedom. The disdain for property and the breaking of the law tell us very little. Instead, they are constitutive acts, making the world into a space able to accommodate a new humanity.

BALTIMORE

The Black Lives Matter movement's most controversial moments have centered around destruction of property. While the movement for Black lives—from the events in Ferguson, MO in the late summer and fall of 2014, the Oakland BART train shutdown on Black Friday, 2014, to the uprising in Baltimore—many of Black Lives Matter's most notable actions have involved direct interference with the normal operations of businesses.

Freddie Gray was killed in Baltimore by Police on April 19, 2015. A CVS was looted. On the 27th, what the media reported as a "riot" began at the Mondawmin Mall, not long after Gray had been buried. At the end of the school day, riot police began assembling at the mall where they heard rumor of an attack against people was being planned.

> When the police shut down the public transportation system near the mall, effectively preventing students from getting home, the tinderbox exploded. By that evening, Sandtown, as it is known locally, was on fire, with police cars, a drug store, and various storefronts set ablaze. Politicians denounced the violence as a riot that needed to be controlled immediately: the governor called in the National Guard, the mayor declared a curfew, and the media largely focused on the looting of liquor and drug stores and the cost of the property damage.[25]

That the uprising began at Mondawmin Mall is not merely coincidence. According to N.D.B. Connolly,

> it actually sits in the middle of three big narratives about the city's history. One is the most recent riot. The second is the story of prices and the everyday life of living in Baltimore and what this mall represents for everyday people trying to shop here. And the third is that this mall actually began as one of the city's first shopping malls that used to primarily serve white

---

[25] Anjali Kamat, "The Baltimore Uprising," in *Policing the Planet: Why the Policing Crisis Led to Black Lives Matter*, eds. Jordan T. Camp and Christina Heatherton (London and New York, Verso, 2016).

customers. And it suffered white flight, and had to basically repurpose itself to deal with a black clientele. And so the history of segregation, the history of price gouging, and the more recent history of the riot are all built here, around the Mondawmin Mall. So at the Mondawmin Shopping Center, the experience of being a customer here is actually a little bit different than it is shopping anywhere else in the region.[26]

Connolly explains further that the prices at the mall aren't fixed and require haggling. This tends to result in inflated prices, upwards of 15%. As a result, the experience of shopping at the mall produces precariousness, both in financial terms as well as in terms of what it means to be a human consumer. David Harvey, in a chapter about Baltimore, explains the predicament this way.

> Those who have the money power are free to choose among name-brand commodities (including prestigious locations, properly secured, gated, and serviced), but the citizenry as a whole is denied any collective choice of political system, of ways of social relating, or of modes of production, it is simply because there is indeed [as Margaret Thatcher said] "no alternative." It is the supreme rationality of the market versus the silly irrationality of anything else. And all those institutions that might have helped define some alternative have either been suppressed or—with some notable exceptions, such as the church—been brow-beaten into submission. We the people have no right to choose what kind of city we shall inhabit.[27]

Name-brand commodities are one thing. But, not too long ago, commodities had Names. For most of the history of this country, people brought here from Africa and their descendants were owned by white people. Black people *were property* and were used to increase the wealth of white America to which they had no access. Property destruction—while not unique to any particular movement—is nevertheless the most impressive feature of the Black Lives Matter movement because of this historical relationship between Blackness and property; between racism and colonial exploitation. Who would understand property destruction better than a movement for people whose ancestors *were* property?

---

[26] Paul Solman, "Why the Freddie Gray Riots Began at a Shopping Mall," PBS's website. May 29, 2015 http://www.pbs.org/newshour/makingsense/answersbaltimoreseconomicrecoverystartsshoppingmall/.
[27] David Harvey, *Spaces of Hope* (Berkley and Los Angeles: University of California Press, 2000), 154.

Property destruction is an inherently decolonial act. In the movement for Black lives, such acts force us to choose which we value more: human life or property. The destruction of property by people whose ancestors had been owned should be understood as a direct and obvious reclaiming of their very humanity. But far from being nihilistic, in its direct acknowledgment of the relative valuelessness of property in relation to human life, property destruction is an *affirmation* of life. Riots are thus theological and property destruction is a deeply theological act.

David Graeber recognizes the theological quality of the colonial matrix of power when he writes that, "capitalism's unlimited demand for growth and profit is related to the transcendent abstraction of the corporate form. In any society, the dominant forms are considered transcendent from reality in much the way value forms tend to be and when these transcendent forms encounter 'material' reality, their demands are absolute."[28] Property destruction is a kenotic, theological act, which empties the abusive transcendence of capital. It is an inversion of the kenotic act of God (who took "the form of a slave, being born in human likeness"[29]). The Baltimore uprising, in its destructiveness of the transcendent, absolute demands of capital, was an iconoclasm in its original, material sense. Broken windows are a symbol of resisting theology. They are an apophatic symbol, whether in Zurich and the Netherlands in the sixteenth century, or in Baltimore in April, 2015.

---

[28] Graeber, 85.
[29] Philippians 2:7.

CHAPTER 8

Conclusion: Standing Rock

This morning, Oceti Sakowin is on fire. It is being ceremonially destroyed. A few hundred people there are marching home, praying and singing together, ahead of the Army Corps of Engineers' deadline for the camp at the Standing Rock Sioux reservation in North Dakota to be cleared. A few months ago, there were tens of thousands there, protecting the water and blocking the construction of the Dakota Access pipeline. Energy Transfer Partners, the pipeline developer, has announced that the pipeline will be complete and full of oil within the next month.[1] The pipeline will be built. In their most direct goal, the Water Protectors have failed. But, beginning in the summer and lasting into the first full month of the new White House administration, the movement at Standing Rock has awakened a spirit of resistance in the United States and invigorated it for the twenty-first century.

I live in Newport, Rhode Island. In the fifteenth and sixteenth centuries, Europeans sailed here, to the land called America but whose real name is Turtle Island, and they took lives and gold for their own glory. The value accumulated and was concentrated in some places, in some families more than others. The gold began to accumulate here in Newport.

---

[1] Morgan Winsor and James Hill, "Authorities Move into Dakota Access Pipeline Protest Camp," February 22, 2017. ABC News. Accessed February 22, 2017. http://abcnews.go.com/US/deadline-looms-dakota-access-pipeline-opponents-evacuate-protest/story?id=45654213.

It gilded our city. Today, the colonial streets here see some of the most foot traffic out of any city in the country. And at their crowning intersection of Memorial Boulevard and Bellevue Avenue stands a monument to the man who first started taking the gold. Christopher Columbus stands there holding the Earth in his right hand.

In 1851 and 1868, treaties were signed at Fort Laramie that created the Great Sioux Reservation. It included more than double the amount of land that the Sioux control today. Especially important to the Sioux back then was that the Black Hills were included—one of the Sioux's most sacred sites. In 1874, General Custer rode from Bismarck to the Black Hills where someone discovered gold. The public announcement brought miners. The miners skirmished with the Sioux. The army defended the miners. The conflict grew into a war. In 1877, the US Army defeated the Sioux and annexed their land—including the Black Hills. Because of the gold. Black Hills gold. In 1890 at Wounded Knee, the US Army killed 98 Lakota Sioux men, 65 Lakota Sioux women, and 24 Lakota Sioux children, wounding 52 more. Some put the total number as high at 400 dead. In 1990, Congress expressed "deep regret" for the massacre.

In 2015, Dakota Access began plans to build a pipeline to bring oil from the Bakken oil fields through the Dakotas and Iowa to Illinois. Soon after, the people of Bismarck, the origin of Custer's ride to the Black Hills, began registering their concerns about the proposal to run the pipeline through their town. Bismarck, North Dakota: population 71,000; 92% white. This route would have crossed what federal pipeline regulators call a "high consequence area" where the most significant adverse consequences would occur in an accident. So Dakota Access moved the pipeline to Sioux land reclaimed through eminent domain.

Every new movement of whiteness's impact on this continent has reinforced white disrespect for Native people. White only seems to respect profit. In the beginning, when white people came to Turtle Island and explored indigenous land, they took gold and lives. In the middle, when white people explored indigenous land in the Dakotas, they took the Black Hills gold and lives. Today, when the white corporation explores possible routes for its black gold, it heeds the concerns of good white folks at the expense of Native people. It once was about gold in the Black Hills. Now it is about black gold moving under the river. So while we say that water is life, we must never forget that oil is death.

In September 2016, District Courts denied a petition by the Standing Rock Sioux to halt construction of the pipeline. The court sided with a 3.8-billion-dollar project. The Justice Department issued a memo requesting that Dakota Access voluntarily halt construction on less than 3% of the project—the lands specifically in dispute as cultural sites. The Justice Department wrote, "we request that the pipeline company voluntarily pause all construction activity within 20 miles east or west of Lake Oahe." But not only that. Justice also noted "this case has highlighted the need for a serious discussion" and plans to "invite tribes to formal, government-to-government consultations." Meanwhile, the militarized police continued to assemble and Dakota Access kept digging.

Serious discussion. Consultation. And the instruments of death kept plunging into the Earth. The corporation's wishes are enforced by police and National Guard. Profit has turned public servants into corporate security. The presence of militarized police at Standing Rock should be understood as a military invasion of a sovereign nation on behalf of a foreign oil company.

The Justice Department asked the Sioux to be patient, to talk, and to listen. Dakota Access kept building. Donald Trump quietly invested in the pipeline, but said nothing. Dakota Access kept building. Hillary Clinton said that she thinks all voices should be heard and all views considered in federal infrastructure projects. Dakota Access kept building. The Army Corps of Engineers put a moratorium on building at the end of Obama's term. A couple months later, the new chief executive gave the Army Corps of Engineers the green light to let the construction commence. So Dakota Access is building again. We continue to talk and they continue to build.

Solidarity is empty when it's talk. If our current election cycle has taught us anything it should be that talk is cheap.

What has been happening at Standing Rock is not a historical event. It is not new. It did not begin in the summer of 2016. It is merely a single moment in a 500-year-long and unbroken process of white people extracting resources from Native land a people for profit. Its name is colonial exploitation. Columbus, Custer, and Citi Bank are its perpetrators.

It is important to note here in my colonial city that Oliver Perry, whose statue stands in front of our court house, once remarked that, "we have met the enemy and they are ours." It is our colonial history which continues to make us our money, but which stands in opposition to the interests of Native people and Standing Rock. From Columbus, who physically stands over the city, to the gilded age which still serves as its principal tourist draw, to the colonial downtown built on the slave trade, to the city's current investment in the banks that fund the war against Standing Rock, Perry was right. We have met the enemy and they are ours.

Water is life. Oil is death.

BENEDICTION

Theology, after Paul Tillich, shows what concerns us. After Charles Winquist, it describes our most insatiable desires. If the racial, political, economic, or environmental history of the United States were to generate a theology, it would be a theology of death. But it is not enough to denounce death. We must endeavor to conquer it. Desiring life is resisting theology that emerges from that American tradition. On this day of the destruction of the encampment at Standing Rock, I am reminded of Qohelet, who said,

> On the day that the guards of the house will quake and the stalwart men be twisted, and the maids who grind grow idle, for they are now few, and those who look from the casements go dark. And the double doors close in the market as the sound of the mill sinks down, and the sound of the bird arises, and all the songstresses are bowed. Of the very height they are afraid, and terror is in the road. And the almond blossoms, and the locust tree is laden, and the caper-fruit falls apart. For man is going to his everlasting house, and the mourners turn around in the market. Until the silver cord is snapped, and the golden bowl is smashed, and the pitcher is broken against the well, and the jug smashed at the pit.
>
> And dust returns to the earth as it was, and the life-breath returns to God Who gave it.
>
> Merest breath, said Qohelet. All is mere breath.[2]

When one starts a fire, one blows on embers to cause it to catch. Broken windows let the spirit breath into a room. Spirit ignites. This is an opportunity to radicalize a generation. May the ceremonial fire of Oceti Sakowin—a sacred fire—at the end of the Standing Rock occupation, like the self-immolation of Mohamed Bouazizi, or the fire that produced the ashes of the bodies of David Wojnarowicz's friends, the mystic's soul which burns so much it roars, the tongues of flame that were the Spirit of Occupy, or the fire that damaged the CVS in Baltimore serve like the tongues of fire that bestow spiritual gifts. Let it be a fire of both destruction and inauguration. May we become arsonists and illuminators. It is not enough to be an advocate or an ally. Any theology that is not life's accomplice—any theology that does not commit to resistance on behalf of life and Earth and risk God and theology in the process—any theology that does not risk itself is an instrument of death. It must build a world that resists at every turn. It must be a resisting theology.

---

[2] Robert Alter, translator, *The Wisdom Books: Job, Proverbs, and Ecclesiastes* (New York: W.W. Norton and Co., 2010), Ecclesiastes 12:3–8.

BIBLIOGRAPHY

ACT UP NY. 1993. Tim Bailey's Political Funeral. Held on July 1, in Washington, DC. *ACT UP NY*. http://actupny.org/divatv/netcasts/tim_bailey.html. Accessed 12 November 2014.

———. 2003. *Interview with Joy Episalla*. Conducted by Sarah Schulman for the ACT UP Oral History Project, December 6. http://www.actuporalhistory.org/interviews/images/episalla.pdf. Accessed 12 November 2014.

———. ACT UP's Statement of Purpose. *ACT UP NY*. http://actupny.org. Accessed 12 November 2014.

———. Political Funerals. *ACT UP NY*. http://actupny.org/diva/polfunsyn.html. Accessed 12 November 2014.

Adbusters. *Occupy Wall Street*. http://www.adbusters.org/campaigns/occupy-wallstreet.

Agamben, Giorgio. 1993. *The Coming Community*. Trans. M. Hardt. Minneapolis, MN and London: University of Minnesota Press.

———. 1998. *Homo Sacer: Sovereign Power and Bare Life*. Trans. D. Heller-Roazen. Stanford, CA: Stanford University Press.

———. 1999. On Potentiality. In *Potentialities: Collected Essays in Philosophy*. Ed. and Trans. D. Heller-Roazen, 177–184. Stanford, CA: Stanford University Press.

———. 2004. *The Open: Man and Animal*. Trans. K. Attell. Stanford, CA: Stanford University Press.

———. 2005. *State of Exception*. Trans. K. Attell. Chicago, IL and London: Chicago University Press.

———. 2011. *The Kingdom and the Glory: For a Theological Genealogy of Economy and Government*. Trans. L. Chiesa and M. Mandarini. Stanford, CA: Stanford University Press.

Agamben, Giorgio, Alain Badiou, Daniel Bensaïd, Wendy Brown, Jean-Luc Nancy, Jacques Rancière, Kristin Ross, and Slavoj Žižek. 2011. *Democracy in What State?* Trans. W. McCuaig. New York: Columbia University Press.

Allen, Peter Lewis. 2000. *The Wages of Sin: Sex and Disease, Past and Present.* Chicago, IL: University of Chicago Press.

Almond, Ian. 2004. *Sufism and Deconstruction: A Comparative Study of Derrida and Ibn 'Arabi.* London and New York: Routledge.

Al-Qushayri. 1990. *Principles of Sufism.* Trans. B.R. von Schlegell. Oneonta, NY: Mizan Press.

Alter, Robert. 2010. *The Wisdom Books: Job, Proverbs, and Ecclesiastes: A Translation with Commentary.* New York: W. W. Norton & Company.

Althaus-Reid, Marcella. 2000. *Indecent Theology: Theological Perversions in Sex, Gender, and Politics.* New York: Routledge.

———. 2004. *From Feminist Theology to Indecent Theology.* London: SCM Press.

Altizer, Thomas J.J. 1966. *The Gospel of Christian Atheism.* Philadelphia, PA: The Westminster Press.

———. 1968. Radical Theology and Political Revolution. *Criterion* 7 (Spring): 5–10.

———. 2006. *Living the Death of God.* Albany, NY: State University of New York Press.

———. 2012. *The Call to Radical Theology.* Ed. L. McCullough. Albany, NY: SUNY Press.

———. 2017. *Satan and Apocalypse: And Other Essays on Political Theology.* Albany, NY: SUNY Press.

Altizer, Thomas J.J., and William Hamilton. 1966. *Radical Theology and the Death of God.* Indianapolis, IN and New York: Bobbs-Merrill Company, Inc.

Altizer, Thomas J.J., Max A. Myers, Carl A. Raschke, Robert P. Scharlemann, Mark C. Taylor, and Charles E. Winquist. 1982. *Deconstruction and Theology.* New York: The Crossroad Publishing Company.

Alves, Rubem. 1992. Theopoetics: Longing and Liberation. In *Struggles for Solidarity: Liberation Theologies in Tension*, ed. Lorine M. Getz and Ruy O. Costa, 159–171. Minneapolis, MN: Fortress Press.

Arendt, Hannah. 1998 [1958]. *The Human Condition.* Introd. M. Canovan. Chicago, IL and London: University of Chicago Press.

Aristotle. 2006. *Metaphysics Theta.* Trans. S. Makin. Oxford: Oxford University Press.

Armstrong, Amaryah. 2014. On Ferguson and Property. In the *Women in Theology* Blog, November 24. https://womenintheology.org/2014/11/26/on-ferguson-and-property/.

Asad, Talal. 2003. *Formations of the Secular: Christianity, Islam, Modernity.* Stanford, CA: Stanford University Press.

Attar, Farid ud-Din. 1998. *The Conference of the Birds*. Trans. C.S. Nott. Accord, NY: Pir Press.
Augustine. 1991. *Confessions*. Trans. H. Chadwick. Oxford: Oxford University.
Badiou, Alain. 2012. *The Rebirth of History: Times of Riots and Uprisings*. Trans. G. Elliott. London and New York: Verso.
Beaumont, Justin, and Christopher Baker, eds. 2011. *Postsecular Cities*. London and New York: Continuum.
Bellah, Robert. 2011. *Religion in Human Evolution: From the Paleolithic to the Axial Age*. Cambridge, MA: Harvard University Press.
Benjamin, Walter. 1978. *Reflections: Essays, Aphorisms, Autobiographical Writings*. Ed. P. Demetz. New York: Harcourt Brace.
———. 2007. *Illuminations: Essays and Reflections*. Ed. H. Arendt and Trans. H. Zohn. New York: Schocken Books.
Bennett, Drake. 2011. David Graeber, the Anti-Leader of Occupy Wall Street, October 26. http://www.businessweek.com/printer/magazine/david-graeber-the-antileader-of- occupy-wall-street-10262011.html.
Berger, Peter L. 1966. *The Sacred Canopy: Elements of a Sociological Theory of Religion*. Garden City, NY: Doubleday.
———., ed. 1999. *The Desecularization of the World: Resurgent Religion and World Politics*. Grand Rapids, MI: Wm. B. Eerdmans Publishing Company.
Bergo, Bettina. 2005. Levinasian Responsibility and Freudian Analysis: Is the Unthinkable an Un-Conscious? In *Addressing Levinas*, ed. Eric Sean Nelson, Antje Kapust, and Kent Still, 257–295. Evanston, IL: Northwestern University Press.
Bergson, Henri. 1963. *The Two Sources of Morality and Religion*. Trans. R. Ashley Audra, C. Brereton, and W. Horsfall Carter. Westport, CT: Greenwood Press.
Berkowitz, Richard, and Michael Callen. 1983. *How to Have Sex in an Epidemic: One Approach*. With Medical and Scientific Consultation from Joseph Sonnabend, M.D. New York: Tower Press, N.Y.C.
Berlinger, Joshua. 2015. Baltimore Riots: A Timeline. *CNN's* Website, April 28. http://www.cnn.com/2015/04/27/us/baltimore-riots-timeline/.
Berman, Marshall. 1988. *All That Is Solid Melts into Air: The Experience of Modernity*. New York: Penguin.
Bernasconi, Robert. 1999. The Third Party: Levinas on the Intersection of the Ethical and the Political. *Journal of the British Society for Phenomenology* 30 (1): 76–87.
Bersani, Leo. 1988. Is the Rectum a Grave? In *AIDS: Cultural Analysis/Cultural Activism*, ed. Douglas Crimp and Leo Bersani. Cambridge, MA: MIT Press.
Blanton, Ward. 2014. *A Materialism for the Masses*. New York: Columbia University Press.
Blanton, Ward, Clayton Crockett, Jeffrey W. Robbins, and Noelle Vahanian. 2016. *An Insurrectionist Manifesto*. New York: Columbia University Press.

Blauner, Robert. 1969. Internal Colonialism and Ghetto Revolt. *Social Problems* 16 (4, Spring): 393–408.
Bonhoeffer, Dietrich. 1997. *Letters and Papers from Prison.* Ed. E. Bethge. New York: Touchstone.
Bray, Mark. 2013. *Translating Anarchy: The Anarchism of Occupy Wall Street.* Winchester: Zero Books.
Brecher, Jeremy, Tim Costello, and Brendan Smith, eds. 2000. *Globalization from Below: The Power of Solidarity.* Cambridge, MA: South End Press.
Brown, Robert McAfee. 1988. *Spirituality and Liberation: Overcoming the Great Fallacy.* Louisville: Westminster John Knox Press.
Buber, Martin. 1996. *I and Thou.* Trans. W. Kaufmann. New York: Simon and Schuster.
Burke, James, and Robert Ornstein. 1997. *The Axemaker's Gift: Technology's Capture and Control of Our Minds and Culture.* New York: Penguin Putnam Inc.
Butler, Anthea, Elizabeth Drescher, Peter Laarman, Sarah Posner, and Nathan Schneider. 2011a. God Dissolves into the Occupy Movement: A Revealing Roundtable on the Role of Religion in the Occupy Movement. *Religion Dispatches*, October 16. http://www.religiondispatches.org/archive/politics/5268/. Accessed 5 December 2012.
Butler, Judith, Jürgen Habermas, Charles Taylor, and Cornel West. 2011b. *The Power of Religion in the Public Sphere.* Ed. E. Mendieta, J. VanAntwerpen, and C. Calhoun. New York: Columbia University Press.
Caffentzis, George, and Silvia Federici, eds. 2001. A Brief History of Resistance to Structural Adjustment. In *Democratizing the Global Economy.* Ed. K. Danaher. Monroe, ME: Common Courage Press.
Calhoun, Craig, Mark Juergensmeyer, and Jonathan VanAntwerpen, eds. 2011. *Rethinking Secularism.* Oxford and New York: Oxford University Press.
Camus, Albert. 1956. *The Rebel: An Essay on Man in Revolt.* Trans. A. Bower. New York: Vintage Books.
———. 1995. *Resistance, Rebellion, and Death.* New York: Vintage.
Canning, Peter. 2001. God Is of (Possibility). In *Secular Theology: American Radical Theological Thought*, ed. Clayton Crockett, 233–246. London and New York: Routledge.
Caputo, John D. 1997. *The Prayers and Tears of Jacques Derrida: Religion Without Religion.* Bloomington and Indianapolis, IN: Indiana University Press.
———. 2001. *On Religion.* London and New York: Routledge.
———. 2013. *The Insistence of God.* Bloomington, IN: Indiana University Press.
Caputo, John D., and Jacques Derrida. 1997. *Deconstruction in a Nutshell: A Conversation with Jacques Derrida.* Ed. and with a Commen. J. D. Caputo. New York: Fordham University Press.

Cavanaugh, William T. 1995. 'A Fire Strong Enough to Consume the House': The Wars of Religion and the Rise of the State. *Modern Theology* 11 (4): 397–420.
———. 2007. Does Religion Cause Violence? *Harvard Divinity Bulletin* 35 (Spring/Summer): 2–3. http://www.hds.harvard.edu/news-events/harvard-divinity-bulletin/articles/does-religion-cause-violence.
Chappell, Bill. 2011. Occupy Wall Street: From A Blog Post to a Movement. *National Public Radio's* Website, October 20. http://www.npr.org/2011/10/20/141530025/occupy-wall-street-from-a-blog-post-to-a-movement.
Clover, Joshua. 2014. Propaganda, Deed. *The Nation*, December 9. http://www.thenation.com/article/propaganda-deed/.
———. 2016. *Riot. Strike. Riot. The New Era of Uprisings*. London and New York: Verso.
Comte, Auguste. 1896. *The Positive Philosophy of Auguste Comte: Freely Translated and Condensed by Harriet Martineau*. London: George Bell & Sons.
Cone, James. 1997. *Black Theology and Black Power*. Maryknoll, NY: Orbis Books.
Cox, Harvey. 1971. *Secular City: Secularization and Urbanization in Theological Perspective*. New York: Macmillan.
Crawford, Matthew B. 2009. *Shop Class as Soulcraft*. New York: Penguin.
Critchley, Simon. 1999. *The Ethics of Deconstruction: Derrida and Levinas*. 2nd ed. West Lafayette, IN: Purdue University Press.
———. 2012. *The Faith of the Faithless: Experiments in Political Theology*. London and New York: Verso.
Crockett, Clayton. 2001a. Contact Epistemology for the Sites of Theology. In *Secular Theology: American Radical Theological Thought*, ed. Clayton Crockett, 198–211. London and New York: Routledge.
———, ed. 2001b. *Secular Theology: American Radical Theological Thought*. London and New York: Routledge.
———, ed. 2006. *Religion and Violence in the Secular World: Toward a New Political Theology*. Charlottesville, VA: University of Virginia Press.
———. 2011. *Radical Political Theology: Religion and Politics After Liberalism*. New York: Columbia University Press.
Crowfoot, Brad. 2013. Flash Mob Round Dance at West Edmonton Mall. *Windspeaker* 30 (10). http://www.ammsa.com/publications/windspeaker/flash-mob-round-dance-west-edmonton-mall#sthash.Q6bCW1VR.dpuf.
Dahrendorf, Ralf. 1968. Homo Sociologicus: On the History, Significance, and Limits of the Category of Social Role. In *Essays in the Theory of Society*. Stanford, CA: Stanford University Press.
De Certeau, Michel. 1988. *The Practice of Everyday Life*. Trans. S. Rendall. Berkeley, CA: University of California Press.
Debord, Guy. 1994. *Society of the Spectacle*. Trans. D. Nicholson-Smith. New York: Zone Books.

DeCaro, Louis A., Jr. 1997. *On the Side of My People: A Religious Life of Malcolm X.* New York: NYU Press.
Derrida, Jacques. 1978. *Writing and Difference.* Trans. A. Bass. Chicago, IL and London: Chicago University Press.
———. 1982a. Différance. In *Margins of Philosophy.* Trans. A. Bass. Chicago, IL and London: University of Chicago Press.
———. 1982b. Of an Apocalyptic Tone Recently Adopted in Philosophy. Trans. John P. Leavey, Jr. *Semeia* 23: 63–97.
———. 1995a. *The Gift of Death.* Trans. D. Wills. Chicago, IL and London: University of Chicago Press.
———. 1995b. *On the Name.* Ed. T. Dutoit and Trans. D. Wood, J.P. Leavey, Jr., and I. McLeod. Stanford, CA: Stanford University Press.
———. 2002. *Acts of Religion.* Ed. G. Anidjar. London and New York: Routledge.
———. 2005. *Rogues: Two Essays on Reason.* Trans. P.-A. Brault and M. Naas. Stanford, CA: Stanford University Press.
Dery, Mark. 1993. *Culture Jamming: Hacking, Slashing and Sniping in the Empire of Signs.* Westfield, NJ: Open Media.
Detienne, Marcel. 2006. The Gods of Politics in Early Greek Cities. Trans. J. Lloyd. In *Political Theologies: Public Religions in a Post-secular World*, ed. Hent de Vries and Lawrence E. Sullivan, 91–101. New York: Fordham University Press.
Dōgen, Eihei, and Thomas F. Cleary. 1991. *Shōbōgenzō: Zen Essays by Dōgen.* Honolulu: University of Hawaii Press.
Dostoevsky, Fyodor. 2003. *The Grand Inquisitor.* Ed. A. Fremantle. New York: Continuum.
Douglas, Mary. 1966. *Purity and Danger: An Analysis of The Concepts of Pollution and Taboo.* New York: Frederick A. Praeger.
———. 1973. *Natural Symbols: Explorations in Cosmology.* Harmondsworth: Penguin.
Duncombe, Stephen, ed. 2002. *The Cultural Resistance Reader.* London and New York: Verso.
Durkheim, Emile. 1995. *The Elementary Forms of the Religious Life.* New York: Free Press.
Eckhart, Meister. 1978. *Meister Eckhart: Mystic and Philosopher.* Ed. R. Schürmann. Bloomington: Indiana University Press.
———. 1994. *Meister Eckhart: Selected Writings.* Ed. O. Davies. New York: Penguin.
Edelman, Lee. 2004. *No Future: Queer Theory and the Death Drive.* Durham, NC: Duke University Press.
Eliade, Mircea. 1987. *The Sacred and the Profane: The Nature of Religion.* Orlando, FL: Harcourt.
Ellison, Ralph. 1980. *Invisible Man.* New York: Vintage International.
Emmer, Pascal. 2012. Talkin' 'Bout Meta-Generation: ACT UP History and Queer Futurity. *Quarterly Journal of Speech* 98 (1): 89–96.

Fanon, Frantz. 2005. *The Wretched of the Earth*. Trans. R. Philcox. New York: Grove Press.
———. 2008. *Black Skin, White Masks*. Trans. R. Philcox. New York: Grove Press.
Feuerbach, Ludwig. 1989. *The Essence of Christianity*. Trans. G. Elliot. Amherst, NY: Prometheus Books.
Fisher, Mark Lowe. Bury Me Furiously. *ACT UP NY*. http://actupny.org/diva/polfunsyn.html. Accessed 12 November 2014.
Foucault, Michel. 1988. *Madness and Civilization: A History of Insanity in the Age of Reason*. Trans. R. Howard. New York: Vintage Books.
———. 1994. The Subject and Power. In *Power*, ed. James D. Faubion. New York: The New Press.
Freud, Sigmund. 1989a. Civilization and Its Discontents. In *The Freud Reader*, ed. Peter Gay, 722–771. New York and London: W. W. Norton and Co.
———. 1989b. Obsessive Actions and Religious Practices. In *The Freud Reader*, ed. Peter Gay, 429–435. New York and London: W. W. Norton and Co.
———. 1989c. *The Future of an Illusion* in *The Freud Reader*. Ed. P. Gay, 685–721. New York and London: W. W. Norton and Co.
———. 2001. *New Introductory Lectures on Psychoanalysis*. New York: Vintage.
Friere, Paulo. 1993. *Pedagogy of the Oppressed*. Trans. M.B. Ramos. New York: Continuum.
Gallup, George H., Jr. 2003. Americans' Spiritual Searches Turn Inward. *Gallup's Website*, February 11. http://www.gallup.com/poll/7759/americans-spiritual-searches-turn-inward.aspx.
Gauchet, Marcel. 1999. *The Disenchantment of the World*. Trans. O. Burge. Princeton, NJ: Princeton University Press.
Geertz, Clifford. 1965. Religion as a Cultural System. In *Anthropological Approaches to Religion*, ed. M. Banton. London: Tavistock. ASA Monograph, no. 3.
———. 1973. *The Interpretation of Cultures*. New York: Basic Books.
Ger, Guliz, ed. 2005. Religion and Consumption: The Profane Sacred. *Advances in Consumer Research* 32. http://www.acrwebsite.org/volumes/v32/acr_vol32_44.pdf.
Gessen, Keith, Astra Taylor, Eli Schmitt, Nikil Saval, Sarah Resnick, Sarah Leonard, Mark Greif, and Carla Blumenkranz, eds. 2011. *Occupy! Scenes from Occupied America*. London and New York: Verso.
Gills, Barry K., ed. 2001. *Globalization and the Politics of Resistance*. New York: Palgrave.
Girard, René. 1977. *Violence and the Sacred*. Trans. P. Gregory. Baltimore: Johns Hopkins University Press.
———. 1979. Mimesis and Violence: Perspectives in Cultural Criticism. *Berkshire Review* 14: 9–19.
———. 1987. *Things Hidden Since the Foundation of the World*. Trans. S. Bann and M. Metteer. Stanford, CA: Stanford University Press.

Gluckstein, Donny. 2011. *The Paris Commune: A Revolution in Democracy.* Chicago, IL: Haymarket Books.
Goodchild, Philip. 2002. *Capitalism and Religion: The Price of Piety.* New York: Routledge.
———. 2009a. Interview for *Rorotoko*, November 30. http://rorotoko.com/interview/20091130_goodchiled_philip_on_theology_of_money/?page=1.
———. 2009b. *Theology of Money.* Durham, NC: Duke University Press.
Gorski, Philip, David Kyuman Kim, John Torpey, and Jonathan VanAntwerpen, eds. 2012. *The Post-Secular in Question: Religion in Contemporary Society.* New York and London: New York University Press.
Graeber, David. 2004. *Fragments of an Anarchist Anthropology.* Chicago, IL and London: University of Chicago Press.
———. 2006. Turning Modes of Production Inside Out: Or, Why Capitalism Is a Transformation of Slavery. *Critique of Anthropology.* 26 (1): 61–85.
———. 2013. *The Democracy Project: A History, a Crisis, a Movement.* New York: Spiegel and Grau.
Gramsci, Antonio. 2000. *The Antonio Gramsci Reader: Selected Writings 1916–1935.* Ed. D. Forgacs. New York: New York University Press.
Greenwald, Glenn. 2006. "An Ideology of Lawlessness" on the Blog. *Unclaimed Territory*, January 6. http://glenngreenwald.blogspot.com.br/2006/01/ideology-of-lawlessness.html.
Grossman, Cathy Lynn. 2010. Survey: 72% of Millennials 'More Spiritual Than Religious. *USA Today*'s Website, October 14. http://usatoday30.usatoday.com/news/religion/2010-04-27-1Amillfaith27_ST_N.htm.
Guerin, Daniel, ed. 2005. *No Gods, No Masters: An Anthology of Anarchism.* Oakland, CA: AK Press.
Gutiérrez, Gustavo. 1988. *A Theology of Liberation.* Trans. Sister C. Inda and J. Eagleson. Maryknoll, NY: Orbis Books.
Habermas, Jürgen. 2008. Notes on Post-Secular Society. *New Perspectives Quarterly* 25 (4, Fall): 17–29.
———. 2010. *An Awareness of What Is Missing: Faith and Reason in a Post-secular Age.* Cambridge and Malden, MA: Polity Press.
Haensch, Anna. 2013. When Choirs Sing, Many Hearts Beat As One, from July 10, on National Public Radio's Shots Health News. http://www.npr.org/blogs/health/2013/07/09/200390454/when-choirs-sing-many-hearts-beat-as-one. Accessed 11 July 2013.
Hall, Stuart, and Tony Jefferson, eds. 1990. *Resistance Through Rituals: Youth Subcultures in Post-War Britain.* London and New York: Routledge.
Hallie, Philip. 1979. *Lest Innocent Blood Be Shed.* New York: HarperCollins.
Hardt, Michael, and Antonio Negri. 2001. *Empire.* Cambridge, MA: Harvard.
———. 2004. *Multitude: War and Democracy in the Age of Empire.* New York: Penguin.

———. 2009. *Commonwealth*. Cambridge, MA: Harvard.
Hargreaves, Steve. 2013. How Income Inequality Hurts America. *CNN Money*, September 25. http://money.cnn.com/2013/09/25/news/economy/income-inequality/.
Harvey, David. 2006. *Spaces of Global Capitalism: Towards a Theory of Uneven Geographical Development*. London: Verso.
———. 2007. *A Brief History of Neoliberalism*. Oxford: Oxford and New York.
———. 2008a. The Right to the City. *New Left Review* (53), September/October.
———. 2008b. *Social Justice and the City*. Athens, GA and London: University of Georgia Press.
———. 2011. The Party of Wall Street Meets Its Nemesis. *The Socialist Worker*'s Blog, October 28. http://socialistworker.org/blog/critical-reading/2011/10/29/david-harvey-occupy-wall-street.
———. 2012. *Rebel Cities: From the Right to the City to the Urban Revolution*. London and New York: Verso.
Heidegger, Martin. 1966. *Discourse on Thinking: A Translation of Gelassenheit*. Trans. J. M. Anderson and E. Hans Freund. New York and London: Harper Perennial.
———. 2009. Question Concerning Technology. In *Readings in the Philosophy of Technology*, ed. David M. Kaplan, 2nd ed. Lanham, MD: Rowman & Littlefield Publishers.
Henry, Michel. 2000. Speech and Religion: The Word of God. In *Phenomenology and the "Theological Turn": The French Debate*, ed. Dominique Janicaud, 217–241. New York: Fordham University Press.
How to Survive a Plague. 2012. Direc. David France. Public Square Films, DVD.
James, William. 1958. *The Varieties of Religious Experience: A Study in Human Nature*. Forw. Jacques Barzun. New York: Mentor/New American Library.
Kamat, Anjali. 2016. The Baltimore Uprising. In *Policing the Planet: Why the Policing Crisis Led to Black Lives Matter*, ed. Jordan T. Camp and Christina Heatherton. London and New York: Verso.
Kant, Immanuel. 1993. *Opus Postumum*. Ed. E. Förster and Trans. E. Förster and M. Rosen. Cambridge: Cambridge University Press.
Kantorowicz, Ernst H. 1997. *The King's Two Bodies*. Princeton, NJ: Princeton University Press.
Keller, Catherine. 2003. *Face of the Deep: A Theology of Becoming*. London and New York: Routledge.
Kestenbaum, David. 2011. Ranking Cute Animals: A Stock Market Experiment. National Public Radio's *Planet Money* Blog, January 14. http://www.npr.org/blogs/money/2011/01/14/132906135/ranking-cute-animals-a-stock-market-experiment?ft=1&f=93559255.
Kierkegaard, Søren. 1944. *Attack upon "Christendom."* Trans. W. Lowrie. Princeton, NJ: Princeton University Press.

———. 1967–1978. *Søren Kierkegaard's Papers and Journals Vol. 1*. Trans. H.V. Hong, E.H. Hong, and G. Malantschuk. Bloomington: Indiana University Press.

———. 2006. *Fear and Trembling*. Ed. C. Stephan Evans and S. Walsh. Cambridge and New York: Cambridge University Press.

King, Martin Luther, Jr. 1986. Letter from Birmingham City Jail. In *A Testament of Hope: The Essential Writings and Speeches of Martin Luther King, Jr*, ed. James M. Washington, 289–302. San Francisco: Harper San Francisco.

———. 1968a. *The Other America*. Speech at Grosse Pointe High School, March 14. http://www.gphistorical.org/mlk/mlkspeech/.

———. 1968b. The Role of the Behavioral Scientist in the Civil Rights Movement. *Journal of Social Issues* 24 (1): 1–12.

———. 1986. *Testament of Hope: The Essential Writings and Speeches of Martin Luther King, Jr*. Ed. J. Washington. New York: HarperCollins.

Kotsko, Adam. 2011. Religious, But Not Spiritual, on the Weblog, *an und für sich*, November 18. http://itself.wordpress.com/2011/11/18/religious-but-not-spiritual/.

Kristeva, Julia. 2009. *This Incredible Need to Believe*. Trans. B. Bie Brahic. New York: Columbia University Press.

Laclau, Ernesto. 2007. *On Populist Reason*. London and New York: Verso.

Lazier, Benjamin. 2008. *God Interrupted: Heresy and the European Imagination Between the World Wars*. Princeton, NJ: Princeton University Press.

Levinas, Emmanuel. 1969. *Totality and Infinity: An Essay on Exteriority*. Trans. A. Lingus. Pittsburgh, PA: Duquesne University Press.

———. 1990. The Pact. In *The Levinas Reader*. Trans. S. Hand, 211–226. Oxford: Basil Blackwell.

———. 1999. *Alterity and Transcendence*. Trans. M.B. Smith. New York: Columbia University Press.

Lewis, Simon L., and Mark A. Maslin. 2015. Defining the Anthropocene. *Nature* 519: 171–180.

Lilla, Mark. 2007. *The Stillborn God: Religion, Politics, and the Modern West*. New York: Knopf.

Locke, John. 1980. *Second Treatise of Government*. Ed. C.B. Macpherson. Indianapolis, IN and Cambridge: Hackett.

Lorde, Audre. 1981. *The Uses of Anger: Women Responding to Racism*. Keynote Presentation at the National Women's Studies Association Conference, Storrs, Connecticut, June. http://www.blackpast.org/1981audrelordeusesangerwomenrespondingracism.

Lowith, Karl. 1957. *Meaning in History: The Theological Implications of the Philosophy of History*. Chicago, IL and London: University of Chicago Press.

Lyotard, Jean-Francois. 2002. *The Postmodern Condition: A Report on Knowledge.* Trans. G. Bennington and B. Massumi. Minneapolis, MN: University of Minnesota Press.

MacIntyre, Alasdair. 2007. *After Virtue: A Study in Moral Theory.* Notre Dame, IN: University of Notre Dame Press.

Marx, Karl. 1998. Theses on Feuerbach. In *The German Ideology*, Coauthored with F. Engels, 569–575. Amherst, NY: Prometheus Books.

Marx, Karl, and Friedrich Engels. 1964. *On Religion.* Atlanta, GA: Scholars Press.

Mathews, Jay. 1993. Robert Rafsky, Writer and Activist in AIDS Fight, Dies. *The Washington Post* and as Found on the ACT UP NY Website, February 23. http://www.actupny.org/divatv/netcasts/rafsky_reads.html. Accessed 12 November 2014.

McCarthy, Timothy Patrick, and John McMillian. 2003. *The Radical Reader: A Documentary History of the American Radical Tradition.* New York and London: The New Press.

McMillan, Stephanie. 2012. *The Beginning of the American Fall: A Comics Journalist Inside the Occupy Wall Street Movement.* New York: Seven Stories Press.

Mertes, Tom, ed. 2004. *A Movement of Movements: Is Another World Really Possible?* London: Verso.

Merton, Robert K. 1936. The Unanticipated Consequences of Purposive Social Action. *American Sociological Review* 1 (6): 894–904.

Merton, Thomas. 1968. *Faith and Violence: Christian Teaching and Christian Practice.* Notre Dame, IN: University of Notre Dame Press.

———. 1979. *Love and Living.* Ed. N.B. Stone and Brother P. Hart. San Diego, CA: Harcourt, Inc.

———. 1992. *Thomas Merton: Spiritual Master: The Essential Writings.* Ed. L.S. Cunningham. New York: Paulist Press.

Mignolo, Walter. 2011. *The Darker Side of Western Modernity: Global Futures, Decolonial Options.* Durham, NC: Duke.

Mignolo, Walter, and Rubén Gaztambide-Fernández. 2014. Decolonial Options and Artistic/Aesthetic Entanglements: An Interview with Walter Mignolo. *Decolonization: Indigeneity, Education & Society* 3 (1): 196–212, 199.

Morris, I.I.I., and E. Charles. 2012. ACT UP 25: HIV/AIDS, Archival Queers, and Mnemonic World Making. *Quarterly Journal of Speech* 98 (1): 49–53.

Mouffe, Chantal. 2005. *The Return of the Political.* London and New York: Verso.

———. 2009. *The Democratic Paradox.* London and New York: Verso.

———. 2013. *Agonistics: Thinking the World Politically.* London and New York: Verso.

Muñoz, José Esteban. 2009. *Cruising Utopia: The Then and There of Queer Futurity.* New York and London: New York University Press.

Nancy, Jean-Luc. 1991. *The Inoperative Community.* Ed. P. Connor and Forew. C. Fynsk. Minneapolis, MN and London: University of Minnesota Press.

Navarro, Marysa. 1989. The Personal Is Political: Las Madres de Plaza de Mayo. In *Power and Popular Protest: Latin American Social Movements*, ed. Susan Eckstein, 251. Berkeley, CA: University of California Press.

Negri, Antonio. 2013. *Spinoza for Our Time: Politics and Postmodernity.* Trans. W. McCuaig. New York: Columbia University Press.

Nicholas of Cusa. 1986. Cibratio Alkorani. In *Nicolai de Cusa Opera Omnia*, ed. Ludwig Hagemann. Hamburg: Felix Meiner Verlag.

———. 1997. *Selected Spiritual Writings.* Trans. H. Lawrence Bond. Mahwah, NJ: Paulist Press.

Nicolin, F. 1967. Unbekannte Aphorismen Hegels aus der Jenaer Periode. *Hegel-Studien* 4: 9–19. Quoted in R. R. Williams. 2012. *Tragedy, Recognition, and the Death of God: Studies in Hegel and Nietzsche.* Oxford: Oxford University Press.

Niebuhr, H. Richard. 1993. *Radical Monotheism and Western Culture.* Louisville, KY: Westminster/John Knox Press.

———. 1996. *Christ and Culture.* New York: Harper Collins.

Niebuhr, Reinhold. 2002. *Moral Man and Immoral Society.* Louisville, KY: Westminster/John Knox Press.

Nietzsche, Friedrich. 1974. *The Gay Science.* Trans. W. Kaufmann. New York: Vintage.

———. 1997. *On the Genealogy of Morality.* Ed. K. Ansell-Pearson and Trans. C. Diethe. Cambridge: Cambridge University Press.

———. 2000. *The Antichrist.* Trans. A.M. Ludovici. Amherst, NY: Prometheus Books.

Norris, Pippa, and Ronald Inglehart. 2004. The Secularization Debate. In *Sacred and Secular: Religion and Politics Worldwide*, 3–32. New York and Cambridge: Cambridge University Press.

Nunberg, Geoffrey. 2002. *The History of 'Protest': The Syntax of Resistance.* Fresh Air Commentary, National Public Radio, March 11. http://bit.ly/ADMSg5.

NYC General Assembly. 2011. *Declaration of the Occupation of New York City*, September 29. http://www.nycga.net/resources/documents/declaration/.

Ortiz, Erik, and NBC News. 2015. Freddie Gray: From Baltimore Arrest to Protests, a Timeline of the Case. *NBC's* Website. http://www.nbcnews.com/storyline/baltimore-unrest/timeline-freddie-gray-case-arrest-protests-n351156.

Pan, David. 2012. Political Theology for Democracy: Carl Schmitt and John Dewey on Aesthetics and Politics. *Telos* 2012 (161, Winter): 120–140.

Pareene, Alex. 2011. A New Declaration of Independence: 10 Ideas for Taking America Back from the 1%. AlterNet.org. October 31. http://www.alternet.org/story/152912a_new_declaration_of_independence%3A_10_ideas_for_taking_america_back_from_the_1?akid=7799.250815.H41J8b&rd=1&t=8.

Pascal, Blaise. 1958. *Pensées*. Ed. T.S. Eliot. New York: E. P. Dutton & Co., Inc.
Peretti, Jonah. *Ordering My Own 'Nike Sweatshop' Shoes: Culture Jamming*. http://depts.washington.edu/ccce/polcommcampaigns/peretti.html. Accessed 12 June 2012.
Peterson, Daniel J., and G. Michael Zbaraschuk, eds. 2014. *Resurrecting the Death of God*. Albany, NY: SUNY.
Pew Research Center's Forum on Religion & Public Life. 2012. Nones on the Rise, October 9. http://www.pewforum.org/2012/10/09/nones-on-the-rise/.
Postman, Neil. 1992. *Technopoly: The Surrender of Culture to Technology*. New York: Vintage Books.
Pseudo-Dyonysius. 2001. The Divine Names. In *Light from Light: An Anthology of Christian Mysticism*, ed. Louis Dupré, James A. Wiseman, and O.S.B., 82–85. New York and Mahwah, NJ: Paulist Press.
———. 2001a. The Divine Names. In *Light from Light: An Anthology of Christian Mysticism*, ed. Louis Dupré, James A. Wiseman, and O.S.B., 82–85. New York and Mahwah, NJ: Paulist Press.
Quijano, Anibal, and Immanuel Wallerstein. 1992. Americanity as a Concept, or the Americas in the Modern World-System. *International Social Science Journal* 134: 549–557.
Rafsky, Bob. 2012. As quoted in "'How to Survive a Plague': As ACT UP Turns 25, New Film Chronicles History of AIDS Activism in U.S." Democracy Now, March 23. http://www.democracynow.org/2012/3/23/how_to_survive_a_plague_as.
Rakia, Raven. 2013. Black Riot. *The New Inquiry* (45), November 14. http://thenewinquiry.com/essays/blackriot/.
Ramnath, Maia. 2011. *Decolonizing Anarchism: An Antiauthoritarian History of India's Liberation Struggle*. Oakland, CA: AK Press and the Institute for Anarchist Studies.
Rancière, Jacques. 2009. *Hatred of Democracy*. Trans. S. Corcoran. London and New York: Verso.
Rappaport, Roy A. 1979. *Ecology, Meaning, and Religion*. Berkeley, CA: North Atlantic Books.
———. 1999. *Ritual and Religion in the Making of Humanity*. Cambridge: Cambridge University Press.
Ratzinger, Joseph and Jürgen Habermas. 2006. *The Dialectics of Secularization: On Reason and Religion*. Ed. F. Schuller. San Francisco: Ignatius Press.
Rawls, John. 1971. *A Theory of Justice*. Cambridge MA and Oxford: Harvard University Press.
Reder, Michael, and S.J. Josef Schmidt. 2010. Habermas and Religion. In *An Awareness of What Is Missing: Faith and Reason in a Post-secular Age*, ed. Jurgen Habermas. Cambridge and Malden, MA: Polity Press.

Richard, Alan Jay. 2012. The Theo-Politics of Radical Democracy: An Interview with Jeffrey W. Robbins (Part 2), on the *Political Theology* journal's Website, January 9. http://www.politicaltheology.com/blog/?p=1488.

Robbins, Jeffrey W. 2011. *Radical Democracy and Political Theology*. New York: Columbia University Press.

———. 2016. *Radical Theology: A Vision for Change*. Bloomington, IN: Indiana University Press.

Robbins, Jeffrey W., and Neal MaGee, eds. 2008. *The Sleeping Giant Has Awoken: The New Politics of Religion in the United States*. New York: Continuum.

Robert Rafsky, Writer and Activist in AIDS Fight, Dies. 1993. *The Washington Post*, February 23. As found at http://www.actupny.org/divatv/netcasts/rafsky_reads.html.

Rocker, Rudolph. 2004. *Anarcho-Syndicalism: Theory and Practice*. Trans. R.E. Chase. Oakland, CA: AK Press.

Rodkey, Christopher D., and Jordan E. Miller, eds. 2018. *The Palgrave Handbook of Radical Theology*. New York: Palgrave Macmillan.

Rorty, Richard. 1989. *Contingency, Irony, and Solidarity*. Cambridge and New York: Cambridge University Press.

Rubenstein, Richard L. 1992 [1966]. *After Auschwitz*. 2nd ed. Baltimore and London: Johns Hopkins University Press.

Rushkoff, Douglas. 2011. Think Occupy Wall St. Is a Phase? You Don't Get It, on CNN Opinions Website, October 5. http://www.cnn.com/2011/10/05/opinion/rushkoff-occupy-wall-street/index.html.

Santner, Eric L. 2011. *The Royal Remains: The People's Two Bodies and the Endgames of Sovereignty*. Chicago, IL and London: University of Chicago Press.

Sawyer, Eric. 2002. An ACT UP Founder 'Acts Up' for Africa's Access to AIDS. In *From ACT UP to the WTO: Urban Protest and Community Building in the Era of Globalization*, ed. Benjamin Shepard and Ronald Hayduk, 88–102. Verso: London and New York.

Scarry, Elaine. 1985. *The Body in Pain: The Making and Unmaking of the World*. Oxford and New York: Oxford University Press.

Schmitt, Carl. 2006. *Political Theology: Four Chapters on the Concept of Sovereignty*. Trans. G. Schwab. Chicago, IL and London: University of Chicago Press.

———. 2007. *The Concept of the Political*. Trans. G. Schwab. Chicago, IL and London: University of Chicago Press.

Schneider, Nathan. 2011. Occupy Wall Street: FAQ, on *The Nation*'s Website, September 29. http://www.thenation.com/article/163719/occupy-wall-street-faq.

———. 2013. *Thank You, Anarchy: Notes from the Occupy Apocalypse*. Berkeley, CA: University of California Press.

Schweizer, Albert. 2003. *The Albert Scweizer—Helen Bresslau Letters: 1902–1912*. Ed. R. Schweitzer Miller and G. Woytt and Trans. A. Bultmann Lemke with N. Stewart. Syracuse: Syracuse University Press.

Seligman, Adam B., Robert P. Weller, Michael J. Puett, and Bennett Simon. 2008. *Ritual and Its Consequences: An Essay on the Limits of Sincerity*. Oxford and New York: Oxford University Press.

Shepard, Benjamin, and Ronald Hayduk, eds. 2002. *From Act Up to the WTO: Urban Protest and Community Building in the Era of Globalization*. London and New York: Verso.

Simon, David. 2002. The Detail. *The Wire*. Direc. C. Johnson. HBO. Originally aired on June 9.

Simpson, J.A., and E.S.C. Weiner. 1991. *The Oxford English Dictionary*. 2nd ed. Oxford: Clarendon Press.

Smith, Mychal Denzel. 2015. The Rebirth of Black Rage: From Kanye to Obama and Back Again. *The Nation*, August 13. http://www.thenation.com/article/the-rebirth-of-black-rage/.

Solman, Paul. 2015. Why the Freddie Gray Riots Began at a Shopping Mall. *PBS's Website*, May 29. http://www.pbs.org/newshour/makingsense/answersbaltimoreseconomicrecoverystartshoppingmall/.

Spinoza, Baruch. 2001. *Theological-Political Treatise*. Trans. S. Shirley. Indianapolis, IN: Hackett Publishing.

Stevens, Wallace. 1997. Final Soliloquy of the Interior Paramour. In *Collected Poetry and Prose*, ed. Frank Kermode and Joan Richardson, 444. New York: The Library of America.

Stoppard, Tom. 1993. *Arcadia*. New York: Faber and Faber, Inc.

Strauss, Leo. 1997. *Spinoza's Critique of Religion*. Trans. E.M. Sinclair. Chicago, IL and London: University of Chicago Press.

Swatos, William H., Jr., and Daniel V.A. Olson, eds. 2000. *The Secularization Debate*. Lanham, MD and Oxford: Rowman and Littlefield Publishers, Inc.

Taubes, Jacob. 2003. *The Political Theology of Paul*. Trans. D. Hollander. Stanford, CA: Stanford University Press.

———. 2009. *Occidental Eschatology*. Trans. D. Ratmoko. Stanford, CA: Stanford University Press.

———. 2013. *To Carl Schmitt: Letters and Reflections*. Trans. K. Tribe. New York: Columbia University Press.

Taylor, Mark C. 1987. *Erring: A Postmodern A/theology*. Chicago, IL and London: University of Chicago Press.

Taylor, Diana. 1997. *Disappearing Acts: Spectacles of Gender and Nationalism in Argentina's "Dirty War"*. Durham, NC: Duke University Press.

Taylor, Charles. 2007a. *A Secular Age*. Cambridge, MA: The Belknap Press of Harvard University Press.

Taylor, Mark C. 2007b. *After God*. Chicago, IL and London: University of Chicago Press.
Taylor, Mark L. 2011. *The Theological and the Political: On the Weight of the World*. Minneapolis, MN: Fortress Press.
Tillich, Paul. 1959. *Theology of Culture*. Ed. R.C. Kimball. Oxford: Oxford University Press.
Timeline: Freddie Gray's Arrest, Death and the Aftermath. *The Baltimore Sun*. http://data.baltimoresun.com/news/freddie-gray/.
De Tocqueville, Alexis. 1956. *Democracy in America*. Ed. R.D. Heffner. New York: Mentor Books.
Treichler, Paula A. 1999. *How to Have Theory in an Epidemic: Cultural Chronicles of AIDS*. Durham and London: Duke University Press.
Ture, Kwame, and Charles V. Hamilton. 1992. *Black Power: The Politics of Liberation*. New York: Vintage Books.
Turner, Victor. 1964. "Symbols in Ndembu Ritual" in "Closed Systems and Open Minds: The Limits of Naivete". In *Social Anthropology*, ed. M. Gluckman and E. Devons. Chicago, IL: Aldine.
———. 1967. *The Forest of Symbols: Aspects of Ndembu Ritual*. Ithaca, NY: Cornell University Press.
———. 1969. *The Ritual Process*. Chicago, IL: Aldine.
Vahanian, Gabriel. 1961. *The Death of God: The Culture of Our Post-Christian Era*. New York: George Braziller.
Vasquez, Manuel, and Marie Marquardt. 2003. *Globalizing the Sacred: Religion Across the Americas*. Piscataway, NJ: Rutgers.
Vattimo, Gianni. 1999. *Belief*. Stanford, CA: Stanford University Press.
Vattimo, Gianni, and John D. Caputo. 2007. *After the Death of God*. Ed. J.W. Robbins. New York: Columbia University Press.
De Vries, Hent, and Lawrence E. Sullivan, eds. 2006. *Political Theologies: Public Religions in a Post-Secular World*. New York: Fordham University Press.
Wark, McKenzie. 2011a. *The Beach Beneath the Street: The Everyday Life and Glorious Times of the Situationist International*. London and New York: Verso.
———. 2011b. How To Occupy an Abstraction, from the Verso Books Blog, October 3. http://www.versobooks.com/blogs/728-mckenzie-wark-on-occupy-wall-street-how-to-occupy-an-abstraction.
———. Preoccupying: McKenzie Wark. http://theoccupiedtimes.org/?p=6451.
Warner, Michael, Jonathan VanAntwerpen, and Craig Calhoun, eds. 2010. *Varieties of Secularism in a Secular Age*. Cambridge, MA: Harvard University Press.
Wartofsky, Michael Gould. 2015. When Rioting Is Rational. *Jacobin Magazine*, January 2. https://www.jacobinmag.com/2015/01/whenriotingisrationalferguson/.

Wearden, Graeme. 2014. Oxfam: 85 Richest People as Wealthy as Poorest Half of the World. *The Guardian*, January 20. http://www.theguardian.com/business/2014/jan/20/oxfam-85-richest-people-half-of-the-world.
Weber, Max. 1930. *The Protestant Ethic and the Spirit of Capitalism*. New York: Scribner.
———. 1975. *Economy and Society*. Berkeley, CA: University of California Press.
Weigel, David, and Lauren Hepler. 2011. Everything You Need to Know About Occupy Wall Street Entry 3: A Timeline of the Movement, from February to Today, on Slate.com, November 18. http://www.slate.com/articles/news_and_politics/politics/features/2011/occupy_wall_street/what_is_ows_a_complete_timeline.html.
West, James. 2012. 365 Days of Occupy Wall Street—An Anniversary Timeline, on *Mother Jones*'s Website, September 17. http://www.motherjones.com/mojo/2012/09/occupy-wall-street-anniversary-timeline.
Wignaraja, Ponna, ed. 1993. *New Social Movements in the South: Empowering the People*. London: Zed Books.
Williams, Robert R. 2012. *Tragedy, Recognition, and the Death of God: Studies in Hegel and Nietzsche*. Oxford: Oxford University Press.
Wilson, Bryan. 1966. *Religion in Secular Society: A Sociological Comment*. London: C.A. Watts.
Winquist, Charles E. 1986. *Desiring Theology*. Chicago, IL and London: University of Chicago Press.
———. 2001. Postmodern Secular Theology. In *Secular Theology: American Radical Theological Thought*, ed. Clayton Crockett, 26–36. London and New York: Routledge.
———. 2003. *The Surface of the Deep*. Aurora, CO: The Davies Group, Publishers.
Winsor, Morgan and James Hill. 2017. Authorities Move into Dakota Access Pipeline Protest Camp. *ABC News*, February 22. http://abcnews.go.com/US/deadline-looms-dakota-access-pipeline-opponents-evacuate-protest/story?id=45654213. Accessed 22 February 2017.
Wojnarowicz, David. Ashes Action. *ACT UP NY*. http://actupny.org/reports/reportashes.html. Accessed 12 November 2014.
———. David Wojnarowicz Readings. *ACT UP NY*. http://www.actupny.org/diva/synWoj.html. Accessed 12 November 2014.
———. Political Funerals. *ACT UP NY*. http://actupny.org/diva/polfunsyn.html. Accessed 12 November 2014.
World's Largest Shopping Centers. http://web.archive.org/web/20120305041824/http://nutmeg.easternct.edu/~pocock/MallsWorld.htm.
Žižek, Slavoj. 2009. Dialectical Clarity Versus the Misty Conceit of Paradox. In *The Monstrosity of Christ: Paradox or Dialectic*, Co-authored with J. Milbank and Ed. C. Davis, 234–306. Cambridge, MA and London: MIT Press.

———. 2011a. Occupy First. Demands Come Later. *The Guardian*'s Website, October 26. http://www.guardian.co.uk/commentisfree/2011/oct/26/occupy-protesters-bill-clinton.

———. 2011b. Žižek in Wall Street, October 11. http://criticallegalthinking.com/2011/10/11/zizek-in-wall-street-transcript/.

———. 2012a. If There Is a God, Then Anything Is Permitted. *ABC's Religion and Ethics* Website, April 17. http://www.egs.edu/faculty/slavoj-zizek/articles/if-there-is-a-god-then-anything-is-permitted/.

———. 2012b. *The Year of Dreaming Dangerously*. London and New York: Verso.

———. 2013. The Simple Courage of Decision: A Leftist Tribute to Thatcher. *New Statesman*, April 17. http://www.newstatesman.com/politics/politics/2013/04/simple-couragedecision-leftist-tribute-thatcher.

INDEX

NUMBERS AND SYMBOLS
#BlackLivesMatter, xii, 4, 11, 15, 67, 79, 80, 153–164
15-M, 4, 15, 128

A
Abraham, 75n7
Abyss, 136
Academia, academic, academy, x, xi, 3, 7, 9, 15, 53, 79, 91, 95, 96, 135
Act, action, 7, 9, 13–16, 19, 21, 23, 25, 27, 31, 32, 37–39, 41, 47, 49, 52, 53, 60–62, 64, 66–68, 71, 74, 76, 78, 80, 89, 94, 95, 104n87, 108, 109, 111–113, 115–118, 122, 123, 125, 127, 128, 131, 133, 141–143, 146, 149, 150, 155, 157–160, 161n24, 162, 164
Acts, book of, 71
Adbusters, 127n1, 128, 128n2, 129, 129n3, 129n4, 134, 134n21
Agamben, Giorgio, 58, 61, 62, 134, 141

AIDS, 111–118, 114n8, 121, 123, 123n29, 124, 124n35, 126
AIDS Coalition to Unleash Power (ACT UP), xii, 11, 14, 67, 75, 77, 79, 80, 111–126
Allen, Peter Lewis, 123n29
Alter, Robert, 168n2
Althaus-Reid, Marcella, 95–97, 153
Altizer, Thomas J. J., viii, x, xi, 8n11, 10, 10n15, 35, 35n40, 41, 69, 105, 106, 145–149, 147n58, 159
America, 81, 85, 133, 134, 155–157, 159, 163, 165
Anarchy, anarchism, anarchic, x, 4, 14, 15, 29, 71, 79, 80n20, 97–101, 129, 134, 137
Anger, 112
Anthropocene, 81, 81n22
Anthropology, anthropological, anthropologist, 6, 10, 21, 60, 66, 73, 79, 154
Apocalypse, apocalypticism, 45
Apophasis, apophatic, 11, 15, 25, 28, 31, 34, 37, 71, 142, 144, 146, 149, 164

Arab Spring, xi, 2, 4, 15, 59, 128, 146, 147
Arendt, Hannah, 142
Asad, Talal, 3, 4, 76
Ashes, 113, 168
As if, 7, 9, 43n64, 66, 72, 76
　See also Subjunctive, subjunctivity, subjunctively
Atheism, x, 40, 45, 47, 71, 143, 147
Attar, Farid ud-Din, 28, 28n24, 35, 69
Augustine, St., 29, 30
Authority, x, 10, 12, 27–29, 33, 45, 52, 53, 53n7, 59–65, 70, 71, 82–84, 86, 87, 89, 116, 129

B
Badiou, Alain, 4n4
Bailey, Timothy (Tim), 121–123
Baltimore, MD, 15, 162–164, 168
Beginning, 7, 8n11, 15, 25, 31n32, 42, 49, 74n7, 107, 113, 114, 128, 132n13, 142, 144, 153, 165, 166
Benjamin, Walter, 58
Berger, Peter, 2n1, 3n2
Bergson, Henri, 32
Berkowitz, Richard, 116n11
Berman, Marshall, 81, 81n21, 84
Bersani, Leo, 120n24
Bethge, Eberhard, 10n15, 35n40
Bible, 12, 31, 49
Black power, 154
Blanton, Ward, ix
Bonhoeffer, Dietrich, 8n11, 10, 10n15, 35, 35n40, 69, 80, 146, 150
Bouazizi, Mohammed, 127, 128, 147n58, 168
Bray, Mark, 4n4
Buber, Martin, 12, 12n17, 35–41, 67, 69
Buddha, Shakyamuni, 23

Buddhism, 22, 24
Bultmann, Rudolf, 8n11
Burn, burning, 33n35, 121, 168
Bush, George W., vii, 53, 54
Butler, Judith, 3n2

C
Calhoun, Craig, 3n2
Callen, Michael, 116, 116n11
Canning, Peter, 101
Canon, canonical, 31, 33, 60, 61, 64
Capitalism, 2n1, 7, 16, 57, 58, 72, 81, 85, 92, 130, 131, 135, 141, 154–158, 164
Caputo, John D., 92n49, 139n34, 142, 142n46
Cavanaugh, William T., 3n2, 81–85, 84n30, 89, 90
Certeau, Michel de, 13, 14, 73–75, 78, 93, 94, 102–104, 104n87, 108, 143, 148, 149
Chaos, 62, 63, 77
Christ, x, 42, 43n64, 44, 55, 61n32, 84n30, 147, 149
　See also Jesus
Christendom, 81, 85
Christian, x, 2, 12, 41, 47, 55, 67, 70, 82, 83, 133, 159
Christian atheism, 41
Christianity, 44, 58, 69, 133, 147
Church, ix, x, 2n1, 34, 57, 59, 72, 82–84, 86, 90, 117, 122n29, 133, 163
City, 13, 14, 75n8, 78–80, 101–109, 112, 113, 128–130, 132, 134, 143–145, 148–150, 159, 161n24, 162, 163, 166, 167
Civil Rights, viii
Cleary, Thomas F., 11n16, 23, 24
Colonization, 73, 80, 81, 96

Communion, 14, 35–40, 67, 107, 141, 149
Compassion, 23
Comte, Auguste, 1n1, 2n1
Cone, James, 159
Connolly, N.D.B., 162, 163
Contemporary, viii, ix, 5, 8, 13, 25, 37n43, 44, 48, 55, 58, 66, 73, 74, 79, 90, 91, 131, 148, 154
Craft, 11, 12, 15, 19, 27, 30, 66, 67, 72, 73, 79, 145
Craftsman, 30
Crawford, Matthew B., 27, 30, 35, 48, 69
Creation, 8, 14, 15, 31, 36, 37, 40, 42, 47, 49n84, 50, 65, 66, 78, 81–83, 101, 102, 104, 106, 107, 144, 145, 157, 158, 160
Creator, x, 31, 51, 106, 117, 131, 158
Critchley, Simon, 52, 54
Crockett, Clayton, ix, xiii, 3n2, 87, 90
CVS, 162, 168

D

Dahrendorf, Ralf, 28n23
Daiichi Pharmaceuticals, 124
Dakota Access, 165–167
De Certeau, Michel, 13, 14, 73, 93
De Tocqueville, Alexis, 86, 86n34
de Vries, Hent, 3n2, 101n79
Death, vii, x, 14, 42–44, 42n62, 43n64, 50, 55, 70, 86, 89, 96, 105, 106, 113, 118, 121, 123, 123n29, 124, 126, 145–147, 158, 166–168
Death of God, viii–xi, 7–9, 8n11, 14, 42, 48, 68, 72, 73, 77, 79, 86–91, 98, 99, 105
DeCaro, Jr., Louis A., 154n5
Declaration, 71, 130
Decolonial, 15, 80n20, 159, 164

Deconstruction, viii, ix, 16, 91, 142
Delusion, 22, 23
Democracy, 4, 7, 14, 15, 43, 48, 52, 53, 65, 75, 79, 86, 91, 97–101, 109, 128, 129, 131, 134, 139, 142, 142n46, 144, 151
Depth-dimension, 91, 97, 118
Derrida, Jacques, 137, 139, 139n34, 142, 142n46
Desire, desiring, 5, 6, 8n11, 13, 14, 17, 19, 28, 30, 33–35, 33n35, 39, 41, 43–46, 71, 72, 79, 87–90, 95, 97, 101, 103, 104, 108, 112, 113, 118–122, 162, 168
Detienne, Marcel, 101
Dialectic, dialectical, 38, 45, 57, 100, 149
Difference, 7, 22, 38, 61, 64, 83, 87n37, 93, 105, 137, 138, 142, 146
Disappoint, 13, 17, 88, 89, 95, 97, 118, 119
Disorder, disordering, 13, 62, 63, 85, 89, 90, 157
Dōgen, 11, 11n16, 22–24, 35, 37, 69
Dogmatic, 90
Dostoevsky, Fyodor, 44n71
Douglas, Mary, 21
Durkheim, Emile, 2n1, 21

E

Earth, vii, 7, 24, 64, 70, 130, 156n11, 161n24, 166–168
Ecclesiastes, book of, *see* Qohelet
Ecclesiastical, 82
Eckhart, Meister, 29, 30, 40
Economics, vii, viii, 4, 5, 8, 15, 56, 58, 59, 71, 75n8, 82, 91, 96, 102, 103, 129, 131, 133, 134, 138, 141, 150, 153–155, 168

Economy, 92, 95, 96, 121, 128, 154
Edelman, Lee, 120n24
Emancipation, 99, 100, 106
Embodiment, 48, 71, 99
Empire, 55, 145
Emptiness, 23, 24, 37, 43n64, 73, 141, 148
Engels, Friedrich, 1n1, 11n16, 20n3
Enlightenment, the, 1, 1n1, 24, 42, 81
Episalla, Joy, 118n16, 121n27
Erasmus, 104, 144, 150
Ethical, 2n1, 74, 96
Ethics, 30, 72, 139
The exception, 43, 45, 51, 52, 54, 58–62, 61n32, 64, 65, 69, 70, 91, 140, 163
Existential, 8n11, 23, 25–27, 50, 88, 106
Existentialism, 27
Ezekiel, book of, 158

F
Faith, 25, 26, 28, 39, 42, 48–50, 79, 82, 83, 88, 99, 126, 137, 142, 156
Fanon, Frantz, 153, 157
Feminine, 158
Feminist, 153
Ferguson, MO, 162
Feuerbach, Ludwig, 1n1
Fire, 107, 127, 155, 162, 165, 168
Fisher, Mark Lowe, 117, 118
Flowers in the sky, 23, 24
Foucault, Michel, 104n87
France, David, 123n34
Freedom, 42–44, 50, 84, 90, 99, 105, 146, 156, 157, 162
Freud, Sigmund, 1–2n1, 11, 11n16, 20–22, 24, 105
Futurity, 120, 122, 125

G
Garner, Eric, 158
Geertz, Clifford, 115
Genealogy, 96
General assembly, 130, 131, 134, 140, 141
Genesis, book of, 31, 31n32, 37, 84
Ghost, 122–125
Gift, 168
Girard, René, 12, 36, 40–45, 67
Globalization, xi, 4, 72
God, vii, x, 7, 8n11, 9, 11, 12, 15, 17, 25–31, 26n18, 29n26, 31n32, 33–45, 33n35, 47, 48, 50, 54, 55, 58, 61, 64–67, 69–71, 77–80, 82, 86–90, 95, 96, 98, 101, 102, 104–106, 104n87, 108, 115, 144–147, 158, 159, 164, 168
God, death of, viii–xi, 7–9, 8n11, 14, 42, 48, 68, 72, 73, 77, 79, 86–91, 98, 99, 105, 144–148, 147n58, 150
Goodchild, Philip, 97
Gorski, Philip, 3n2
Gospel, Gospels, 25, 31n32, 40–42
Graeber, David, 149, 150, 150n65, 154, 156, 157, 164
Gray, Freddie, 15, 162, 163n26
Greenwald, Glenn, 53, 53n7

H
Habermas, Jürgen, 3n2
Hallie, Philip, 35n40
Hamilton, Charles V., 154, 154n5
Hamilton, William, 35, 69, 145, 147, 148
Hardt, Michael, 63, 64, 148
Harvey, David, 13, 56, 57, 103, 107, 108, 134, 148, 149, 163
Haunt, 112, 113, 122–124, 126
Hayduk, Ronald, 112n4

Heaven, 48, 67, 70
Hebrew, 159n19
Hedges, Chris, 137
Hegel, Georg Wilhelm Friedrich, 9, 9n12, 134, 134n20, 147n58
Hegemony, 59, 85, 142, 151
Heresy, vii, xi, 29, 32
Hermeneutics, 10, 14, 96
Heterodoxy, 32
History, xii, 8, 10, 45, 46, 56, 81n22, 106, 108, 134, 134n20, 140, 147, 162, 163, 167, 168
HIV, 111, 112, 114, 123, 124, 126
Holiness, 64
Holy Spirit, 15, 133, 134, 149
Hope, xii, 5, 16, 19, 25, 42, 77, 116, 133, 138, 141, 142, 159
How to Survive a Plague, 124, 124n36

I
Iconoclast, iconoclasm, iconoclastic, 12, 15, 28, 34, 35, 69, 71, 155, 164
Identity, 33, 41, 46n77, 93, 107, 119, 150, 158
Ideology, 53, 96, 97, 136, 145, 145n54, 150
Idle No More, 4
Idol, 12, 29, 133
Illusion, 11, 19, 20, 22–25, 35, 48, 66, 125, 140
Imagination, 16, 17, 100, 125
Immanence, 37, 44, 109, 148
Immanent, 26, 65, 148
Immediacy, 26, 32, 159
Imperative, 9, 17, 47, 66, 72, 74, 95, 97, 111, 112, 115, 146
Impotence, 30
Infinite, 46, 119n19
Injustice, 4, 99, 100, 130, 147n59, 160

Interdisciplinary, 10, 11, 15, 16, 60, 65, 78
Invisible, 58
Irony, 34, 37, 139, 140, 156
Islam, *see* Sufism

J
James, William, 38, 48
Jesus, x, 25, 26n18, 40, 42, 50, 69–71
 See also Christ
Jew, Jewish, Judaism, 34, 46n77, 47, 67, 74n7, 105
Job, book of, 42
John, book of, 31n32
Jones-Armstrong, Amaryah, 155n9, 156
Joy, 107, 109
Judgment, x, 26, 27, 70
Judson Memorial Church, 117
Juergensmeyer, Mark, 3n2
Justice, 26, 84, 86, 99, 100, 142, 167

K
Kant, Immanuel, 17
Kantorowicz, Ernst H, 3n2
Kaposi's sarcoma, 124
Kenosis, kenotic, kenotically, 70, 97, 147, 148, 164
 See also Emptiness
Kierkegaard, Søren, 9
Kill, 15, 42, 96, 112, 115, 123n29, 124, 158, 161n24, 162
Kim, David Kyuman, 3n2
King, Jr., Martin Luther, 160, 161n24

L
Labor, viii, 62, 72, 79, 103, 109, 149, 156

Language, xi, 10, 11, 13, 14, 16, 16n23, 21, 22, 25, 27–31, 36, 37, 37n43, 39, 46, 49, 49n84, 50, 60, 67, 73, 87, 93–95, 101, 114, 115, 119, 121, 125, 141, 143, 144, 149, 159, 160
Latin America, 96
Law, legal, 26n18, 41, 47, 51–54, 59–64, 69–71, 73, 94, 153, 154, 156, 161, 162
Legitimate, legitimacy, 33, 51, 60, 61, 63, 66, 70, 71, 86, 115
Letters and Papers from Prison (Bonhoeffer), 10n15, 35n40
Levinas, Emmanuel, 43, 139, 139n33
Lewis, Simon L., 81n22
Liberal, liberalism, 13, 15, 27, 43, 52, 53, 55, 56, 59, 81, 85, 86, 98, 134, 138, 156, 160
Liberation, 21, 24, 29n26, 42, 91–97, 115, 116, 123, 124, 153, 157
Life, vii, x, 6, 13, 15, 19, 20, 23, 31, 31n32, 33, 37, 46, 49–52, 50n84, 55, 60, 64, 65, 69, 74n7, 76, 77, 79, 80, 82, 84, 85, 88, 89, 93, 96, 97, 102, 103, 106, 107, 109, 111, 118, 118–119n19, 122, 123, 138, 143, 145, 146, 149, 150, 155–159, 159n19, 161n24, 162, 164, 166–168
Light, 4, 5, 11, 31n32, 33n35, 37, 40, 58, 68, 143, 148, 167
Literature, 78, 92–94
Locke, John, 156, 156n11
Long, Iris, 123
Lord, x, 31
Love, vii, 12, 25, 26, 26n18, 28, 29, 29n25, 32, 39n51, 40, 70, 71, 106, 107, 118, 121, 133, 150, 159
Lowith, Karl, 3n2
Luke, book of, 25n16, 50n89
Luther, Martin, 82

M

Machiavelli, Niccolo, 63
MacIntyre, Alasdair
Madison, WI, 128
Madman (Nietzsche's), 86, 147n58
Mahayana Buddhism, 24
Maimonides, Moses, 33n35
Make, remake, 7, 11, 12, 15, 17, 21–25, 27, 30–33, 36, 42, 43, 45, 46, 50, 53, 53n7, 54, 62, 66, 72, 74, 75n7, 79, 82, 84, 88, 89, 93–95, 103, 106–108, 111, 112, 114, 118, 121, 125, 126, 131, 132, 136–138, 140, 141, 143, 146, 150, 151, 154, 156–159, 156n11, 167
Mall, shopping mall, Mondawmin Mall, 15, 162, 163
Manhattan, xi, 129, 130, 133
Manufacture, manufacturing, 17, 27–34, 107
Mark, book of, 25n16, 50n89, 146
Marx, Karl, 2n1, 11, 17, 20–22, 24, 72, 100, 105, 134
Marxism, 43
Mask, 149
Maslin, Mark A., 81n22
Materialism, 100
Matthew, book of, 27
McCullough, Lissa, 10n15, 35n39
McMillan, Stephanie, 129
Meaning-making, 13, 14, 89, 99, 111n1, 120
Medieval, 12, 22, 28, 78, 81–83, 104
Memory, 8, 144
Mendieta, Eduardo, 3n2
Merton, Robert K., 107
Merton, Thomas, 13, 14, 74, 103–108
Metaphysics, 87, 138
Middle Ages, 73
Mignolo, Walter, xv

The Milagro Beanfield War, 65, 73
Mimesis, mimetic, 41, 42, 43n64
Misogyny, 4
Modern, modernity, 1, 2n1, 4, 12, 13, 26, 54, 55, 58, 65, 71, 78, 81–91, 94, 98, 102, 148, 154, 156
Moral Majority, 147
Moses, 33n35
Mouffe, Chantal, 5n4
Movement for Black lives, 15, 155, 159, 162, 164
Multiplicity, 146
Multitude, 55, 63, 65, 73, 79, 98, 109, 129, 150
Muñoz, José Esteban, 120–126, 120n25
Muslim, *see* Islam
Myers, Max A., 8n11
Mystery, 38
Mysticism, 11, 28, 29, 31–34, 47, 67, 73, 149

N

Name of God, 25, 29, 47, 88
Nancy, Jean-Luc, 143
Negation, 159
Negative, 12, 25, 28, 30, 45, 61, 100, 120, 144
Negativity, 100, 101
Negri, Antonio, 8, 85, 144, 148
Neoliberalism, 4, 5, 55, 57–59, 72, 79, 148
New Testament, 48
New York, 112, 118, 122n29, 129, 132, 134
Niebuhr, H. Richard, 3n2
Niebuhr, Reinhold, 24, 25
Nietzsche, Friedrich, 34, 69, 86, 147n58
Nihil, 15

Nihilism, 30
North Atlantic, 96
North Dakota, 4, 165, 166
Nostalgia, nostalgic, viii, 44, 45, 64, 137, 147
Nothing, 2n1, 9, 22, 29, 30, 31n32, 32, 37, 39, 44, 48, 50, 51, 56, 71, 75n7, 100, 106, 114, 115, 157–159, 167
Nothingness, 29

O

Oakland, CA, 80n20, 132
Occupation, xi, 15, 55, 105, 129–133, 132n13, 140, 141, 143–145, 149, 150, 168
Occupy, xi, 15, 37n43, 77, 104, 129, 131–151
Occupy Wall Street, 4n4, 11, 15, 55, 67, 75, 79, 80, 127–151
Ontology, 124
Order, ordering, xi, 6, 13, 16n23, 19, 22, 33, 34, 36, 42, 48, 60–63, 69–73, 78, 79, 81, 82, 85, 89, 90, 95, 101n79, 103, 108, 116, 134, 145, 153, 154, 157, 158
Orthodoxies, 32

P

Pain, 137n29, 139
Parable, 23
Paradox, 23, 30, 34, 36, 44, 47
Paris, 150
Pascal, Blaise, 99
Pathology, 24
Patriarchy, 96
Peace, 48, 82, 129
People's microphone, people's mic, 75, 137, 139, 149

Performance, 5, 9, 13, 16, 25, 27, 73, 74, 76, 78, 79, 117, 122, 125, 149, 160
Peterson, Daniel J., ix
Phenomenology, 37
Philosophy, vii, viii, 4, 5, 9, 10, 16, 34, 53, 71, 80n20, 87, 98, 156
Pneuma, 159n19
Poetry, 117–118
Poiesis, 158
Police, policing, viii, 15, 82, 113, 127, 128, 130, 132, 133, 154n5, 155, 155n9, 159, 161n24, 162, 167
Political funeral, 14, 113, 118, 118n16, 120–125, 121n27
Portland, OR, 132
Postindustrial, 86
Postmodern, x, 87, 91, 119
Postsecular, 91
Potentiality, potentialities, 5, 19, 120, 125, 134, 142, 150
Power, x, 4, 5, 7, 11, 13, 15, 16, 22, 24, 29, 29n26, 31, 33, 34, 37, 38, 43, 46, 47, 49–55, 62–65, 70, 73, 74, 75n8, 82–85, 91–95, 98–101, 103, 104, 106, 107, 109, 115, 122, 125, 126, 128, 129, 134–136, 144, 145, 148, 154, 155, 157, 159, 161n24, 163, 164
Primordial, 158
Profane, 3n2, 37, 45
Property, 15, 56, 74, 87, 94, 102, 150, 155–164, 155n9, 156n11, 161n24
Property destruction, 15, 92n50, 155–164
Prophet, prophetic, viii, 34, 42, 58, 64, 70, 85, 158, 159
Protest, xi, 20, 59, 113, 122n29, 124, 124n36, 127–131, 136, 138, 145n54, 160
Protestantism, 24, 81
Puett, Michael J., 6, 6n7, 22, 22n7, 66

Q
Qohelet, 168
Queer, 116, 119, 120, 120n25, 122, 124–126
Queer futurity, 120, 120n25, 122, 125
Queer theory, 120, 124
Qushayri, 28, 35, 69, 149

R
Racism, 4, 155, 157, 158, 163
Radical democracy, 7, 14, 48, 75, 79, 97–99, 98n70, 129, 139, 142, 144
Radical, radicalize, radicalization, vii–xi, 5–12, 16, 21, 31, 34–36, 48, 58, 68–71, 73, 75, 78–80, 80n20, 86n34, 90, 92n49, 96–99, 105, 111, 129, 137, 138, 144, 145, 147, 147n58, 148, 150, 168
Radical Theology and the Death of God (Altizer and Hamilton), 8n11, 10n15, 35n40, 145n56
Rafsky, Robert (Bob), 124, 124n35, 124n36
Rage, 118
Rakia, Raven, 156, 157
Ramnath, Maia, 14, 80n20, 98–101, 99n72
Rancière, Jacques, 98, 109
Rappaport, Roy A., xiv, xv, 11, 14, 15, 21, 22, 25, 27, 36, 41, 48–50, 59–64, 66, 78, 100
Raschke, Carl A., viii, 8n11
Rawls, John, 16n23, 134, 142n41
Real, vii, 10, 20, 23–25, 39, 47, 48, 51, 53, 55, 59, 66, 67, 72, 76, 102, 114, 115, 119, 121, 123, 126, 129, 130, 135, 140, 158, 159, 165
Rebel, (noun) rebellion, 4, 63, 129, 148, 149, 155

INDEX   195

Redemption, 134
Reich, Robert, 135
Religion, vii, 1, 2, 19–27, 56, 72, 114, 133, 145
Religiosity, 26, 34, 69
Repair, 19, 27, 76
Repetition, 51, 60, 137, 146
Resisting theology, vii, viii, xii, 1–17, 67–109, 116, 150, 151, 153, 158, 164, 168
Resist, resisting, resistance, vii, xi, xii, 1, 4–7, 9–17, 19, 29, 45, 47, 48, 59, 63–66, 68–81, 80n20, 88, 89, 91–95, 97–101, 103, 104n87, 107, 109, 112, 117, 119, 122, 123, 125, 126, 132–136, 141, 144, 145n54, 146, 148, 150, 153–155, 165, 168
Responsibility, x, 40, 41, 56, 122, 124, 139
Resurrection, 44
Retribution, 161n24
Reversal, xi, 57
Revolution, revolutionary, x, 2, 4, 43n64, 61, 64, 81, 81n22, 90, 98, 128, 145, 147, 156, 158
Richard, Alan Jay, xiv, 111n1
Riot, 15, 132, 133, 155, 159–164, 161n24
Risk, vii, x, 26, 48–50, 52, 77, 79, 88, 95–97, 99, 123, 125, 161n24, 168
Ritual, 1, 2n1, 6, 6n7, 9, 10n14, 12, 19, 21, 22, 22n6, 22n7, 27, 27n21, 36, 42, 49, 59, 62–68, 62n33, 62n34, 64n41, 67n43, 72–79, 74n6, 74n7, 75n9, 99, 101n77, 107, 109, 121–123, 149
Robbins, Jeffrey W., viii, ix, xiii, 7, 14, 16, 17, 63, 65, 90, 97–99, 98n70, 109, 129, 129n5, 144, 148, 151
Rodkey, Christopher D., ix

Romans, book of, 26n18, 70, 71
Rorty, Richard, 137, 138
Ruach, 159n19
Rubenstein, Richard L., 8n11, 105
Rushkoff, Douglas, 138

S

Sacred, 3n2, 37, 46, 49, 64, 87, 161n24, 166, 168
Sacrifice, 29, 42, 44
Salvation, 21, 48, 82, 134
Scapegoat, 41, 42, 43n64, 44
Scarry, Elaine, 137, 137n29
Scharlemann, Robert P., 8n11
Schmitt, Carl, 5, 8, 16, 41, 51–62, 60n27, 71, 72, 78, 91, 144
Schneider, Nathan, 132n13
Schulman, Sarah, 118n16
Schweizer, Albert, 34n37
Science, xi, 1, 2n1, 15, 43, 45, 78, 87, 91, 114, 115, 123, 124, 160
Seattle, WA, 59
Secular, secularism, secularist, secularity, 2–5, 3n2, 7, 10, 14, 16, 26, 36, 45–47, 49, 71, 76, 79, 80, 82–84, 89, 91, 93, 96, 97, 111, 113, 119, 122, 126, 133, 144, 145, 147, 148
Self-consciousness, 6, 14, 28, 79, 99, 148
Self-emptying, *see* Kenosis, kenotic, kenotically
Self-referential, 25, 27, 29, 31, 33, 50, 59–61, 64, 65, 104, 145
Seligman, Adam, xiv, 6, 22, 66, 74, 74n7, 75, 75n9, 78
September 11, 2001, 9/11, viii, 147
Shepard, Benjamin, xiv, 112, 112n4
Silence, 28, 37, 38, 138, 141–151
Simon, Bennett, 6, 6n7, 22, 22n7, 66
Simon, David, 136n27

Sin, 30
Sincerity, sincere, 87
Sioux, 166, 167
Slave, slavery, slave trade, 81, 85, 154, 156, 157, 164, 167
Socialism, 2n1, 4, 56
Social, social movement, vii, viii, x, xi, 2n1, 4–6, 8–10, 8n11, 12, 13, 15, 19, 21, 22, 26, 33, 36, 38, 49, 50n84, 56–60, 60n27, 62–64, 66, 71–73, 78–80, 82, 84, 85, 88, 89, 92, 96, 99, 102, 103, 106, 107, 114, 122, 144, 146, 148, 149, 153, 154, 158, 160, 163
Solidarity, vii, 12, 15, 36, 56, 57, 59, 63, 66, 78, 96, 117, 122, 132, 138, 139, 148, 167
Sovereignty, x, 1, 5, 7, 10–13, 29, 43, 45, 51–65, 67, 69–71, 73, 81–87, 84n30, 91, 93, 98, 101n79, 109, 145, 147, 148, 150, 167
Spain, xi, 4, 15, 128
Speech, 31, 33n35, 37, 38, 64, 104n87, 123, 124n35, 133, 133n17, 137, 141, 143, 144, 160
Spinoza, Baruch, 63, 85–87
Spirit, 8, 9, 14, 20, 45, 46, 70, 79, 119n19, 126, 133–142, 144, 146, 147, 156, 159n19, 165, 168
Spirituality, spiritual, 19–27, 33, 37, 46, 49, 50, 50n84, 82, 118–119n19, 168
Standing Rock, 4, 165–168
State-making, 13, 85
State of exception, 52, 54, 58, 61, 62
State (political organization), 14, 149
Strategy, 75n8, 93, 94
Strauss, Leo, 85
Subject, 10, 45, 47, 48, 52, 54, 61, 62, 70, 75n8, 78, 82, 102, 111n1, 155

Subjectivity, 11
Subjunctive, subjunctivity, subjunctively, 5–9, 11–13, 15–17, 19–50, 62–68, 71, 72, 74–80, 88, 89, 95, 97–102, 99n72, 104–109, 114–122, 125, 126, 129, 132–134, 137, 142, 145, 148, 150
Substance, 46, 49, 50n84, 119n19, 137
Suffering, viii, 21, 130
Sufi, 28, 67n44
Sufism, 28n22, 35n40, 149n62
Sunyata, *see* Emptiness
Supernatural, 157
Systematic, 54, 60n27

T

Tactics, 28, 47, 75–77, 91–97, 99, 128, 132, 144, 154n5
Taubes, Jacob, 26n18, 91n47, 134, 134n20
Taylor, Charles, 3n2
Taylor, Mark C., viii, 8n11
Taylor, Mark L., xv, 117, 118, 122, 125, 126
Tea Party, 59, 137
Technology, 1, 15, 20, 37, 67
Terror, 70, 142, 168
Thatcher, Margaret, 52n4, 56, 133, 163
Theism, 11
Theological-political, theopolitical, 86n33
Theology, 1–17
  death-of-God theology, viii, ix, 8, 8n11, 88, 144
  desiring theology, 118, 122, 125
  indecent theology, 95n61, 153, 153n1
  liberation theology, 96, 124, 153
  negative theology, 28, 61
    (*see also* Apophaticism)

political theology, vii, x, 4, 5, 7–13, 16, 17, 35, 51–69, 71–73, 78, 79, 86n34, 89, 90, 95–98, 102, 126, 145, 150
radical theology, viii–xi, 5, 6, 8, 10, 12, 16, 34–36, 66, 69–71, 75, 78–80, 90, 92n49, 105, 144, 145, 147, 148, 150
resisting theology, vii, viii, xii, 69–109
secular theology, xii, 93, 125
Theopoetics, xii, 125
Theravada Buddhism, 24
Tillich, Paul, 8n11, 10–12, 25–27, 34–36, 39, 45–50, 67, 69, 72, 78, 87, 88, 91, 97, 105, 106, 118, 118n19, 119, 146, 168
Time, vii, viii, xi, xii, 4, 13, 15, 20, 26, 33n35, 39, 42, 52, 54, 57, 58, 76, 78, 81, 82, 90, 96, 99, 113, 122, 127n1, 132n13, 135, 136, 142, 145, 145n54, 146, 158, 160
TIME Magazine, viii
Torpey, John, 3n2
Totalitarianism, 33, 89
Totality, 49, 76, 87n37, 92, 139, 141, 142, 144
Trace, 126
Transcendence, 26, 36, 37, 44, 100, 148, 164
Treichler, Paula A., 114, 115
Trinity, 147
Ture, Kwame, 154

U
Ultimate, ultimacy, x, 12, 25, 26, 29, 34–36, 39, 43, 46–50, 49–50n84, 52, 69, 72, 88, 97, 99, 111, 118–119n19, 119
Unconscious, 42, 47

Uprising, 128, 134, 155, 160, 162, 164
Utopia, utopian, utopianism, 43, 62, 102, 108, 112, 120n25, 121, 125–126

V
Vahanian, Noelle, ix
Van Buren, Paul, 8n11
VanAntwerpen, Jonathan, 3n2
Vattimo, Gianni, 144, 144n52
Victim, 40, 42
Violence, 2, 4, 41–43, 51, 55, 65, 92n50, 128, 141, 157, 159, 161n24, 162
Void, 19, 77, 114, 137, 144, 145, 150

W
War
  Iraq war, viii, 132
  Vietnam War, viii
  War on Terror, viii
Wark, McKenzie, 55, 55n13, 55n14, 57, 77, 77n14, 145, 145n55, 150
Washington, D.C., 113, 121, 121n27
Weakness, 98
Weber, Max, 1–2n1, 33, 33n36
Weller, Robert P., xiv, 6, 22, 66
West, 167
West, Cornel, 137, 149
Western, 37, 39
Winquist, Charles E., viii, 8n11, 10, 10n15, 69, 87, 87n39, 87n40, 88, 91–97, 92n48, 92n50, 93n51, 93n52, 93n53, 94n58, 95n59, 95n60, 95n62, 96n64, 118, 118n18, 119n20, 121, 125, 125n40, 168
Wisdom, 1, 30, 114
Wojnarowicz, David, 113, 123, 125, 168

Word, 23, 24, 28–30, 29n26, 31n32, 32–35, 33n35, 37, 38, 45, 46, 59, 64, 65, 70, 71, 73, 73n4, 79, 82, 97, 98, 103, 108, 116, 117, 119n19, 122, 123, 125, 131, 136, 137, 143, 144, 149, 150, 159
Work, vii, x, xi, 2n1, 6–11, 8n11, 14, 17, 19, 22, 30, 31, 34, 36, 41, 45, 60, 66, 71, 72, 75n9, 76–79, 86n33, 92n50, 97, 98n70, 100, 106–108, 114, 116, 129n5, 135, 138, 145, 147n59, 149, 156n11, 158, 160
World, 1, 19, 55, 69, 115, 130, 154
World Trade Organization (WTO), 59
Writing, 4n4, 16, 26n18, 53, 58, 86, 87n37, 92, 100, 103, 104n87, 125, 153

Z

Zapatistas, 4, 148, 149
Zbaraschuk, G. Michael, ix
Zen Buddhism, 22, 24
Žižek, Slavoj, 5n4, 15, 40n56, 44, 44n67, 52n4, 131–136, 131n11, 131n12, 132n14, 133n17, 135n26, 136n28, 139n33, 141, 141n40, 142, 142n42, 145, 145n54, 147, 147n58
Zuccotti Park, xi, 15, 130, 149